JEAN-LUC GODARD

SON+IMAGE

1974–1991

JEAN-LUC GODARD

SON + IMAGE

1974–1991

EDITED BY RAYMOND BELLOUR
WITH MARY LEA BANDY

The Museum of Modern Art, New York
Distributed by Harry N. Abrams, Inc., New York

Published on the occasion of the exhibition *Jean-Luc Godard: Son+Image 1974–1991*, October 30–November 30, 1992, organized by Mary Lea Bandy, Director, Laurence Kardish, Curator, and Barbara London, Assistant Curator, Video, Department of Film, The Museum of Modern Art, New York, and Colin MacCabe, Guest Curator

This publication is made possible by a generous grant from Celeste Bartos and Pinewood Foundation.

ISBN 0-87070-348-X (MoMA/T&H)
ISBN 0-8109-6114-8 (Abrams)

Produced by the Department of Publications
The Museum of Modern Art, New York
Osa Brown, Director of Publications

Edited by Alexandra Bonfante-Warren
Designed by Emsworth Design, New York, New York
Production by Vicki Drake
Printed by Litho Incorporated, St. Paul, Minnesota
Bound by Midwest Editions, Inc., Minneapolis, Minnesota

Printed in the United States of America

Published by The Museum of Modern Art
11 West 53 Street, New York, N.Y. 10019

Distributed in the United States and Canada by
Harry N. Abrams Inc., New York
A Times Mirror Company

Distributed outside the United States and Canada by
Thames and Hudson Ltd., London

Rachel Bowlby translated "The Declension," by Jean-Louis Leutrat; "Three Questions about *Six fois deux*," an interview with Gilles Deleuze; and "The Medium," by Jacques Aumont. Georgia Gurrieri translated "Godard Makes [Hi]stories," an interview with Godard by Serge Daney. Lynne Kirby translated "The Other Side of the Bouquet," by Alain Bergala; "Excerpts from a document . . ."; "Video Thinks What Cinema Creates," by Philippe Dubois; and "(Not) Just An Other Filmmaker," by Raymond Bellour.

Frontispiece: *Prénom Carmen* (1983)

TABLE OF CONTENTS

Hanns Zischler, Nathalie Kadem

Eddie Constantine

**ALLEMAGNE ANNEE
90 NEUF ZERO**

1991

PREFACE

Jean-Luc Godard is widely recognized as one of the filmmakers who has most influenced the modern art and language of the medium. He is less well known in the United States as a videomaker, although he has been creating some of the most beautiful and provocative imagery for television for nearly two decades.

The retrospective *Jean-Luc Godard: Son+Image*, which this publication accompanies, is a comprehensive presentation of Godard's oeuvre from 1974, when, with *Ici et ailleurs*, he first incorporated video technology into his work, through 1991, when he wrote and directed a film for television, *Allemagne année 90 neuf zero*, a meditation, in Berlin, on the art and politics of a Europe in transition.

Godard's work is as visually and verbally dense with meaning through these years, as his revolutionary films of the sixties—in certain ways, more so. In the various "episodes" of his career, as identified in Colin MacCabe's introductory essay, Godard has focused, intensely and intently, on politics, history, and communication, anxiety, sex, and desire, art, aesthetics, and music, and the history of the movies. And from the moment he began what Jean-Louis Leutrat refers to as his "shuttle between cinema and video," with *Ici et ailleurs* (1974) and *Numéro deux* (1975), Godard initiated an investigation of video as medium, and television as subject, that has yet to be exhausted.

Included in the retrospective are Godard's collaborative video experiments of the seventies and eighties with Anne-Marie Miéville: *Six fois deux* (1976), *France/tour/détour/deux/enfants* (1977–78), and *Soft and Hard* (1986), in which they explore the roles and influences of television as mass communicator, its impact on the daily lives of adults and children, and the intertwining of their personal lives and their creative work. Godard returned to filmmaking with *Sauve qui peut (la vie)* (1979) and *Passion* (1982), accompanying both with video-essays, or *scénarios*: if *Passion* is an exploration of the natures of film and painting, *Scénario du film Passion* is a reflection on the creative processes of filmmaking itself, on screenwriting and the making of imagery—at a remove of almost twenty years from that other film within a film, *Le Mépris*, of 1963.

Godard is an artist obsessed by many of the arts: as a writer, he began his career documenting his views of filmmaking for *Cahiers du Cinéma*; he has continued writing about cinema, for print journals, while writing his own cinema, alone or in collaboration. His application of words—his own or appropriated texts—over and between images established other dimensions of meaning in his work; it is an important element in his evolution as essayist and historian in video, begun with Miéville, and recently most interestingly revealed in his *Histoire(s) du cinéma* (1989–). Godard conceived this project as a history of the movies and of history through movies, structured in video "chapters"; he has so far completed two segments, which will be shown in the retrospective. Published in this volume are selections from his notebook on the *Histoire(s)*, pages of film images and words he composed for the video screen, interspersed with his commentaries; it is followed by an interview with Serge Daney that preceded the first telecast and probes Godard's role as historian.

As one who identifies with the artist as painter or sculptor, Godard has queried, in *Passion* and other works, the creative process and the iconography of the work of Titian and Tintoretto, El Greco, Goya, and Rembrandt, Maillol and Rodin. Godard still makes his versions of the filmmaker's traditional preparatory storyboards, in which he plots a work frame by frame; these may be pages of photo layouts, with annotations, or series of frames of images and words, broadly stroked in black, accompanied by typed dialogue or commentary. In his sketchbooks, or *dossiers*, Godard assembles collages of stills of his own or others' films, with reproductions of famous paintings and drawings; two *dossiers* are reprinted here, one announcing a selection of JLG Films productions, the other, the *Histoire(s) du cinéma* project.

Like Picasso, Godard reveals to us throughout his work his world as source and subject: the artist's studio, the objects of his daily life, the references to and repetitions of his own works, the layering of words and images, the women he has loved, the horrors of war. But it is in the aspect of his work as collages, the filmmaker's montages of suggestive textures, themes, and images, his play with "found objects" of art, television, and film, that he evokes the sly wit, eroticism, and provocative disjunctions of other surrealist collagists, like Max Ernst in his Picture-Poems. Godard's *Puissance de la parole*, a powerfully charged work in video of 1988, juxtaposes sequences portraying nature in explosion or movement with those of passionate discussions between two couples, one a variation on James Cain's lovers in *The Postman Always Rings Twice*, the other speaking the words of Edgar Allan Poe. The twenty-five-minute video is as suggestive as Ernst's collage "novel," *Une Semaine de bonté*, organized as chapters on each of the "seven deadly elements," depicted from Sunday to Monday, that mix epigraphs of Eluard, Tzara, and Breton with imagery from wood-engravings of late-nineteenth-century French pulp novels of *crimes passionels* and catalogue illustrations.

Citing Godard's return to the classics in recent years, Peter Wollen compares Godard to Jean Cocteau, noting their similarly "contradictory reverence for the art of the past and a delinquent refusal to obey any of its rules." Godard as musician reveres the classics, first quoting Bach, Handel, Beethoven in his films in the midfifties, as he admires the rhythms of jazz artists, the music of Stockhausen, Cage, Bob Dylan, and The Rolling Stones. No longer restricted to the background, music becomes text, as intriguing as the imagery of nature, film, and television, and it is in this sense that he takes collage where the painter and printmaker cannot follow. He achieves a sensory intricacy by overlapping dialogue, music, and electronic and other sound effects with visually rhythmic variations of slow takes and rapid cuts, in juxtapositions as rich as the Titian, Mozart, and Coltrane compositions he knows so well.

Beethoven, in particular the late string quartets, has ever fascinated Godard. First heard in the "Nouveau Monde" sketch in *Rogopag* (1962), in *Une Femme mariée* (1964), and in *Deux ou Trois Choses que je sais d'elle* (1966), they are a principal subject in *Prénom Carmen* (1984), as Godard films his musicians rehearsing and criticizing their approaches to the quartets; "music," Godard writes in his notes on the film, "which usually announces catastrophe." In subsequent works of the eighties and early nineties, including, in the retrospective, *Je vous salue Marie, Détective, Grandeur et décadence . . .*, "Armide," *Puissance de la parole*, and *Allemagne année 90 . . .*, Godard frequently quotes classical compositions, by Beethoven, Wagner, Chopin, Liszt, Franck, or Stravinsky, as well as the more contemporary music of jazz and rock musicians.

A curious, periodically unsettling problem for historians and curators, in our efforts to analyze and categorize the visual arts through their various eras, is how to redefine and expand upon what the French christened,

shortly after its birth, the seventh art. *Cinema, film, the motion picture*—these terms have been in use for nearly one hundred years. *Television* came into use in the twenties, followed by *video, (mass) media, media arts*, and most recently, *the moving image*. All denote imagery seen on a screen; we have only *the silent movie, the talkies, the sound film* (or, on the French side, *le film muet, le film parlant, le film sonore*) to distinguish the traditionally demarcated periods of the motion picture without, then with, recorded sound. Trust Godard to solve the problem, with clarity and simplicity, when in 1972 he and Miéville established their production and distribution company, Sonimage. There is, unfortunately, no satisfactory equivalent in English; *audiovisual*, though accurate, reminds us of our lessons in grade school.

In choosing Sonimage, Godard made a key point, presaging what would be of increasing importance through his subsequent work: his obsession with the possibilities of manipulating imagery and sound, imbuing each and the whole with amassed content and meaning. And in setting image against image, image against sound, sound against sound, he creates discontinuities of text and art that disturb us to new discoveries, new perceptions.

Raymond Bellour, noted scholar and writer, served as guest editor of *Jean-Luc Godard: Son+Image*, giving shape and focus to a dialogue on the issues and directions of this period of Godard's work. The Department of Film gratefully acknowledges his unstinting efforts and collaboration, and extends thanks to him and to Colin MacCabe, guest curator, as well as to the other distinguished authors who contributed essays to this volume: Jacques Aumont, Alain Bergala, Janet Bergstrom, Gilles Deleuze, Philippe Dubois, Jean-Louis Leutrat, Elisabeth Lyon, Laura Mulvey, Constance Penley, Jonathan Rosenbaum, and Peter Wollen. We acknowledge, too, the critical perspective of the late writer and editor Serge Daney, in his fine interview with Godard on the making of (hi)stories.

MARY LEA BANDY
DIRECTOR
DEPARTMENT OF FILM

ACKNOWLEDGEMENTS

Jean-Luc Godard: Son+Image is both a publication and a retrospective. The organizers of the project are Raymond Bellour, guest editor; Colin MacCabe, guest curator; and Mary Lea Bandy, Director, Laurence Kardish, Curator, and Barbara London, Assistant Curator, of the Department of Film, The Museum of Modern Art, New York.

First and foremost, the organizing committee thanks Jean-Luc Godard, an equal partner, for his participation and assistance at every phase of research and planning. We are particularly grateful to him for making it possible for the Department of Film to establish the Jean-Luc Godard Collection, and for providing photographs and *dossiers* for the publication.

We owe our sincere gratitude to Celeste Bartos, Chairman of the Trustee Committee on Film, and Pinewood Foundation, whose generous support has made possible this publication. James Niven, Vice-Chairman of the Committee, merits our warm thanks for his kind contribution, which has enabled us to acquire key films by Godard.

For their loans of films and videotapes for the retrospective, we thank, above all, Jean-Luc Godard, and Dan Talbot and New Yorker Films, Gaumont, Rod Stoneman and Channel 4, Lori Zippay, Stephen Vitiello, and Electronic Arts Intermix, Darty, Erato Compagnie, Marithé and François Girbaud, France Télécom, and Télévision Suisse Romande. We are grateful to Sony Corporation of America for the loan of equipment for the retrospective.

For her invaluable assistance, advice, and support, we thank Catherine Verret-Vimont, Executive Director of the French Film Office\Unifrance Film. We also thank our fellow members of the International Federation of Film Archives for their help and support, for loans of works to the retrospective and photographs and documents for the publication, and for sharing their research with us: we particularly acknowledge Michelle Aubert and the Archives du Film, Centre National de la Cinématographie, Bois d'Arcy; Freddy Buache and André Chevallier, the Cinémathèque Suisse, Lausanne; Jean-Paul Gorce and the Cinémathèque de Toulouse; Dominique Païni, Alain Marchand, and the Cinémathèque Française, Paris; Jayne Pilling, Esther Johnson, Bridget Kinally, and Alan Gregory and the British Film Institute, London. We also are especially grateful to the following for providing photographs for the publication: Erwan Depenanster, Philippe Dubois, Catherine Fröchen and *Cahiers du Cinéma*, Anne-Marie Faux, Jean Narboni, Marc-Emmanuel Melon, Paul-Emmanuel Odin, Catherine Schapira, and Electronic Arts Intermix and Marita Sturken.

We are most grateful to Annie Cohen-Salal, Cultural Counselor to the French Embassy, for her tireless efforts on our behalf. We also thank Patrick Vittet-Philippe, Cultural Attaché, and Jacques Soulillou, Head of the Visual Arts Department, of the French Cultural Services.

We deeply appreciate the support and participation of the staff of the Department of Film, particularly Ron Magliozzi, who prepared the List of Works and Selected Bibliography, and Joan Jansen, who was most helpful at every phase. We also thank Robert Beers, Sally Berger, Eileen Bowser, Mary Corliss, Rachel Gallagher, Terry Geesken, Andy Haas, Stephen Harvey, Jytte Jensen, Anne Morra, and Charles Kalinowski, Anthony Tavolacci, Gregory Singer, and Edmund D'Inzillo. In addition, we especially thank Jeanne Collins, Director, and Barbara Marshall, Film Press Representative, of the Department of Public Information.

Other Museum colleagues to whom we owe a special debt are Richard E. Oldenburg, Director of the Museum; Sue B. Dorn, Deputy Director for Development and Special Affairs; Daniel Vecchitto, Director of Development; and John Wielk, Manager, Exhibition and Project Funding.

In the Department of Publications we offer our thanks to Alexandra Bonfante-Warren, Associate Editor, for her expert editing of this publication, her mastery of the nuances and subtleties of texts translated from French, and her skills as a researcher. To Vicki Drake, Associate Production Manager, go our thanks for her perceptive and skillful supervision of production and printing. In the same department we also thank Osa Brown, Director; Harriet Schoenholz Bee, Managing Editor; Nancy Kranz, Manager of Promotion and Special Services; and Jessica Altholz, Assistant

Editor. Special thanks go to Michael Hentges, Director of Graphics, and most particularly to Antony Drobinski of Emsworth Design, who once again has brought his sensitivity and design expertise to bear on a complex publication.

Of greatest importance have been our translators, whose skillful efforts in the field of French critical writing are deeply appreciated. To Rachel Bowlby, Georgia Gurrieri, and Lynne Kirby go our thanks and our respect for difficult tasks well performed.

Finally, we acknowledge a special debt to Yse Marguerite Tran, who collaborated with Raymond Bellour throughout the project, in particular on the selection of illustrations, and to Serge Daney, to whose memory we dedicate this volume.

RAYMOND BELLOUR
AND
MARY LEA BANDY

Eddie Constantine, Claudia Michelsen

Eddie Constantine

**ALLEMAGNE ANNEE
90 NEUF ZERO**

1991

Jean-Luc Godard on the set of
DETECTIVE
1985

JEAN-LUC GODARD
A Life in Seven Episodes (to Date)

COLIN MYLES MACCABE

From Hollywood to the Third World, from the mainstream to the avant-garde, Godard's name is perhaps the only one that occurs wherever cinema is discussed or produced. And yet he lives a life as far removed from the conventional image of a moviemaker as it is possible to imagine. For over a decade now he has based himself in the small Swiss village of Rolle, halfway between Lausanne and Geneva. Here, in a nondescript modern building, he occupies two apartments; he lives in one, the other houses his video equipment. There are no secretaries, no assistants, none of the panoply of power and success with which one associates the cinema. The phone rings from Los Angeles or Paris, and it is Godard himself who answers to set up whatever complicated financing is necessary for the next movie.

Godard is physically small and talks in the softest and most unemphatic of voices. However, even the briefest meeting leaves one astonished by the force of his presence. Like a shaman he alternates between almost total withdrawal from the world and sudden blazes of interest. What enables him to escape his intense privacy is his obsession with the images and sounds of the cinema.

It is this intensity of Godard's commitment to the cinema that makes his life more than just the record of an extraordinary individual but also, inevitably, a history of European culture since World War II. To talk of Godard is to talk of *Cahiers du Cinéma* and the Nouvelle Vague, of militant politics and '68, of domestic politics and feminism. Perhaps most crucially it is to talk of the relationship between the traditional culture of Europe and the popular culture of the United States—to try and understand what the cinema might be and what it is, to understand its potential and its limitations.

Jean-Luc's life takes us through almost every possible position with regard to Hollywood—the devotion of the early years, the ferocious opposition of the Dziga Vertov period, the attempt to use video in the seventies to carve out a completely different kind of audiovisual production, the reconciliation of the early eighties with an office in Coppola's Zoetrope studios and a filmed *King Lear* (1987) for Cannon. Today he engages across the entire range of audiovisual production, alternating

a feature and an experimental video, interrupting his long project of a televised history of the cinema to make a commercial.

Godard's life contains an extraordinary plurality of lives: as he has changed lives he has changed worlds, leaving behind a complete set of relationships in order to start a new life. And starting a new life for Godard has always been starting a new relationship to the image.

To give an account of Godard's life one could simply write an account of his films, for he is the most autobiographical of filmmakers. There can be no other director who has so thoroughly used the medium to analyze his own obsessions. His relationships with women, his political evolution, his sexual obsessions— all are laid bare in the most intimate detail.

Life 1: The Tale of Two Countries: A Bourgeois Idyll

Godard's childhood is remarkable both for its mobility —he moved between Switzerland and Paris with the frequency of a contemporary executive—and its stability—his grandfather's huge and wealthy estate provided a constant backdrop for the rest of the family's activities. Jean-Luc was born on December 3, 1930. His elder sister, Rachel, had been born at the beginning of the same year, and his parents were to have two other children, Claude and Véronique, both considerably younger than Jean-Luc. His father, Paul-Jean Godard, a brilliant doctor, qualified in both England and France, was the son of a jeweler and the first of his family to go to college, but Jean-Luc's mother, Odile, came from a very rich family, the Monods. Her father, Julien Monod, had founded the Banque de Paris et des Pays-Bas.

Godard's parents met at medical school, but Odile abandoned her medical studies to marry. It may be that Odile was happy to abandon her medical studies, because for Godard she is identified with the classic literature that she loved and to which she introduced him at a very early age. However, when her third child, Claude, was born, she tried briefly to resume her medical studies. The details of the parents' marriage are shrouded by the veil that covers all such private negotiations, but it rarely seems to have been the blissful union that Godard himself recalls. There seems to have been a continuous tension between the grande bourgeoisie from which Odile came and the petit-bourgeois world of the Godards—a tension that crystallized in part around money. Both parents, however, were enormously talented. Godard's father was a brilliant scientist, and his mother was deeply versed in European culture.

Both Godard's parents were from Protestant families, which may have been a factor in the decision his father took shortly after Jean-Luc's birth to move to Switzerland and to set up a private clinic in the town of Nyon. Godard's early years were thus spent in Switzerland, but the link to his mother's large family (she was one of seven) and particularly to his mother's twin sister meant that his childhood was one of travel as he commuted between Paris and Switzerland. Indeed, in 1940 Jean-Luc was trapped in Paris and had to be sent to school in Brittany until, after a few months, he returned to Nyon, where he graduated from the Collège de Nyon at the end of the war.

Godard's memories of his childhood are of a paradise full of affection and wealth. Everything centered on Julien Monod and his large estate on the French side of Lake Geneva, the site of endless family gatherings, as the pious Protestant banker commemorated the feasts of the year with his numerous children and grandchildren.

Godard's account of his childhood contains no moment of revelation at the cinema—his thoughts were dominated by the literature of his beloved mother. The Swiss context is not, however, without significance. Most important, it places Godard both inside and outside French culture, totally familiar with a national culture that is not his own. Swiss cinemas presented him, from the start, with films from a range of countries. One of his few childhood memories of film reflects this Swiss setting—during the war he was able to watch German and British newsreels in the same cinema recounting different versions of the same battle. For the rest, Godard's childhood seems unremarkable. The predominant memories are of sports, particularly skiing and football, and of the pleasures of the Swiss countryside. The impression one gets is of a rather dreamy child, charming and spoiled, the apple of his mother's eye, but from early on in considerable conflict with his father.

Life 2: I Want to Make Movies: A Troubled Adolescence

Godard moved to Paris after the war and went to the Lycée Buffon to take his *baccalauréat*. Jean-Luc seems to have been adopted by the whole of his mother's family, lodging with his mother's twin sister and taking his meals around Paris with the Monods. His life at this point was becoming increasingly troubled, and he finally took his *baccalauréat* after a further period of schooling in Switzerland. Although he fulfilled the family's demands by registering as an anthropology student, his life at this time seems curiously undirected. An early interest in mathematics had been replaced by a vague desire to become an artist. Attempts at writing and painting were quickly followed by a determination to get into the cinema, but Godard has no exact memory of the motivation for this decision. It did, however, coincide with his parents' separation and divorce, and, although Godard's memory gives these events little importance, it is difficult not to read the problems of the next few years as being, in part, a reaction to his parents' divorce.

It is at this point that he started his training as a filmmaker—not by making films but by watching them. Godard has never ceased to stress the debt that he owes to Henri Langlois, the legendary curator of the Cinémathèque Française, who was, in the late forties, busy showing, to any who would come to his programs, the entire history of the cinema up to that time. His most assiduous patrons were to become famous ten years later as the Nouvelle Vague: Godard, Truffaut, Rivette, Chabrol, Rohmer. If, in retrospect, their interest in the cinema was justified by their success as critics and filmmakers, it is well to remember that at this stage they seemed more like social misfits. Particularly Truffaut, who tangled with the juvenile courts, and Godard, who was, by now, regularly stealing small amounts of money from his Parisian aunts and uncles. The dreamy, charming child had turned into a shy and uncharming adolescent.

His father, however, was concerned about more than Jean-Luc. He was worried about the Cold War in Europe, and, as he had British as well as French medical qualifications, he decided to emigrate to Jamaica. Jean-Luc accompanied his father, remaining behind after his father abandoned his plan and returned to Switzerland. For the next eighteen months Jean-Luc traveled extensively in South America, in Peru, Bolivia, Argentina, Chile, and Brazil; for most of this period he stayed with members of his father's family. It seems probable that one reason for the long trip was to avoid military service: his father had advised him to opt for Swiss citizenship at the age of twenty-one to avoid the risk of being called up to fight for the French in Indochina, but Swiss citizenship required its own military service, which Godard was unwilling to fulfill. The South American journey came to an end when Godard's father once again refused to support his son

Rachel, Claude,
Véronique, and
Jean-Luc Godard

Jean-Luc Godard (first row,
third from left)

Jean-Luc Godard

any longer. A few nights on the beach at Copacabana and a pathetic failure to raise money as a homosexual prostitute were the prelude to a return to Switzerland and Paris, where Godard contributed to the first issues of *Cahiers du Cinéma*.

If for many years the Nouvelle Vague was seen as a unified intellectual position, what always marked Godard out from the rest of the group was the fundamental importance he accorded to the image. For the others, the image was important insofar as it revealed reality—for Godard image and reality could never be separated, reality was always already an image. Whereas Truffaut, for example, was always willing to use the generic conventions he so brilliantly analyzed as a critic, Godard was always trying to push a genre to the moment it would break down to reveal the operations of the cinema. Much of this is clear as early as 1952 and the first long article that Godard published in *Cahiers du Cinéma*, "Défense et illustration du découpage classique."

If, in retrospect, we can read Godard in 1952 setting out one of the great artistic manifestos of the twentieth century, this was not so evident to his family. An understandable weariness with his presence as a guest was compounded by his continual stealing (on one occasion he even stole from the *Cahiers* office). In 1952 his father summoned him home and his mother found him a job in the then nascent Swiss television service. Once again Godard stole money, but this time it was not his family's and the consequences were more serious—three or four days in a Zurich jail before his father managed to bail him out. By now he evidently constituted a major problem for his father, who committed him to a psychiatric hospital for a considerable period.

His mother now made her last effort on her son's behalf. In 1954, just before her death in a traffic accident, she found work for him with a construction company building a dam in the Valais. Jean-Luc applied himself with a purpose—with the money he earned from this project he shot his first film, *Opération Béton*, a documentary about the dam he had helped to construct. The sale of the film to the construction company financed both his first short fiction, *Une Femme coquette* (1955), and his return to Paris in 1956. The next three years were to see him write increasingly for both *Cahiers* and *Arts* magazines, take Chabrol's place in the publicity department at Fox, and make three more shorts.

By now the *Cahiers'* critics' contempt for French cinema and their polemic defense of their favorite American auteurs were beginning to find a wider audience. Truffaut, in particular, waged continuous war against the French cinema in the pages of the popular magazine *Arts*. Truffaut not only enraged the organizers of

Anna Karina and Jean-Luc Godard on the set of *Alphaville* (1965)

The Dziga Vertov Group (Jean-Pierre Gorin and Jean-Luc Godard) in *Vladimir et Rosa* (1971)

the Cannes Film Festival, from which he was banned in 1958, but also his father-in-law—for Truffaut had married Madeline Morgenstern, daughter of one of the biggest French distributors. Enraged by one of his son-in-law's more scornful attacks on a favored film, Morgenstern *père* challenged him to do better. Truffaut accepted the wager, and the father-in-law found he had financed the hit movie *Les Quatre Cent Coups*.

Suddenly, and for perhaps the only time in the history of the cinema, producers were looking for untried young critics to direct movies. Godard, with a Truffaut scenario to hand, persuaded a young documentary producer called Georges de Beauregard to raise the money. Shooting took place in the summer of 1959. Beauregard was obviously terrified by the unorthodox rushes (Godard used the jump cut as his major editing device), but Truffaut and the elder director Jean-Pierre Melville turned up on a daily basis to reassure him, and the movie, *A bout de souffle*, was finally ready for release in March 1960. It was immediately an enormous hit.

Life 3: The Nouvelle Vague: Success in the World

The critical and commercial success of *A bout de souffle* transformed the conditions of Godard's life. He was no longer a penurious critic but a famous filmmaker. The relaxed and private world of the *Cahiers'* critics exploded as they found themselves the center of what quickly became known as the Nouvelle Vague. Although Godard was totally absorbed by his work, a side of him reveled in finally entering the glamorous world of filmmaking that he and his friends had observed from the outside for so long.

It is impossible to imagine Godard's subsequent career without the commercial success of *A bout de souffle*, but, as Godard himself noted, this "success was a misunderstanding; through a concatenation of circumstances, it became much too successful." In retrospect the film rehearses many of Godard's abiding preoccupations: the characters are caught up in systems of representations that produce the reality in which they live. Belmondo's imitation of Bogart is only the most obvious example of the film's concern with the production and dissemination of images and information. The film's success, however, comes from its classic love story, abbreviated by Godard's jump cuts, but a compelling narrative just the same. Godard never used such a narrative again, and in hindsight it can be seen as an unimportant part of the film for him. But another reason for the film's popularity—the almost documentary accuracy of its social observation—proved to be a more enduring feature of Godard's work. For the first time we really see the Champs-Elysées and the place de la Concorde on film; the Paris of 1959, its styles and idioms, are projected on the screen to produce a new image of France.

It is, in fact, the documentary strength of Godard's image that is the most important unifying thread through the hectic next seven years of moviemaking. At a rate of almost two a year, Godard produced a string of classic movies, among them, *Le Mépris* (1963), *Une Femme mariée* (1964), *Alphaville* (1965), *Pierrot le fou* (1965), *Deux ou Trois Choses que je sais d'elle* (1966). Each film has its own power and each one has already generated a considerable interpretative literature but each one gives us a different image of the new France being produced under de Gaulle. Godard himself holds his anthropological training of little account, but it is difficult not to read this decade of filmmaking as an extended anthropological survey of contemporary France—a survey that has no parallel in the history of moviemaking. Most anthropologists position themselves at the margin of their society, but Godard's analysis focuses increasingly on his own activity as a filmmaker. As France embarked on a late—compared to the United States and Britain—but rapid shift toward a consumer society, and the centrality of the image to that society became more and more evident, Jean-Luc's studies in the Cinémathèque looked less like the marginal activities of a connoisseur and more like fundamental research into contemporary society.

This period was marked by two pivotal collaborations, one with Raoul Coutard, his cinematographer, and the other with Anna Karina, his star in so many of these films and also, for much of the period, his wife. She was the female lead in *Le Petit Soldat* (1960), which Godard made immediately after *A bout de souffle*. Halfway through the shooting of the film, and despite the fact that her boyfriend was the unit photographer, Godard and Karina became lovers. According to Godard, this was his first proper relationship as, to use his own words, "I started very late with girls." Typically, his relationship with her started as a relationship with an image—he cast her after seeing her picture in a magazine.

In the early films, the forms of cinema seem to offer Godard infinite possibilities. But as he progresses through the decade, the forms become more limiting and constricting. By October 1965 Godard could say in an interview, "The only great problem is . . . when and why to start a shot and when and why to end it." His dissatisfaction, indeed, his despair with the existing forms of cinema followed from two different but complementary developments.

In the public sphere, the war in Vietnam was coming to dominate the international scene. Godard's increasing disgust with the United States' involvement there was crucially linked to developments within his own culture. Whereas at the Cinémathèque in the late forties American films had seemed to offer a host of new possibilities, the culture from which those films had sprung was no longer foreign exotica but the daily reality of France. The United States' attempt to impose a political system on Vietnam, and the daily imposition of their cultural system in France, became for Godard aspects of the same process. But privately as well the cinema was failing Godard. His marriage with Karina, a relationship articulated entirely in terms of the cinema, was breaking up. Her infidelities rendered Godard prey to the most terrible jealousy—Karina's other lovers were known to him. There was for Godard now no escape from the cinema. It would seem that his and Karina's social life was entirely dominated by work. Godard can hardly remember if they even went on holiday. He also saw his relationship with Karina in terms of earlier examples from the history of the cinema: Sternberg and Dietrich, the director and his star.

The final films of this period, *La Chinoise* (1967) and *Week-end* (1967), sketch a series of impasses, both personal and cinematic, that are frightening in their finality. But socially and culturally France was also at the end of a certain phase. Ten years of Gaullist rule were to culminate in the events of May 1968.

Life 4: The Dziga Vertov Group: Godard as Revolutionary

Godard was ready for 1968, ripe for its denunciation of consumer society and its embracing of different models of development: a different society and a different cinema. For three years Godard made films addressed to small groups of militants rather than aimed at a mass market. Such films were not guaranteed by star names but by revolutionary credentials. "Godard" was left behind, the Dziga Vertov Group appeared. The political posturing among filmmakers in this period was truly grotesque, but Godard never really participated in it. His break from the cinema had come from within and though he abandoned the Maoist political rhetoric three years later, he never abandoned the critique that it had enabled him to make.

Godard's first contact with the young Maoists who had split from the Communist party and were busy preaching doctrines of revolutionary purity came during the making of the film *La Chinoise* in 1967. This film, with uncanny prescience, sketched many of the discourses and emphases that were soon to dominate French life. At the time, it seemed to many a personal aberration, and the film was comprehensively attacked by both Maoists and the orthodox Left. For Godard,

however, it marked the beginning of two relationships that were to replace those with Coutard and Karina. The star of *La Chinoise*, Anne Wiazemsky, became Godard's second wife. Jean-Pierre Gorin, one of the young Maoists whom Godard had talked with during the course of his research for the film, became his closest collaborator. Godard had first seen Karina in a publicity photograph; he first saw Wiazemsky in a Bresson film. The complex interplay between image and reality is not, for Godard, an abstract theoretical question but characterizes his very existence: over the next three years Wiazemsky appeared in almost all his films.

Week-end marked the end of one kind of relationship to the image—Godard embarked on another immediately on its completion. At the end of 1967 he started shooting for the main French television station a film called, after Nietzsche, *Le Gai Savoir* (*The Gay Science* [1968]). Narrative is reduced to a vanishing point, and the content of the image is pruned to the minimum of two characters in a studio. It is the verbal sound track and the graphics that become the dominant elements in a desperate attempt to analyze the functioning of image and sound, the real politics of the cinema. Before *Le Gai Savoir* could be edited, politics entered Godard's life more directly. Early in 1968 Langlois, the spiritual godfather of the Nouvelle Vague, was fired as curator of the Cinémathèque by de Gaulle's minister of cultural affairs, André Malraux. Godard was one of the organizers of the groups that sprang to Langlois's defense and led the series of demonstrations and riots that forced the government to back down. These events, in retrospect, were some of the most important precursors of the much bigger riots and demonstrations that marked May of the same year.

More than twenty years after the events it is still difficult to analyze them fully. Whether they are more important as the end of one revolutionary tradition, stretching back to the Bastille, or as the beginning of a new kind of life-style politics is still difficult to determine. What is certain is that for two years France exchanged the comfortable securities of the late fifties and early sixties for a period of deep social uncertainty. Perhaps more than any other filmmaker Godard participated in that deep uncertainty. The first obvious casualty was his name. Defined within a whole system of cinema that he now wished to repudiate, he abandoned his patronym in order to work under the name of a revolutionary Soviet filmmaker: the Dziga Vertov Group was born. "Group" was a slight exaggeration, for it never really comprised more than Godard himself and Jean-Pierre Gorin.

Godard had got back in touch with Gorin early in 1968 and as the year progressed Gorin introduced him

Anne-Marie Miéville
and Jean-Luc Godard in *Soft
and Hard* (1986), co-directed
by Anne-Marie Miéville

Hanna Schygulla and
Jean-Luc Godard on the
set of *Passion* (1982)

fully to the Maoist discourses that he had merely observed in *La Chinoise*—*Le Gai Savoir* became a model for the films that they made in this period. Funding came from television companies rather than film distributors. The money that Godard's name guaranteed was used to carry further the experiments in sound and image that had been begun in *Le Gai Savoir*. It was impossible to use images until one really understood how they worked, understood how they articulated a whole social organization. The methods of analysis were largely drawn from contemporary intellectual debates in Paris, in which a version of Althusserian Maoism was used to criticize the consumer society. In some sense the films of that period, *British Sounds* (1969), *Pravda* (1969), and *Vent d'est* (1969), to mention only the better known, are rebarbative and didactic. In another, they mark an unparalleled attempt to investigate the operations of the image.

If Godard's disgust with the cinema was a disgust with the fundamental relationship between film and audience, the political situation in France offered the brief opportunity of another way of addressing an audience. But the genuine political upheaval of '68 did not last all that long. By 1970 the period of genuine uncertainty was past and if the lessons of '68 were still to be learnt, the brief possibility of reaching an audience directly through politics had passed. At the same time, his relationship with Wiazemsky came to a conclusion—in exactly the same fury of jealousy that had marked his separation from Karina.

It was in this context that Godard and Gorin determined to make a political film within the commercial structures that had proved more durable than the revolution. The result, *Tout va bien* (1972), with Yves Montand and Jane Fonda, is perhaps the single best cinematic description of France in the aftermath of '68; it makes a striking coda to all Godard's work of the sixties.

Life 5: The Personal and the Political: From Godard to Jean-Luc

Six months before the making of *Tout va bien*, Godard was very seriously injured in a motorcycle accident. The woman who nursed him through the two and a half years of intermittent hospital treatment that followed was Anne-Marie Miéville. For the first time Godard found himself involved with a woman who was on the same side of the camera as himself (she was a stills photographer) and who was unwilling to simply accept the findings of his intellect. Karina, Wiazemsky, Gorin: for all of them Godard had been a great public name of the contemporary cinema. For Anne-Marie he was simply Jean-Luc. She relentlessly criticized the

assumptions of the Maoist revolutionary discourse and argued that it had continuously ignored the reality of daily life in France. The response to the inadequacies of the commercial cinema was to be found in the analysis of how the image functioned in daily life, not in didactic revolutionary films. Together with Godard she set up a small atelier in Paris, in which the new resources of video were harnessed to investigate the intersection of the political and the personal in everyday life and the place of the image in that intersection. Gorin soon tired of this venture and departed for California; Godard and Miéville moved their atelier to Grenoble in order to escape the metropolitan isolation of Paris.

The culmination of the work of the Dziga Vertov Group was to have been a film about the Palestinian revolution titled *Jusqu'à la victoire*, and in late 1969 Godard and Gorin had traveled to Lebanon and Jordan to shoot footage of the fedayeen. The project had come to nothing when the Palestinian revolution collapsed in the carnage of the Jordanian civil war of September 1970; when that project was given up the Dziga Vertov Group ceased to exist. It was this footage that Godard and Miéville used to dramatize their debates in the little-seen *Ici et ailleurs* (1974), and it was these debates that informed Godard's *Numéro deux* (1975), which combined film and video to examine the intersection of sex and politics in the home. Further collaborative work followed for French television: *Six fois deux/Sur et sous la communication* (1976), a series of programs on communication, and *France/tour/détour/deux/enfants* (1977–78), an investigation of the world of children. These programs are demanding and challenging and constitute a whole new use of television—they are among the most beautiful of Godard's many essays.

Life 6: *Sauve qui peut (la vie)*: A Postmodern Survival Course

In 1976 Godard's life reached another crisis. His sexual relationship with Miéville came to an end, and the Grenoble experiment was breaking down, as it became clear that it was not viable to run the kind of small studio they had envisaged in a media economy that would not provide resources for such experiments. Miéville was determined to return to Switzerland—she, too, was Swiss—with her child, and Godard decided to accompany her. He thus began what, compared with every previous phase of his life, is a period of prolonged stability. Installed on the banks of Lake Geneva in the surroundings of his childhood, Godard resumed his earlier commuting between Paris and Geneva. After they finished the second of the television commissions, Miéville urged him to return to the cinema and to use what he had learned from their experiments. The first result of this was the film *Sauve qui peut (la vie)* (1979). More frankly autobiographical than his earlier work and shot with a tiny crew, this film returned again to the questions of art, sexuality, and politics that had obsessed him for twenty years. Now, however, the mood was much gentler and the concerns less resolutely contemporary. In this film and the two that followed it, *Passion* (1982) and *Prénom Carmen* (1983), Godard's meditations on traditional culture and religion come to the fore. It is as though we were revisiting the earlier films *sub specie aeternitatis*. If in some ways the mood was gentler, the making of the films was tougher. The smallness of the crews and Godard's determination that every technician should bring his or her whole experience to the film made for very difficult productions.

Godard's solution was to reduce even further the size of the crews, to use even more flexible shooting schedules, and to base the productions even more securely in Rolle. Both *Je vous salue Marie* (1985) and *King Lear* were shot in this fashion. At the beginning of this period, Godard had been involved with Coppola's experiments at Zoetrope, and preliminary scenes for *Passion* were shot on the Zoetrope lot, but Zoetrope's collapse led to the annulment of these plans. In 1985, at Cannes, Menachem Golan, head of Cannon, and Godard roughed out a contract for a filmed version of *King Lear* on a napkin over lunch and signed it at the end of the meal. For a moment it looked as though Godard's dream of a Hollywood movie might finally come to fruition. Two years later, the film Godard brought to Cannes related his failed attempt to make the film—an extravagant Hollywood saga involving Norman Mailer, Faye Dunaway, and a host of aborted shooting dates—hardly what either Golan or Godard could have anticipated at the original lunch.

Life 7: Solitude

It is too soon to say whether Godard's life since *King Lear* is a new chapter in his life or merely an intensification of the options he has pursued since 1979. He has given up trying to run a production company from a tiny Swiss village, and functions as a jobbing director. He continues to work across an impressive variety of genres and media, from features and corporate work to experimental videos. The crews have become ever more minimal and the images simpler—what has become more and more complex is the editing, particularly the construction of meticulously layered sound tracks. The films of this period, *Soigne ta droite* (1987) and *Nouvelle Vague* (1990), require multiple viewings. They defy conventional analysis as their narratives become more and more impoverished, and the relation between sound and image richer and rich-

er. What is striking about these films is that they seem to hesitate between merely indulgent obsession and an even more intense investigation of the workings of the image that has obsessed Godard for forty years now.

Walter Benjamin, in talking to Theodor Adorno about his Arcades project on nineteenth-century Paris, said that each idea had to be wrested away from a realm in which madness reigns, a realm in which the distinction between the nonsensically individual and the significantly collective disappears. It is this realm that Godard is currently exploring, and his masterpiece of this period is his *Histoire(s) du cinéma* (1989–), which has absorbed the greater part of his resources over the last five years. He has so far completed two of a projected eight episodes.

These episodes reject the conventional distinctions between fiction and documentary, indeed, between history and representation. What Godard is producing is a history of the cinema that is also a history of the twentieth century, an account of the development of the image that is both intensely personal and steadily objective. Crossing over from documentary to fiction, these themes erupt into *Allemagne année 90 neuf zéro* (1991), as Eddie Constantine reruns *Alphaville* through the Stalinist cityscapes of East Germany, and Godard reflects on the end of an idea that coincides with the waning of his own life. If the emphasis of these latest works is on an ever more intense solitude, it is still the image that continues to hold out the hope of an ever more necessary, though ever more difficult, communication.

NOUVELLE VAGUE

1990
Alain Delon

THE DECLENSION[1]

JEAN-LOUIS LEUTRAT

Poetry, speech, and thought are but one name beneath the apparent duality of the words. But if we need two names, several names, in order to name what is accomplished singly in research, it is because the only center this has is a unity without unity.

—Maurice Blanchot[2]

There exists a machine-type Godard apparatus. This apparatus, however, has been continually modified and diversified, especially in relation to the partners associated personally with Jean-Luc Godard, and to all kinds of issues. The history of this apparatus consists of connections, disjunctions, different rhythms. We can give an abbreviated description of it in the following pages. In his first phase, Godard devoted himself, within a family (that of the Paris cinema fans, who got together at the Cinémathèque in the rue de Messine, and who later formed the team of the yellow-covered *Cahiers du Cinéma*), to all sorts of writing projects: articles, make-believe interviews, scripts, editing, production of shorts, and so on. This start-up lasted nine years, from 1950 to 1958. It was followed by the fireworks of the sixties, produced in collusion with a group of associates, including Raoul Coutard, Agnès Guillemot, Michel Legrand, Anna Karina, and others. This second period extended from 1959 to 1966. The mechanism jammed in 1967, between *Week-end* and *La Chinoise*, over a play on words, between "a film being made" and "a film found in the scrap heap."[3] After this, from 1968 to 1972, Godard started traveling and working with partners of many different nationalities: Britons, Americans, Italians, Germans, and others. He attempted an experiment in which the notion of author would blur. Then, from 1974 to 1979, he worked in pairs (especially with Anne-Marie Miéville), set up Sonimage, and began his shuttle between cinema and video—*Sauve qui peut (la vie)* (1979). In his sixth period, Godard wanted to be one against all, and made a film, *Passion* (1982), that was to be continually disseminated in other works. After 1984, Godard's aesthetic investment was as great in commissioned video works as in full-length films.

This summary, like any summary, obviously is debatable at every point. In particular, we are well aware that the dates we propose to mark the passage from one period to another are accommodations that we have allowed ourselves; that more rigorous, or different, criteria would result in a different breakdown; and that the very identity of the periods, their unity and coherence, is an invention after the fact. We must bear all this in mind before trying to relate what we shall henceforth call the first period (1959–1966) to the last (the 1980s). The work of the eighties can only be evaluated in light of everything that preceded it, even though all the periods are related by atemporal coexistence, as well as by chronological succession.

Relating the first and last periods is a discursive act that Godard himself helped make possible when he designated *Sauve qui peut (la vie)* as the first work of a new period. Certainly, this film could appear in its author's eyes as a second beginning, and we can draw more than one analogy between this period and that of the sixties. The end of Michel Poiccard and the end of Paul Godard are equally interminable. The film within the film in *Le Mépris* (1963) can be considered a prefiguration of the one in *Passion*. The flight of the couple in *Pierrot le fou* (1965) can herald that of another couple, in *Prénom Carmen* (1983). There are common references from one era to the other, and the distances can be measured for each of them. Passages from *Bérénice* are spoken in *Une Femme mariée* (1964) and in *Soigne ta droite* (1987), but Racine's play is already mentioned in an article of December 1958.[4] Another article, of February 1959, quotes the end of Giraudoux's *Electre*, which reappears in *Prénom Carmen*. There is an allusion to *Aucassin et Nicolette* in *Pierrot le fou* and in connection with *Nouvelle Vague* (1990); the chantefable is mentioned as early as April 1959 in connection with Douglas Sirk's film *A Time to Love and a Time to Die*. Shakespeare, Queneau, Beethoven, and Picasso are references in both periods. *Le Dernier Mot* (1988) reprises the example of Vaugelas ("I'm going or I'm off, for the pair of them is, or are, French . . . and is said, or are said"), spoken by Emile Récamier to his wife in *Une Femme est une femme* (1961), in response to her question "Why is it women who suffer?" He replies, "Because it is they who cause suffering, or they are the ones, for the pair of them is, or are, French, and is said or are said." More generally, Godard's taste for elaborate, dislocated credits, for dedications, and for the colors blue, white, and red; his work on the signs of modern life; the search for what is discontinuous and fragmentary are all constants that serve to bridge time, allowing identical interests and thematic clusters to be established—in a word, allowing an authorial identity to emerge. But it is easy to imagine that what is discontinuous and what is fragmentary, for instance, serve somewhat different ends in each of the periods under discussion. Godard suggests other directions for research as well when, in March 1985, he considers that *Sauve qui peut (la vie)*, *Passion*, *Prénom Carmen*, and *Je vous salue Marie* (1985) "are like four rungs on the same ladder, whereas before 1968 each film was a rung on a different ladder."[5] He distinguishes between two kinds of forward movement in his oeuvre, one, a dispersed order, the other, a more coherent one, and so he invites discussion of how each period develops in itself.

It seems as though we can go from one of the sixties' works to another by a multiplicity of routes. Each film appears to branch off from a number of others that precede it, while functioning itself as an intersection for others. Thus, *Le Mépris* is "heralded" by *Les Carabiniers* (1963), in that the latter film includes a character named Ulysses, a photograph of Brigitte Bardot, and parodies of *Déjeuner de Bébé* and of *L'Entrée d'un train en gare de la Ciotat*. On the other hand, *Les Carabiniers* (1963) recalls *Vivre sa vie* (1962) in its reference to Brecht and the allusion to Nana (by means of a reproduction of Manet). *Vivre sa vie* is "programmed" by *Le Petit Soldat* (1960) (Dreyer and *Pickpocket* being references common to both these films), just as *Bande à part* (1964) is programmed by *Vivre sa vie* (the visit to the Louvre and the oval portrait are present, "incised" in the final tableau of *Vivre sa vie*). Camille, the name of a character in *Le Mépris*, may refer back to Musset, to the Camilla of *La Carrosse d'or*, or to Paul and Camille from *Les Malheurs de Sophie*. With Musset, a network is formed from *Une Femme est une femme* to *Bande à part* and *Pierrot le fou*, because of these films' references to *On ne badine pas avec l'amour* and *Les Caprices de Marianne*. Another network is set up with the work of Jean Renoir, associating *Une Femme est une femme* and *Les Carabiniers*, and so on. These kinds of crossovers can be multiplied indefinitely. They always occur at points of detail, whether in the direction, editing, or other. In the laundromat scene in *Masculin Féminin* (1966), Jean-Pierre Léaud is framed seated with the circular black opening of a machine behind him on either side of his head—which gives him Mickey Mouse ears. The detail,

if unintended (which would remain to be proved), did not escape Godard, who named the character played by the same actor in Godard's next film, *Made in U.S.A.* (1966), "Little Donald." Clearly, this haphazard and rhizomatic development can only account for some of the way in which the filmmaker's work progressed through time at this stage.

The period begins and ends with pairs of intersecting works: *A bout de souffle* (1960) and *Le Petit Soldat* on the one hand, and *Made in U.S.A.* and *Deux ou Trois Choses que je sais d'elle* (1966) on the other. *A bout de souffle* and *Made in U.S.A.* allude to what Godard calls a narrative of the "Alice in Wonderland" type, that is, deriving from the film-noir genre, with its alternate reality of codes and stereotypes—indeed, there is an explicit reference to Humphrey Bogart in both cases. But the route that leads from *A bout de souffle* to *Made in U.S.A.*, taking in *Bande à part* and *Pierrot le fou* on the way, demonstrates a progressive and ineluctable distancing from the American model. On the other hand, *Le Petit Soldat* is a film in which, Godard claimed, he "wanted to reconnect with the realism that [he] had failed to attain in *A bout de souffle*," and to give up everything he had "in [his] belly" at that point in his existence. *Deux ou Trois Choses* and *Le Petit Soldat* both deal with questions of burning current interest that are close to the filmmaker's heart. Godard wanted to take on the theme of brainwashing; the Algerian war drew him toward that of torture. The structural improvements carried out in the region of Paris enable him to talk about "the woman prostituted like a piece of territory that she sells abroad, whose momentary occupation she accepts."[6] What is more, the relation between the four works is one of chiasmus: from one point of view, *A bout de souffle* and *Deux ou Trois Choses* describe Paris and its suburbs (the center losing itself in the periphery), whereas the other two films (the first and the last to be made with Anna Karina) broach political questions concerning North Africa and France, but from an excentric place (Geneva or Atlantic City). The initial opposition between fiction ("Alice in Wonderland") and documentary becomes more complicated; in fact, the entire period can be considered the complication of these two series, whether within a single film or from one film to another, for example, between *Une Femme est une femme* and *Vivre sa vie*, *Bande à part* and *Une Femme mariée*, and *Pierrot le fou* and *Masculin Féminin*. This perspective organizes one strong series into a predominantly documentary mode (*Vivre sa vie*, *Une Femme mariée*, *Masculin Féminin*), and another into a predominantly fictional mode, with both series indexed to the present. This is admittedly an approximate division; there is a third series, where the present is mixed up with imaginary temporalities: either the future (*Alphaville* [1965]), the past (the overlaying of the story of Ulysses onto that of Paul Javal in *Le Mépris*), or the time of an imaginary kingdom (*Les Carabiniers*). Though in each case the present is transparently disguised, nevertheless, Godard felt the need to use this device. *Made in U.S.A.* partakes in part of this third series, which encourages us to think that the questions at issue in the fiction-documentary mix were changing. *La Chinoise*, a film from the documentary series, and *Week-end*, a film from the fictional series, both prefigure, in equal degrees, the near future and the advent of a new problem: how to make political films politically. Thus, in this period, three series are displaced and modified in parallel fashion around an interlacing of common themes: love, betrayal, torture, prostitution, cinema, industrial society, among others.

This type of development, characterized both by rhizomatic expansion and by an intentional resonance between series, is entirely different from that of the eighties. In the latter period, everything seemed to indicate that one work, and one work alone, exercised a seminal function. Concerning *Passion*, we can cite Eugène Fromentin's line, which comes in this film behind the images of the re-creation of *The Night Watch*: "It is a composition full of holes, of badly occupied spaces," or what is said (also in this film) about light: "It goes nowhere, it comes from nowhere." These lines recall Roland Barthes's supplement to *The Pleasure of the Text*:

If the book is not conceived of as the arguing through of an idea or the exposition of a destiny, if it refuses to investigate itself, to anchor itself outside the signifier, it must be perpetual: no full stop to the text, no last word. And what is infinite in that book is not only its end; at every point the supplement is possible: something new can always grow later on in the interstices of the fabric, of the text. The book has holes, and therein lies its productivity . . . ; it is not going somewhere, it is going away, it never stops going away.[7]

Passion would thus be a centerless text, in a state of expansion by "supplementarity."

We can observe how *Passion* continually "goes away," both upstream and downstream. "For *Passion* I had wanted to do something on Beethoven and Rubens, and that didn't happen. An idea remained for a future film: to make a film on the Ninth Symphony, and then I came back to an earlier idea, about a quartet." This was to be *Prénom Carmen*, and it is easy to see that what distinguishes the incomplete projects of the first period from those of the eighties is precisely their incompleteness. *Pour Lucrèce*, *Ubu*, and *Eva* were never produced; at best, we can pick up traces here and there (the adaptation of *William Wilson* with Sami Frey is reabsorbed into a "story" recounted by Pierrot-Ferdinand in *Pierrot le fou*). On the other hand, the project on psychoanalysis, "Freud and Dora" ("A young girl has problems, until the moment the treatment, or its possibility, is discovered, and until the moment her relationship to the father's name is discovered, or just to his name, because I have my doubts about the father"), was simply displaced to give *Je vous salue Marie*.

Prénom Carmen develops, in its way, the singular substantive—without a determinative—that makes up the title *Passion*, and the idea of the first name [*prénom*] that precedes the [family] name. *Je vous salue Marie* also develops *Passion*. And isn't the plane that takes off at the end of *Scénario du film Passion* (1982) the trace of another trace at the start of *Passion*? There is an annunciatory plane in *Je vous salue Marie*—a film that also borrows from Françoise Dolto's book *L'Evangile au risque de la psychanalyse*. *Grandeur et décadence d'un petit commerce de cinéma* (1986) reprises a line from *L'Histoire de l'art* by Elie Faure in *Passion*: "What plunges into the light is the reverberation of what the night submerges; what the night submerges extends into the invisible what plunges into the light." We can find supplements to *Passion* because the film itself is only a supplement. The title *Sauve qui peut (la vie)* no doubt derives "from the desire to call the film 'life,' too, or to call it 'joy' or to call it 'the sky,' 'passion,' or something like that. . . . To give it a double title was also to suggest a third title, yet to be born. . . ."

In *Grandeur et décadence*, the commentaries on pictures are so many supplements to *Passion*. The Bacchus theme was present in the re-creations that the film showed: "The day I wanted to re-create a Titian bacchanalia with young people dancing naked, the camera fell off its crane, like a bad omen, and the set designer left." Tintoretto's *Ariadne and Bacchus* is in *Scénario du film Passion*: "I was talking to them about Tintoretto, about a love scene in the film, and the only idea I had about this love scene was, actually, it was Tintoretto's, that it would have something to do with the three characters in the film, a guy and two women. But while I was showing it to them, they were already seeing the final image. . . ." The same painting, a little later in the same film (through a superimposition), serves to demonstrate the similarity between the gestures of work and those of love: "The Holy Trinity, those three, mightn't there be, in the film, something to do with the Holy Trinity, with love, work, and something between the two? . . ." In connection with the same painting, in *Grandeur et décadence*, Jean-Pierre Léaud asks the question "How many characters are there in this painting?" The correct answer is two (Bacchus and

Ariadne), not three! Similarly, in *L'Origine de la voie lactée*, there is just one character, the Origin, there has never been more than just one character. The questions in *Passion* and *Scénario du film Passion* really address the origin of the film, in fact, of works of art generally. The philosophical reference is certainly more Heidegger than Merleau-Ponty.

Even in this summary form, these descriptions of different modes of deployment imply not only that something was displaced in Godard's work, but also that what appears identical from one film to another, and is taken to be the mark of the Godardian style, the art of his discontinuities, necessarily underwent a modification, so that the component forces became somewhat different.

In the first period, discontinuity seemed to be paraded for its own sake, as the hallmark of a cinema of modernity anxious to break away from the idea of totality (the word "total" appears frequently, whether as the well-known brand of gasoline, which hoists the tricolor—blue, white, and red—or whether adverbially, as in the formula "I love you totally"; but to say "total" in the latter case is tantamount to lying). This continuity is explicit, for instance, in the subtitle of *Une Femme mariée*, *Fragments d'un film tourné en 1964*, and in the division of *Masculin Féminin* into fifteen specific events. Barthélemy Amengual's remarks on this notion of the fragment in Godard, though no longer new, are still cogent: like the pop artists, Godard assembles everything he finds in our world that seems to him apt for creating some jarring and accusatory encounters. It is true that he does not confine himself to just the debris, he is equally capable of taking on works of art or of the mind, but first he turns them into debris: fragments that are badly read, badly spoken, botched, wrecked; corners of images; reproductions of reproductions.[8] In *Bande à part*, there is a reference to Raymond Queneau's novel *Odile*; in fact, a passage from the novel is read out loud by Franz, book in hand: the story of M. Delouit, told by Anglarès. In reality, the character in the novel whose name is Anglarès never does give this absurd little narrative, which is taken from *Nadja*. But Queneau, through the figure of Anglarès, is settling his accounts with Breton. We could see in this no more than simply a knowing wink, but when the narrator says, "Beneath skies of crystal Arthur, Odile, and Franz crossed bridges suspended over motionless rivers. Nothing moved yet on the palaces' fronts. The water was stagnant. A taste of ashes flew in the air," the spectator recognizes a montage of four of Rimbaud's texts: *Les Ponts*, *Le Bateau ivre*, *Aube*, and *Phrases*.

Similarly, there is a scene in *Alphaville* where Natacha and Lemmy Caution are in a hotel room waiting for the police to arrive. A poem is spoken that is supposed to come from *Capitale de la douleur* (here, too, the book is in the characters' hands): "Your voice, your eyes, your hands, your lips, the silence, our words, the vanishing light, the returning light, . . ." This text is made up of some fifteen fragments borrowed from the following slim volumes: *Le Dur Désir de durer*, *Le Temps déborde*, *Corps mémorable*, and *Le Phénix*. The title, *Capitale de la douleur*, is just one more fragment. Rather than being subsumed under a single figure, each quotation refers to a subject that isn't one, that is dispersed, burst open, scattered. The boundary between text and what is outside the text becomes porous. The inside and the outside become confused; both the text and what is outside the text are smashed, fragmented. For instance, in his first period, the filmmaker surrounded the openings of his films with various declarations and texts, promotional and otherwise (a record album of *Une Femme est une femme*, a handout listing the actor/characters of *Bande à part*, *Feu sur "Les Carabiniers,"* and others), as well as his trailers. These texts form part of the work, even though they are materially dissociated. What Roland Barthes says of Schumann's art could be said of Godard's oeuvre: "Ultimately, there are only intermezzi: what interrupts is interrupted in its turn, then it starts over again."[9] Jean-Luc Godard's cinema is exactly that. *Le Petit Soldat* was made to compensate for a disappointment. Godard saw *Une Femme est une femme* as his "first real film," and he said of *Vivre sa vie*, "That was the equilibrium that makes you feel suddenly good in your life, for an hour, or a day, or a week." When lacks are filled with plenitudes that are then instantly dissolved, the fault line can only grow wider or be kept gaping open. Especially when every film's characters are continually recounting stories, multiplying the ruptures, bits, and digressions. The sensory-motor schema, the basis of the image-action, is broken, the continuity of meaning is subverted, spatial and temporal coordinates are altered, the logical chains are unlinked.

In the eighties, the Godardian text was just as broken, but we perceive in it more of "the link that Dante called *legame musaico*, implying both *mosaical* and *musical*," a link that Roger Dragonetti connects to the notion of *generality* (rather than totality), "the signifying power that opens the particular up to multiple symbolizations, kept together by a rhythm whose reality remains out of reach."[10]

We also see the History of the Cinema enter the picture in the eighties, and History *tout court*, as a revenant coming from beneath, a sub-venant. We might say that

Godard's relation to History in the sixties is of an "existential" type, in the sense that a film like *Le Petit Soldat* is based on a conception of the subject that makes the "I" the locus of its meaning (whence the need for the first person in this work). Going beyond the Maoist positions of the seventies, a video film like *Le Dernier Mot* clearly demonstrates the gap between the two periods. First, it is not about present history; in a way, this is even Godard's first costume film (with the exception of some sections of *Week-end* and *Vent d'est* [1969]). Second, in this film, the particular is caught in a general movement that effectively opens it up to "multiple symbolizations," drawing it into a flow where the power of the diverse is expressed. Thus, the fox the woman asks for is a fur, but it fits with the animal emblems of the film (the hen, the piglet) and it belongs to the Godardian language: "The family is a spirit, a fox spirit." Even when they haven't seen one another for a long time, members of the same family recognize each other, like foxes. This explains why the member of the Resistance rejects it when the woman places the fox on him: he and she don't resemble each other, they aren't from the same family. The whole film is built of disjunctive syntheses condensed by a double series of superimpositions (one joining the German officer and the woman, the other the member of the Resistance and the Visitor), or by the facts that the Bach partitas are played by a Frenchman, and that a German spells out names that represent French culture (Apollinaire, Corot, Nerval . . .). This has to do both with Godard's personal history (his father, the collaboration, the house among the trees by the river, the joining "hyphen" . . .), and with that of Valentin Feldman and the characters with generic names (the Visitor, the Voice . . .)—family affairs. The conjunction–disjunction system that controlled the progression of the works from the first period has become internal to the films themselves. It is History that made this possible.

History is what enables us to grasp Godard as an individual caught within a constellation where the discovery of the concentration camps collides with the assumption of desirable bodies onto celluloid. In a way, the *Histoire(s) du cinéma* (1989–) are an expansion of *Passion*. A theater of memory, this film contains traces not only of Eisenstein, John Ford, and Bresson, but also of all Godard's previous films, those of the first period (among other instances: the traveling shot of the sun through the trees, recalling a citation from Fritz Lang in *À bout de souffle*; the sounds of cars honking offscreen, as in the scene of buying the Maserati in *Les Carabiniers*; the light now lit, now out, as in *Le Mépris* or *Alphaville*) and those of the "political" period (the scene of the union meeting with the sound out of synch). There is no

such recapitulating work in the first period. The advertisement for *Pierrot le fou* ("*Pierrot le fou* is: a little soldier [*petit soldat*] who finds out with contempt [*mépris*] that you have to live your life [*vivre sa vie*], that a woman is a woman [*une femme est une femme*], and that in a new world, you have to keep to yourself [*faire bande à part*] to not find yourself out of breath [*à bout de souffle*]") takes the form of an inventory, but what it is, is a simple end-to-end, another instance of collage, neither mosaic nor musical. More: the whole in which History is caught extends to the formation of the planets. In *Puissance de la parole* (1988) and *Histoire(s) du cinéma*, Godard seemed to have reached a veritable atomism. We have gone from the fireworks of the first period (figured in *Pierrot le fou* and spoken, through "July 14th," in the credits of *Une Femme est une femme*) and one of the wonders of the world, the fountain of Geneva, to volcanic eruptions and tumultuous floods. A continuity of spurting seems to correspond to the atomic discontinuity. This recalls Proust's description of "Hubert Robert's famous fountain": from a distance,

one had the impression of art rather than the sensation of water. . . . But from a closer view one realised that . . . it was a constantly changing stream of water that, springing upwards and seeking to obey the architect's original orders, performed them to the letter only by seeming to infringe them, its thousand separate bursts succeeding only from afar in giving the impression of a single thrust. . . . From a little nearer, one saw that this continuity, apparently complete, was assured, at every point in the ascent of the jet where it must otherwise have been broken, by the entering into line, by the lateral incorporation of a parallel jet which mounted higher than the first and was itself, at a greater altitude, which was however already a strain upon its endurance, relieved by a third. From close to, exhausted drops could be seen falling back from the column of water, passing their sisters on the way up, and at times, torn and scattered, caught in an eddy of the night air, disturbed by this unremitting surge, floating awhile before being drowned in the basin.[11]

Godard tries to render both the view from a distance and the view close up, both the "unremitting surge" and the infinite multiplicity of the drops, like that of atoms. The Godardian leitmotiv of the eighties, "On earth as it is in heaven," evokes somewhat André Comte-Sponville's materialist program, to raise oneself up to the sky. *Histoire(s) du cinéma* and *Puissance de la parole* were produced with strangely identical procedures: telescopings and bombardments of visual and aural atoms, accelerations of particles, phenomena of reverberation and superimposition, some of which techniques are reminiscent of Lucretius or Epicurus.

Le Petit Soldat begins with the phrase "The time for action is past, that of reflection is beginning," which could be translated as: the time of action cinema is past, that of the cinema of reflection is on its way. That profession of faith could cover Godard's entire future oeuvre. The filmmaker's earliest characters observed that one never coincides with oneself, that between our appearance and what we think, between the outside (the exteriority) and the inside, there is a break. Patricia says to Michel Poiccard (M.P., as in Monogram Pictures) in *A bout de souffle*, "You don't know what I'm thinking about. I would like to know what's behind your face. I've been looking at it for ten minutes and I know nothing, nothing, nothing." The question is the same in *Le Petit Soldat*—"There, now, what are you thinking about?"—but the way it is photographed reveals an analogy with the developing process. It was photographic work that showed up the face of Christ on Veronica's veil, and it is to Veronika Dreyer that Bruno Forestier declares, "I have such sensitive film, it's Agfa Record, that when you photograph a face, look at me, you photograph the soul behind it." One has to rely on a technique to get a response; alone, face-to-face with others or with yourself, you no longer know anything: "It's funny, when I look at my face straight on, I feel as if it doesn't correspond to the idea I have of it from the inside. Which is more important in your opinion: the interior or the exterior?" This inside/outside dichotomy has always run through Godard's oeuvre, though expressed in various ways. It can be through wordplay, for instance: to imprint an expression or express an impression. The division into tableaux in *Vivre sa vie* "corresponds to the exterior side of things, which was supposed to enable me to convey the feeling of the inside better, as opposed to *Pickpocket*, which is seen from the inside. How can one render the inside? Well, precisely by remaining respectably outside."

In this connection, we may glance at the leap from *Le Petit Soldat* to *Deux ou Trois Choses que je sais d'elle*. In the former film, there is a long scene in which Bruno Forestier literally turns all the way around in front of Veronika Dreyer, who, in turn, after a moment, moves around, while keeping her distance. The young man either addresses the person facing him, or he breaks into an interior monologue (at which time, particular details of Veronika Dreyer's clothing change and place her temporally out of synch, even though she does not move spatially). Bruno Forestier's trajectory, made up of comings and goings, is clearly intended to render tangible such idiomatic expressions as *"cerner sa pensée"* ["comprehend a thought"], or *"il est cerné* ["he's on the spot"]. This gestural deployment attempts to reconstruct thought, and Godard's phrase concerning *Vivre sa vie*—"I wanted to try to film a thought in progress"—seems completely appropriate. Bruno Forestier is in front of the mirror, then facing the camera, making a gesture with his two hands curving

inward to describe his idea of himself and the image of him the mirror gives back; finally he traces a circular shape that summarizes the whole passage. There is no similar scene in *Deux ou Trois Choses*, because Godard was no longer seeking to film a character's thought. In *Made in U.S.A.* and *Deux ou Trois Choses*, Godard approached the same questions: what is a bar? how can we describe such a place? what objects make it up?, but also: what is the point of the words we use? do they give an exact account of our thoughts? The first angled shot in the café scene in *Deux ou Trois Choses* reveals a four-term structure, made up of Juliette, the man, the woman, and, in the mirror, the woman's reflection. This structure describes a rhombus that also turns up in the woman's earrings. From this set, the object as the "mediator" that enables the exchange is inferred, as are the double gaze upon this object, which "subjectivizes" it, and, inversely, the gaze upon the subject, which transforms the latter into an object (especially the woman, who is an object for the man). Paradoxically, it is by means of this alienating structure that a minimal solidarity (*"mon semblable, mon frère"*) comes to light, even though Bruno Forestier does not admit to being anyone's brother.

From that time on, Godard filmed thought by establishing relationships between, on the one hand, various elements of a set and, on the other hand, the text and images that go with it. The text is not spoken by a character, but by a voice (Godard's) with a special status. We are now inside what Gilles Deleuze defined as the Between method, "which conjures all cinema from the One": between two actions, two mental states, two perceptions, two visual images, two sound images, between the acoustic and the visual; to show the indiscernible, that is, the boundary (*Six fois deux/Sur et sous la communication* [1976]). The whole undergoes a mutation, because it has ceased to be the One-Being, to become instead the "and" that constitutes things, the between-two that constitutes the images. The whole is then inseparable from what Blanchot calls the force of "dispersal of the Outside" or "the vertigo of spacing": this void that is no longer a driving part of the image, and that the latter would have to cross in order to continue, but that is the radical questioning of the image.[12] The eighties brought this method, which was born at the end of the sixties, to a point of incandescence. But before we get to the most recent period of Godard's oeuvre, it may be useful to examine his relationship to the one whom the filmmaker could consider committed to investigations that overlapped his own preoccupations—Alain Resnais.

In 1959, Godard asserted that Resnais was "the second *monteur* in the world, after Eisenstein. For them, using montage means organizing cinematographically, in other words, anticipating dramatically, composing musically, or, in yet other words, the most beautiful ones: *mettre en scène*, to stage."[13] The vision of *Le Chant du styrène* led him to say that Resnais "*invented* the modern traveling shot, its racing speed, its abrupt departure and slow arrival, or vice versa." Godard esteemed Resnais very highly: he ranked *Hiroshima mon amour* among the ten best films of 1959, and *Muriel* among the ten best films of 1963. But he confessed to being bothered, in *Hiroshima mon amour* and in *Nuit et brouillard*, by the "horror scenes," which, shown explicitly, make "you automatically outdistanced by his intention." Now, Godard has often spoken of the concentration-camp film that he thinks should be made, from the point of view of the secretaries or the low-level officials whose grind it was to resolve the humble questions of a practical order. He never made this film, but in *Une Femme mariée*, in which the characters see images from *Nuit et brouillard* in the airport cinema, there is a lot about the camps. Moreover, the entire beginning of *Une Femme mariée* can be thought of as a counterpart to the close-ups of the couple in the opening frames of *Hiroshima mon amour*. As for *Muriel*, Godard has said that the movement started by this film is taken up by *Deux ou Trois Choses* (and indicates as much by showing a poster for Resnais's film at the beginning). The fact that Resnais asked Eluard and Queneau to write commentaries on his work, that he made a film on a work by Picasso, that he has always been interested in science fiction and cartoons, are all points in common (and also of divergence) between the two filmmakers. In the course of the seventies, Godard became very severe toward Resnais: "Alain Resnais is stubborn: he always wears the same uniform. He doesn't want to admit to himself that he's no longer got it. . . . Since *Hiroshima mon amour*, he has only gone backward. . . ."

Another state of mind can be discerned in the last period. In the series of lectures he gave in Canada, Godard related *L'Année dernière à Marienbad* to *Alphaville*. *Passion*, as theater of memory, cites *Hiroshima mon amour* in the "I am forgetting you, I am already forgetting you" passage. A phrase of Lubitsch's—"If you can film mountains, can film water and greenness, then you will be able to film people"—is spoken in *Lettre à Freddy Buache* (1981). This line appears in different forms in two articles of 1958, but Godard's most important use of it is in the debate organized by *Cahiers du Cinéma* in its July 1959 issue on *Hiroshima mon amour*; it is used in his argument to say that Resnais's passage from documentaries to full-length feature films did not present a problem: "Cinema is cinema." The fact that he cites this line again upon the emergence of a new form, part

documentary, part essay, is certainly no accident. Another point of convergence with Resnais appears, if we recall that at the time of *Une Femme mariée*, Godard said that there were a number of ways to make films: "like Jean Renoir and Robert Bresson, who make music," or "like Serge Eisenstein, who made paintings," or even "like Alain Resnais, who makes sculpture."[14]

The first important reference to sculpture in Godard's oeuvre is in *Le Mépris*, less in the statues of the gods than in Camille's body. Everyone has remarked how in the scene where her body appears nude at the beginning of the film, the red and blue filters and the "natural" lighting that emphasizes the yellow color approach a three-color mode "quite close to the actual ancient statuary." Godard likens his character to the Eve in Piero della Francesca's painting *Legend of the Cross*; this is probably, in the panel devoted to the death of Adam, the young woman with the impassive face like a kore's. Elie Faure, Godard's guide in matters of art, writes of Piero della Francesca's figures: "Cylindrical torsos, wide shoulders, rounded arms, necks like columns, spherical heads looking straight ahead. They look like walking statues. . . ."[15] The other film from the same period to refer to sculpture is *Une Femme mariée*, which, earlier than *Prénom Carmen*, links Beethoven to sculpture. Godard shows statues by Maillol in *Une Femme mariée* as counterpoints to the images of the body of Charlotte, a fragmented body contrasted with these exuberant women of stone. In *Prénom Carmen*, sculpture, music, and fragmentation are more closely associated: "Studies of pieces of music and pieces of flesh: the body of melody." "For the love scenes, I had asked the crew and actors to go look at Rodin's sculptures. . . . When I was doing the editing and sound mixing myself, I recovered my idea of Rodin: the image of a sculptor working with his hands at a surface he is hollowing out. He hollows out space, and here musicians would probably speak of sound space. I was interested in finding some way to hollow out sound space. . . ."[16] In a talk he gave in Paris on April 26, 1988, to FEMIS,[17] Godard declared, on the subject of editing and mixing: "At that point, there is a set of things that are closer, I don't know, to architecture, or to an art that I have never really understood, and that I am only just beginning to understand, which is sculpture. There are sculptors who start off from the wing of the nose and sculpt everything from there. Michelangelo, apparently, began with the toes, and then did everything else. Others proceed more by successive approaches, that's more what I do." At that point, Godard rediscovered Resnais, was perhaps only just beginning to understand him. Like Resnais in *L'Amour à mort*, but differently, Godard sculpted with light and shadow and music, and it was in the interstices between seeing and hearing that thought would happen.

Bruno Forestier says of Veronika Dreyer that her eyes are *cernés*, that they have circles under them, that she has Velázquez-gray eyes. Godard's project in the sixties, from *Le Petit Soldat* on, was to do the portrait of the woman he loves. To this project, which he states in a scene from *Vivre sa vie*, he devoted seven films. From the first, Anna Karina was associated with mirrors, and thus with Picasso's *Girl Before a Mirror* (1932) (as in *Pierrot le fou*). It is the mirror's task to say a number of things concerning the woman. If it is invisible, then it is the dissociation between the actress and her character. At the beginning of *Le Mépris*, Camille lists the parts of her body that she asks her husband to look at in a mirror placed offscreen. Where the spectator sees the body of Brigitte Bardot, Paul Javal sees that of the woman he loves, in a forbidden space. The scene of the oval portrait in *Vivre sa vie* offers a complementary apparatus. Godard's voice (supposedly that of the character called "The Young Man") speaks Edgar Allan Poe's text, and present as an image is Nana's face, supposedly reflected in a mirror off camera. The image, as invisible as Godard's body, would be that of Anna Karina. In 1966, the filmmaker said, "The only film I really want to make I will never make, because it is impossible. It is a film on love, or about love, or with love. To speak in the mouth, to touch the breast, for women, to imagine and see the man's body, his sex, to caress a shoulder, things as difficult to show and hear as horror, and war, and illness. I don't understand why, and it makes me suffer."[18]

Passion, of course, also takes up again the idea of the filmmaker doing the portrait of the woman he loves, in the scene where Jerzy and Hanna are looking at the video images that the former has made of the latter. The idea that individual and collective (hi)stories repeat themselves is present in various ways in *Puissance de la parole*, in particular by the superimposition of a couple of angels over the earthly couple (Velma and Frank), or by Mlle Oïnos's repeated demand, "Explain to me, or explain yourself." How can we fail to see in the angel Agathos a melancholic Godard explaining himself to a young woman as "the most turbulent and unhallowed of hearts," when years before he recommended Ramuz's *Jean-Luc persécuté* to Pierre Braunberger? How can we fail to perceive this melancholy through the voice of Leonard Cohen, or in that of the narrator of *Histoire(s) du cinéma*? There is a section of this film that is moving because of the gag in it: Godard shows a fragment of *Bande à part*, a close-up of Anna Karina reciting a poem by Aragon: "*Le malheur au malheur ressemble* ["Sorrow resembles sorrow"]. . . ."

In superimposed images, Godard's face bends toward the hand of a Tex Avery pinup to kiss it and murmur: "Farewell, my lovely." This is followed by Godard's voice saying, "Bonjour tristesse"; a line spoken off-screen is transcribed onto the last frame of Max Ophuls's film *Le Plaisir*, "Happiness is no laughing matter." We see that the tone of melancholy submerges everything at this point. The precise echo of the reference to Anna Karina, in *Puissance de la parole*, is the moment when Agathos and Mlle Oïnos are filmed at a great distance under tall trees, exactly like Marianne and Pierrot in the "line of my hip" sequence of *Pierrot le fou*. What we hear on the soundtrack is the second movement ("Absence") of Beethoven's sonata *The Farewells*, opus 81a. *Histoire(s) du cinéma* and *Puissance de la parole* are definitely two works that resonate with each other. We must listen to Agathos's last words: "This wild star . . . with clasped hands, and with streaming eyes, at the feet of my beloved—I spoke it—with a few passionate sentences—into birth. Its brilliant flowers *are* the dearest of all unfulfilled dreams, and its raging volcanoes *are* the passions of the most turbulent and unhallowed of hearts!"[19] "At the feet of my beloved" is said four times—might the "wild star" pointed out by Agathos not be the very oeuvre that Godard has "spoken into birth"?

From the beginning, Godard has worked within cinema's very flesh, incorporating the images of others with his own; today, he incorporates his own with those of others. The result is this art of superimposing two and three images on top of each other so as to make just one: there is urgency, a hasty and feverish piling up, for History could certainly end, the unspooling of the film on the editing table rollers (an image that belongs to both films) come to a halt. Nothing would then be left but the image and voice of an angel, surrounded by the signs of abandonment, the sphere, the stone, the black sun, and dreaming of the bright bloom of flowers, the incandescence of lava and the tumult of churning water, like matter fusing.

Godard began by letting his voice be heard and showing his writing. His appearances onscreen in his films of the sixties were always brief, whereas in the eighties they were numerous and extended. Like the great comic actors, like Buster Keaton and Jerry Lewis, for whom his admiration remains devoted and steadfast, he will have given his body to cinema—as one gives one's body to science.

Postscript—Some months later
    Did titling a film *Nouvelle Vague* in 1990 mean that everything was starting over again? Godard suggests

this: "For me, the film was a sort of return."[20] As usual, there are numerous allusions to the past in this, his most recent work. The *Naked Maja* is unveiled in the airport scene. She is supposed to be coming from Lebanon, exchanged in some way for "the disasters of war." In *Passion*, the tableau vivant in the style of Goya is side by side with the one of the executed, in "The Third of May." The woman with the parasol is replaced in *Nouvelle Vague* by a man with a little dog. So *Passion* returns through a series of small displacements. In the airport garage, the visible colors are still blue, white, and red, grouped as always. Shortly after, we hear the order "Drink your soup!" which in *Passion* is lashed out at the grandfather, whose leitmotiv utterance is "In principle, the poor are always right." In *Nouvelle Vague*, the question is not to lose sight of what differentiates the poor from the rich, or, by a sort of anticipatory vision, regretting the lost difference: "It was a time when there were rich people and poor people, when there were fortresses to capture, ranks to ascend, desirable things well defended enough to preserve their allure." *Passion* returns not only through the manifest gap between the two films, but also by another gap, in *Nouvelle Vague*, between the recent and the distant past. In this film an intertitle bears the title of a poem from *Capitale de la douleur* (already mentioned in *Alphaville*), "Mourir de ne pas mourir"; it takes on a very precise sense within a story of resurrection that alludes metaphorically to the theme of "the death of cinema." *Nouvelle Vague* thus brings about a resonance, by prolonging it, between the eighties series based on themes with religious overtones (among others, *Passion* and *Je vous salue Marie*), and the sixties series (among others, *Vivre sa vie* and *Une Femme est une femme*). Its construction in the form of an apologue may recall that of Pasolini's films. In fact, Pasolini could serve as Godard's echo, depending upon the decade. In 1963, "La Ricotta" (the third episode of *Rogopag*; Godard produced the second) shows a director making a film (a Passion) out of tableaux vivants and still lifes. The penitent thief is asked, like the grandfather in *Passion*, to "say his line." As for the first shots of the sky in *Passion*, how could they fail to recall the last ones in *Che cosa sono le nuvole?* (a film "framed" by Velázquez, from *Las Meninas* to *Venus at the Mirror*) and their commentary: "Oh, searing and magical beauty of creation."

In 1976, Gilles Deleuze began an insightful commentary on the work of Jean-Luc Godard. More than ten years later, *Nouvelle Vague* appeared, an illustration of *Différence et répétition*. The film is divided into two parts, with situations turned inside out like a glove. The title itself becomes *vague nouvelle* ["vague news"] in the credits, and the dialogue insists: "No copy is possible," "Where there's making, there's faking," "Not the same, another," and so on. One wave follows another. A "new" wave necessarily comes in second, and if it follows another "new" wave, it is in at least third place. In his synopsis, Godard refers to the Old and New Testaments—two waves. Along comes a third, which, with Joachim de Flore, we could call a Third Testament. *Nouvelle Vague* is this movement that envelops two others, and that, in deploying them, cancels them out, when "the exchange is exchanged." The synopsis includes the line "And if man has uttered the mystery, woman has revealed the secret." The film alters its terms: "Men organize the mystery and women find the secret." A small difference externally, but a great one internally. The cries of the birds, a leitmotiv of the later works (*King Lear* [1987], *Puissance de la parole*), are present on the sound tracks of *Nouvelle Vague*, but Godard specified that "it's in fact the first of my films in which the voices are not covered by those of the birds." The director did not put his name on the credits and iterates that he is not the one who made this film. Presumably we are meant to understand that this third phase, "this formlessness at the end of time's form," in Gilles Deleuze's words (the film: "Above them, the past, the present, like the single waves of the same ocean"), is that of *l'éternel retour*, the eternal return, which eliminates the same and the similar in order to affirm difference and chance ("Chance was in on it"). All individuation disappears, any "I," any author's name. There remains "one." *Je est un autre* ["I is another"], "Pif, paf, poum, I'm General Boom Boom!" The director's name appears only on the publicity material, as though to emphasize its commercial value.

The arrangement of Godard's and Delon's names at the top of the poster for *Nouvelle Vague* is the same as Godard's and Bardot's in an advertisement for *Le Mépris*. The 1990 film echoes the 1963 film in more ways than one. A man returns, not like Ulysses coming back to Ithaca, but by way of the resurrection of Richard Lennox, who has himself come from nowhere. His suitcase contains two books, *The Long Goodbye* and *Les Evadés des ténèbres*, an anthology of Gothic novels, of ghost stories, stories of revenants. It is a whole montage using intertitles to recall the sonata *The Farewells* and its three movements ("The Farewells," "Absence," and "Return"), as well as a procedure that had already been employed in *Une Femme est une femme*. Under his double appearance, Richard Lennox wears about his neck the ancient Egyptian sign of life, the ankh, which itself makes a Christianized return. The round trip is the principle of travel. This double movement turns up a number of times in *Le Mépris*: at the beginning, on Brigitte Bardot's body; then Francesca and Paul Javal go back up the street in Cinecittà that Francesca had come down during the credits, followed by the camera and the crew; then Prokosch appears, striding up and down the scenic space he has appropriated for himself, and so on. The doubling is multiplied and repeated like the endless back and forth of the sea. Ebb and flow also inform *Nouvelle Vague*, where the same process, rather than arousing a feeling of weariness, brings with it the mystery of a rediscovery, or a reinvention.

At the beginning of *Nouvelle Vague*, there are in the frame a tree trunk in the foreground, then Alain Delon wearing a white T-shirt, and behind him a red truck and a blue car. The lettering on the truck, "Harsh," prepares for the newspaper headline "Cash," the moment when Richard Lennox is playing squash, and the falls into the water, splash! Godard has long enjoyed playing with onomatopoeia. What is specific to this film is the juxtaposition with equal weight of the knotty trunk, grainy and blight-spotted, like a wave-battered rock, and the body of the star running down the road, suitcase in hand, a shooting star destined to fall. "Film stars represent light, or something that is already past and that we have to use in a certain way."[21] The tree makes the difference from *Le Mépris*, a work in which Godard films colors and not things. This time, he is squarely on the side of things, practicing what he preached at the beginning of his career. "Be quiet. Let things be nameless for a moment." Jacques Chardonnay's line is repeated in the film by a philosopher-gardener, as happens in Giraudoux's plays. This also holds for the film itself, which has to be severed, at least momentarily, from any paternity. The reference to the ancient philosophy of atomism (an intertitle bears the famous title *De rerum natura*) means that we can say that *Nouvelle Vague* is, finally, *Pour Lucrèce*! So the periods are made to resonate, but there is memory as well, in the sense of something that has come from beneath the past, of the whole past, like a wave from the depths, enveloping present and future, "a single wave, of which I am the succeeding sea" (Rainer Maria Rilke, *Sonnets to Orpheus*).

Notes

1   The original French title, "La Déclinaison," carries two meanings. The first, from *décliner*, "to decline," is grammatical, and is rendered by its English equivalent: it means the giving of all the endings of a noun, pronoun, adjective, or other inflected part of speech. Thus, the article attempts to enumerate all of the transformations of Godard's oeuvre. At the same time, *déclinaison* renders the *clinamen* of Lucretius, which describes a fall of atoms and a swerve; so, in the author's view, Godard's work in the eighties conjugated spiritualism and materialism.—Ed.

2   Maurice Blanchot, *L'Entretien infini* (Paris: Gallimard, 1969), p. 442, note 1.

3   The French phrases are "un film en train de se faire" and "un film trouvé à la ferraille." The wordplay is between *faire*, "make," and *ferraille*, "scrap heap."—Trans.

4   Jean-Luc Godard intended to do a production of *Bérénice* for television.

5   Alain Bergala, ed., *Jean-Luc Godard par Jean-Luc Godard* (Paris: Cahiers du Cinéma, 1985), p. 19.

6   Jean-Luc Godard, *Introduction à une véritable histoire du cinéma* (Paris: Editions Albatros, 1980), p. 258.

7   Roland Barthes, "Supplément," *Artpress,* no. 4 (May–June 1973).

8   Barthélemy Amengual, "Jean-Luc Godard et la remise en cause de notre civilisation de l'image," *Etudes cinématographiques*, no. 57–61 (1967), p. 165.

9   Roland Barthes, "Rasch," in *L'Obvie et l'obtus* (Paris: Editions du Seuil, 1982), p. 266.

10 Roger Dragonetti, "Les Notes du général dans les *Géorgiques*," in *Sur Claude Simon* (Paris: Editions de Minuit, 1987), p. 97.

11 Marcel Proust, "Cities of the Plain," *Remembrance of Things Past*, vol. 2, trans. C.K. Scott Moncrieff and Terence Kilmartin (New York: Random House, 1981), pp. 680–81.

12 Gilles Deleuze, *L'Image-Temps* (Paris: Editions de Minuit, 1985), p. 235. See also the interview with him in this volume, pp. 35–41.

13 *Godard par Godard*, p. 163.

14 Ibid., p. 254.

15 Elie Faure, *Histoire de l'Art* (Paris: Le Livre de Poche, Fayard, 1976), vol. 3, p. 121.

16 Cited in "Godard à Venise," *Cinématographe,* no. 95 (December 1983), p. 5.

17 The French national film school.

18 *Godard par Godard*, pp. 294–95.

19 *Puissance de la parole*. English text from *Poe: Poetry and Tales,* Patrick F. Quinn, ed. (New York: The Library of America, Literary Classics of the United States, 1984), p. 825.

20 The texts of Jean-Luc Godard concerning *Nouvelle Vague* are taken from the press conference he gave at Cannes, extracts of which were published in *Cahiers du Cinéma*, no. 433 (June 1990), pp. 10–11.

21 Movie stars also represent a possible financial gold mine that you have to know how to use. In *Le Mépris*, as in *Nouvelle Vague*, the exchange of languages is linked back to negotiation and the world of money. Prokosch has a direct relation to images; the financiers in *Nouvelle Vague*, on the other hand, speak of images as of something from which they are distant. Countess Torlano-Favrini's father knew Joseph Mankiewicz, but those days are gone, and the countess lives only in the universe of financial dealings. The film forgoes any interpreters during the polyglot conversations, as well as any ideal figures in the style of Lang (*Le Mépris* plays on Lang and *langue* ["language"]; Paul Javal speaks too much and thinks too much about money, which is the opposite of Fritz Lang).

SIX FOIS DEUX/SUR ET
SOUS LA COMMUNICATION
co-director: Anne-Marie Miéville
1976
"Leçons de choses"

THREE QUESTIONS ABOUT "SIX FOIS DEUX"*

GILLES DELEUZE

I. Cahiers du Cinéma has asked you for an interview because you are a "philosopher," and we would like that kind of a text, but principally because you like and admire what Godard does. What do you think of his recent TV programs?

Like many people, I was moved—and that's a lasting emotion. I can say how I picture Godard. He's a man who works a lot, so he is, necessarily, completely alone. But his is not just any solitude, it's an extraordinarily populous solitude, populated not by dreams, fantasies, or projects, but by actions, things, and even people. A multiple, creative solitude. It's by drawing on the depths of this solitude that Godard can be a force by himself alone, but also work in tandem with several other people. He can deal on equal terms with anyone, from officials or organizations to a cleaning lady, a worker, or madmen and -women. In his TV programs, Godard's questions are always direct. They disturb us, the audience, but not the people to whom he asks them. When he talks to lunatics, he doesn't talk like a psychiatrist, like another lunatic, or like someone acting crazy. When he talks to workers, he's not a boss, or another worker, or an intellectual, or a producer with actors. This isn't at all because he is trying to impersonate artfully every tone, but because his solitude gives him a great capability, a great populatedness. In a certain sense, it's always about being a stammerer. Not a stammerer in his speech, but a stammerer in language itself. Generally, you can only be a foreigner in another language, but here, it's rather a matter of being a foreigner in your own language. Proust said that the great books are necessarily written in a sort of foreign language. It's the same with Godard's programs; he even perfected his Swiss accent for the purpose. It's this creative stammering, this solitude, that gives Godard his force.

As you know better than I, he has always been alone. There's never been a Godard-success in film, in the sense that the people who say, "He changed after this or that moment, his films don't make it anymore" would have us believe. These are often the same people who hated him right from the start. Godard was ahead of everyone, he left his mark on everyone, but not in ways that would have led to success; instead, he continued along his own line, a vanishing trace, a line always broken, zigzagging, subterranean. Even so, in terms of film, they had more or less managed to shut him up in his solitude, contain him. Then he goes and takes advantage of the vacation period and of a vague appeal to creativity to occupy TV for six times two programs. It may be the only case of someone who hasn't been had by TV. Usually you've lost before you've started. They would have forgiven him for finding a slot for his cinema, but not for making this series, which changes so many things within what most affects TV (asking people questions, getting them to talk, showing images from elsewhere, and so on), even if it no longer does any of it, even if it's been stifled. Naturally, many groups and associations were furious: the statement made by the Association des Journalistes, Reporters-Photographes et Cinéastes† is typical. At least Godard has revived hate. But he has also shown that TV could be "populated" another way.

II. You haven't answered our question. If you had to give a "course" on these programs . . . What ideas have you perceived, or felt? How would you go about explaining your enthusiasm? We can always talk about the rest later, even if the rest is the most important part.

Well, but ideas—having an idea—isn't ideology, it's practice. Godard has a beautiful axiom: Not a correct image, just an image [*Pas une image juste, juste une image*]. Philosophers, too, should say it, and find some way to act on it: not correct ideas, just ideas. Because correct ideas are always ideas that conform to dominant meanings or established passwords; they're always ideas that verify something, even if this something is yet to come, even if it is the future of the revolution. Whereas "just ideas" are a becoming-present, a stammering in one's ideas that can only be expressed in the form of questions, which tend rather to silence their answers, or else show something simple, which shatters all the proofs.

In this sense, there are, in Godard's programs, two ideas that are constantly overlapping, mixing, or sepa-

35

Still from the credit
sequence that opens each
episode

"Ya personne"

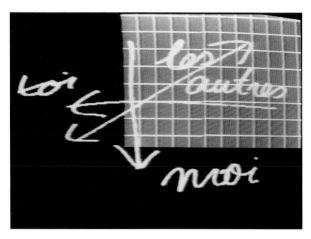

"Nous trois"

rating, segment by segment. This is one of the reasons why each program is divided in two, as in elementary school, the two poles, the lesson about things and the language lesson. The first idea concerns work. I think Godard is always questioning a vaguely Marxist schema that has infiltrated everywhere: you have something fairly abstract, like a "work force," which is sold or bought, under conditions that either define a fundamental social injustice or establish slightly more social justice. Now, Godard asks very concrete questions; he shows images that relate to the following: What is it, in fact, that is bought, and what is sold? What is it that some people are prepared to buy and others to sell, and that is not necessarily the same thing? A young welder is prepared to sell his labor as a welder, but not his sexual force by becoming the lover of an old lady. A cleaning lady is perfectly willing to sell her hours of housework, but doesn't want to sell the moment when she sings a bit of the "Internationale." Why? Because she can't sing? But what if you pay her to talk about precisely what she can't sing? And, inversely, a specialized worker in the watchmaking trade wants to be paid for his watchmaking force, but refuses to be paid for his work as an amateur filmmaker—he calls it his "hobby." The images, however, show that in both cases, the watchmaking assembly line and the filmmaking production, the gestures are strikingly similar, to the point that they could be mistaken for each other. Yet, says the watchmaker, there is a huge difference of love and generosity between these gestures; I don't want to be paid for my filmmaking. But then what about the filmmaker and the photographer, who do get paid? Or, taking it even further, what is a photographer willing to pay for? In some cases he is willing to pay his model, in other cases he is paid by his model. But when he takes pictures of torture or of an execution, he pays neither the victim nor the executioner. And when he takes pictures of children who are sick, injured, or hungry, why doesn't he pay them? Analogously, Guattari proposed at a psychoanalytic convention that those being psychoanalyzed should be paid the same as the psychoanalysts, because the psychoanalyst cannot exactly be said to provide a "service." There is, rather, a division of labor, a development of two types of tasks that are nonparallel: the psychoanalyst's work of listening and sifting, but also the work of the analysand's unconscious. Guattari's proposal seems not to have been taken very seriously. Godard says the same thing: Why not pay the people who watch TV, instead of making them pay, since they are doing real work and providing a public service in their turn? The social division of labor obviously implies that, in a factory, the work on the shop floor is paid, but so is that done in offices and research laboratories. Otherwise, why not imagine the workers having to pay the designers who prepare what the former make? I think all these questions and many others, all these images and many others, tend to destroy the notion of work force. In the first place, the very notion of work force arbitrarily isolates one sector, cuts work off from its relation to love, creation, and even production. It turns work into conservation, the opposite of creation, because it has to reproduce consumer goods, and reproduce its own force, in a closed exchange. From this point of view, it matters little whether the exchange is fair or unfair, since there is always selective violence in an act of payment, and mystification in the very principle that makes us speak of a work force. To the extent that labor could be separated from its pseudo-force, very different, nonparallel flows of production of all sorts could be put into direct relation to flows of money, independently of any mediation by an abstract force.

I am even more confused than Godard. All the better, since what counts are the questions Godard asks and the images he shows, and the viewer's possible feeling that the notion of work force is not innocent, and that it in no way goes without saying, even and especially from the point of view of social criticism. This explains the reactions of the P.C. and of some unions to Godard's programs, as do other, even more visible reasons (he has tampered with the sacred notion of work force . . .). And then there's the second idea, which concerns information. In this case, too, language is presented to us as essentially informative, and information as essentially an exchange. In this case, too, information is measured in abstract units. Now, it's open to question whether the schoolteacher is transmitting pieces of information when she explains a mathematical operation or teaches spelling. She is in charge, so she is, rather, transmitting passwords. In fact, children are provided with syntax in the same way that workers are given tools, to produce statements that conform to the dominant meanings. Godard's phrase must be understood quite literally: children are political prisoners. Language is a system of orders, not a medium of information. On TV: "Now for some fun . . . the latest news, coming up next . . . " Actually, the schema of information science should be reversed. Information science assumes a theoretical maximum of information; at the other pole it posits pure noise, interference; between the two, there is redundancy, which reduces information but enables it to overcome noise. It's the other way around: at the top we should put redundancy, the transmission and repetition of orders or commands; below it, information, always the minimum required for the successful reception of orders; and then below that?? Well, there would be something like silence, like stammering, like a cry, something that would pay out beneath the redundancies and the pieces of information, that would pay out language and make itself heard nonetheless. To speak, even when speaking about oneself, is always to take the place of someone on whose behalf one claims to be speaking, and to whom one refuses the right to speak. Séguy's mouth is open to transmit orders and passwords, but the woman with the dead child is also open-mouthed. An image gets represented by a sound, as a worker is by his shop steward. A sound takes over a series of images. So how does one speak without giving orders, without claiming to represent something or someone, how does one get those who don't have the right to it to speak, and restore to sounds their value of a struggle against power? That must be it: by being like a foreigner in one's own language, marking a sort of vanishing trace of language.

These are "just" two ideas, but two ideas are a lot, are huge, they contain lots of things and lots of other ideas. So Godard questions two accepted notions, that of work force and that of information. He doesn't say we should be giving *true* information, nor that the work force should be *well* paid (these would be "correct" ideas). He says that these notions are very suspect. He writes FALSE next to them. He has been saying for a long time that he wished to be a production office rather than an author, a TV news director rather than a filmmaker. Obviously he didn't mean that he wished to produce his own films, like Verneuil, or to take over TV, but, rather, to make a mosaic of kinds of work, instead of measuring them against an abstract force; rather, to make a juxtaposition of the underlying pieces of information, of all the open mouths, instead of relating them to an abstract kind of information taken as password.

III. If these are Godard's two ideas, do they coincide with the theme of "images and sounds" that is constantly developed in the programs? Does the lesson about things, the images, correspond to kinds of work, and the word lesson, the sounds, to pieces of information?

No, the coincidence is only a partial one: there is also, necessarily, information in the images, and work in the sounds. Random groupings can and must be cut up in a number of ways that only partially coincide. To try to reconstitute the image–sound relation according to Godard, one would have to tell a very abstract story, in several episodes, and realize at the end that this abstract story was simplest and most concrete in a single episode.

1. There are images—things themselves are images—because images are not in the head, in the brain. In fact, the brain itself is one image among oth-

ers. Images continuously act and react on one another, producing and consuming. There is no difference between *images*, *things*, and *movement*.

2. But images also have *insides*, or some images have insides and experience themselves from the inside. These are subjects (cf. Godard's statements about *Deux ou Trois Choses que je sais d'elle* in the collection Belfond published, pp. 393ff.). There is effectively a *gap* between the action undergone by these images and the reaction that is achieved. It is this gap that gives them the power to store other images, in other words, to perceive. But what they store is only what interests them in other images: to perceive is to take away from the image what doesn't interest us; there is always *less* in our perception. We are so full of images that we no longer see outside images as themselves.

3. On the other hand, there are sound-images that appear to be unprivileged. These sound-images, or some of them, do, however, have *reverse sides*, which we can call what we like—ideas, meaning, language, manners of speaking, and so on. These enable the sound-images to contract or capture the other images or a series of other images. A voice takes over a group of images (Hitler's voice). Ideas, acting as passwords, are embodied in the sound-images or soundwaves and tell us what should interest us in the other images: they dictate our perception. There is always a central "collision" that normalizes the images, removes what we must not perceive. What we have in outline, then, thanks to the preceding gap, is, as it were, two currents going in opposite directions: one going from external images to perceptions, the other going from the dominant ideas to perceptions.

4. Thus, we are caught in a chain of images, each in its place, each itself an image, but also part of a web of ideas that act as passwords. So Godard's action, "images and sounds," goes in two directions at once. On the one hand, toward restoring the external images to their fullness, so that we do not perceive less, so that the perception equals the image, so that the images give up everything they have, which is one way, at least, *a* way of fighting this or that power and its collisions. On the other hand, toward undoing language as an assumption of power, making it stammer in the soundwaves, breaking up every set of ideas that claim to be "correct" ideas, so as to extract from them "just" some ideas. These may be two reasons why Godard's use of the *fixed background* is so new. It's a bit like some contemporary musicians: they install a fixed sound background that allows *everything* in the music to be heard. When Godard introduces onto the screen a blackboard on which he writes, he is not making it an object to be filmed, he is making the blackboard and the writing into a new television

"Leçons de choses"

"Jean-Luc"

"Leçons de choses"

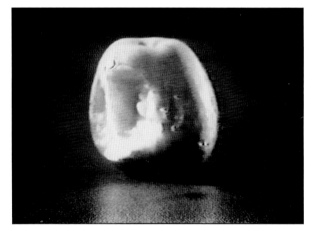

"Leçons de choses" and "René(e)s"

"Marcel"

medium, an expressive substance that has its own current, among other currents on the screen.

This whole abstract story in four episodes has a science-fiction look. It is our social reality today. What is odd is that this story coincides at several points with what Bergson said in the first chapter of *Matter and Memory*. Bergson is considered a sensible philosopher, and one who no longer has novelty value. It would be good if cinema or television gave it back to him (he ought to be in the curriculum at the I.D.H.E.C.[‡]—perhaps he is). The first chapter of *Matter and Memory* develops an extraordinary conception of photography and cinema movement in their relations with things: "Photography, if photography there be, is already taken, already printed in the very inside of things, and for all points in space. . . ." This is not to say that Godard is a Bergsonian. It would, rather, be the reverse, not so much Godard revitalizing Bergson, but Godard finding pieces of Bergson along the way as he revitalizes television.

"René(e)s"

"Louison"

"René(e)s"

IV. But why are there always *two* with Godard? There have to be two for there to be three . . . Fine, but what is the meaning of this two, this three?

You're pretending; nobody knows better than you that it's not like that. Godard is not a dialectician. What counts with him is not two or three, or however many you like, it's AND, the conjunction AND. Godard's use of AND is crucial. It's important because our entire way of thinking is modeled instead on the verb "to be," IS. Philosophy is thick with discussions of the attributive judgement (the sky is blue) and the judgement of existence (God is), their possible reductions, or their irreducibility. But it's always the verb "to be." Even conjunctions are measured by the verb "to be," as we can see clearly in the syllogism. The British and the Americans are practically the only ones to have liberated conjunctions, to have reflected on relations. But when you make the relational judgement into an autonomous type, you realize that it slips in everywhere, penetrates and corrupts everything. The AND is then no longer even a specific conjunction or relation, but implies all relations; there are as many relations as there are ANDs. The AND not only rocks all relations, it rocks being, the verb, and so on. The AND, "and . . . and . . . and . . . ," is exactly the creative stammering, the foreign use of language, as opposed to its conforming and dominant use, based on the verb "to be."

Of course, the AND is diversity, multiplicity, the destruction of identities. The factory gate is not the same when I go in, and then when I come out, and then when I pass by it when I am unemployed. The wife of the condemned man is not the same before and after.

But diversity, or multiplicity, is in no way an aesthetic collection (as when we say "one more," "one more woman" . . .), nor a dialectical schema (as when we say "one gives two, which will give three"). In all these cases there remains a primacy of the One, therefore of being, which is deemed to become multiple. When Godard says that everything can be divided in two, and that day is morning *and* evening, he isn't saying that it's one or the other, nor that one becomes the other, becomes two. For multiplicity is never in the terms, whatever their number, nor in the set, or totality, of them. Multiplicity is precisely in the AND, which does not have the same nature as the elements or the sets.

What is this AND that is neither element nor set? I think it is Godard's force of living and thinking, and of showing the AND in a very new way, and making it operate actively. The AND is neither the one nor the other, it is always between the two, it is the boundary, there is always a boundary, a vanishing trace or flow, only we don't see it, because it is scarcely visible. And yet it is along this vanishing trace that things happen, becomings are made, revolutions are sketched out. "The strong people are not those who occupy one camp or the other; it's the boundary that is powerful." This was Giscard d'Estaing's rueful assessment in the military geography lesson he recently gave the army: the more things find an equilibrium at the level of the large sets—between West and East, the United States–USSR, global agreement, meetings in outer space, world police, and so on—the more they "destabilize" from north to south. Giscard cited Angola, the Near East, the Palestinian resistance, but also all those disturbances that cause "a regional destabilization of security": plane hijackings, Corsica . . . From north to south, you will always find lines that will deflect the sets, an AND, AND, AND that marks a new threshold every time, a new direction of the dotted line, a new mountain pass over the boundary, the border. Godard's aim is "to see the boundaries," in other words, to make the imperceptible visible. The condemned man *and* his wife. Mother *and* child. But also the images *and* the sounds. And the watchmaker's gestures when he is on his watchmaking assembly line *and* when he is at his editing table; they are separated by an imperceptible boundary that is neither the one nor the other, but also draws them both along in a nonparallel development, a trace or flow where we no longer know who is pursuing whom or for what purpose. A whole micropolitics of boundaries, as against the macropolitics of the large groupings. We know at least that that is where things happen, on the boundary between images and sounds, where the images become too full and sounds too loud. This is what Godard has done in *Six fois deux*: six times

between the two, to trace and show this active and creative line, and to drag television along with it.

Notes

* This interview was originally published as "Trois questions sur *Six fois deux*," in *Cahiers du Cinéma*, no. 271 (November 1976).

† Association of Journalists, Photojournalists, and Filmmakers.

‡ The French national film school.

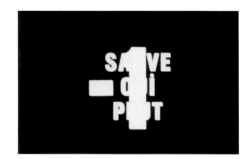

SAUVE QUI PEUT (LA VIE)

1979
Nathalie Baye

SEXUAL DIFFERENCE
AND "SAUVE QUI PEUT (LA VIE)"*

La Passion, c'est pas ça

ELISABETH LYON

The idea of *parole de femme* is one which is new neither to feminism nor to the work of Jean-Luc Godard. Feminists have argued with varying degrees of success for and against the possibilities of a women's language and women's writing, and Godard, in his way, and more recently with the collaboration of Anne-Marie Miéville, has taken up similar issues of women's representation and the representation of women in films such as *Vivre sa vie, Une femme mariée, Deux ou trois choses que je sais d'elle* and *Numéro deux*, among others.

If *Sauve qui peut (la vie)* stands out to us in this context, however, it is because of the way in which the possibility—or here, the impossibility—of sexual relations is figured in the film as explicitly tied to a concept of *parole de femme*, metaphorically as well as in the form of direct citation and appropriation of a figure whose work is as controversial and influential for feminists as Godard's own: Marguerite Duras.

Invoking Duras's work to stand for a *parole de femme*, or the possibility of feminine difference in language, is also to invoke the controversy that surrounds this idea and its relation to her work for feminists. Although the citations from Duras's work may seem in some ways gratuitous, they are embedded in the logic of the film, part of an argument that builds associatively, at times paradoxically, along the two parallel tracks of difference and language which meet in this film in a peculiarly ambivalent notion of *parole de femme*.

In the opening segment of *Sauve qui peut (la vie)*, we see a shot of Denise riding her bicycle in the country. This image and those associated with it—writing at the window-seat in her room in the country, for example—are emblematic of some of the ways in which the film represents difference: here, first in terms of living differently—Denise's decision to leave Paul, the city, her apartment, her work at the television station, in favor of a life in the country; and second, one of the most important aspects of her decision and her new lifestyle—her writing, and perhaps as a woman the possibility of writing differently—this project that is described variously in the course of the film as a novel, or "part of one," and which most probably figures as part of the voice-over narration in the film. There is,

then, at the beginning of the film this idea of difference which is constructed not so much *against* something—men, the city—as it is *for* something else, an attempt to live differently (*vivre autrement*).

The images of the women together—Isabelle and Denise in the car talking, for example, and even the scene of Isabelle-as-pimp, setting up her sister as a prostitute—can also be seen in the context of an attempt on the part of the women in the film to live differently (in economic terms, at least). If there is a logic of difference in the film, it is built across the images of the women, alone or together, and part of this logic of difference in these images comes from the contrast between the kind of interaction that takes place between the women and the aggressiveness of the interaction between the character of Paul Godard (or any of the other men in the film, Monsieur Personne, for example) and any of the women characters.

But it is in relation to language that the aggression between the men and women characters is often expressed, not only in what they say to or about one another, but insofar as what they say often implies (associatively or directly) as much ambivalence towards language as towards the person addressed: Paul condemns Denise's desire to live in the country, and in the same breath his daughter Cécile's passion for soccer, as "just words" ("*la passion, c'est pas ça*": repeated three times in the film, Paul Godard to Denise, Denise to Michel, the printer, M. Personne to Isabelle, reflecting a fundamental—and pervasive—lack of agreement as to the nature of desire). Similarly, in a scene where Denise and Paul are standing at a bar in a cafe, Denise tells an anecdote about a calf she saw that had a hole in its back where everything it ate came out. Paul responds that people are the same way—they have a hole where words come out.

But this kind of general mistrust of language—particularly as it is expressed around Denise's desire to leave—finds perhaps its most dense and suggestive moment in the episode of Marguerite Duras's "visit." The scene occurs immediately after Paul picks up Cécile at the soccer field and begins with Cécile and Paul in the car where we hear Duras's voice in a fragment from *Le Camion*. During the scene in the class-room, after Duras refuses to appear, Paul says a few words in her place, repeating the now familiar citation where she describes the motivation for her filmmaking activity as the attempt to occupy her time, not having the strength to do nothing. Then in a curious appropriation, he tells the students that her statement is true for him as well and, adding a reference to *Le Camion*, that each time a truck passes they should think it is a *parole de femme*.

It is around these issues of the representation of women's desire at stake in the Duras episode that language later becomes a vehicle (quite literally) for aggression—first, in the form of a violent argument between Paul and Denise, who had been waiting for Duras to show up at the television station for a program she was preparing. Paul arrives without Duras, telling Denise that Duras has decided to take an early plane. In the ensuing argument (witnessed by Cécile sitting in the car) Denise accuses Paul of always wanting to think for her, an accusation which turns Godard/*Godard*'s idealized appropriation of women's desire (Duras and the idea of *parole de femme*) into subsequent aggression against the actual possibility of difference in this fiction; here, in the form of Denise and her work. The consequence of Paul's mistrust, his contempt for Denise's desire ("just words"), means that the only way difference can exist for him, for this film, is in its absence, elsewhere, idealized, then taken up and made to speak for him. For Paul, women's desire (*la parole de femme*) is *Le Camion*; for Denise it is her bicycle. *La passion, c'est pas ça.*

The Duras episode is only one example of how the film argues through a logic of associations, coupling an idealized representation of difference with aggression against that difference, an ambivalence which comes out, among other ways, in the form of linguistic and visual puns. For example, during the scene where Isabelle acts as her sister's pimp, telling her how to get into prostitution, we see images of a red truck accompanied by their voice-over discussion of the terms of their business arrangement. The association of sound and image makes a visual play on words between one idea of commerce—trucking—and another—sex (in fact this section of the film is entitled "Le Commerce"). But also, on another level, remembering the scene where Paul instructs the class on the relation between a *parole de femme* and a truck, this particular image of a truck seems to represent the deeper ambivalences of the film, seeming at once self-parodic on the part of Godard and an aggression against the idealized image of women's desire that *Le Camion* has come to represent here. Similarly, the scene between Isabelle and M. Per-sonne presents the same kind of coupling (finally indissociable in this film) of aggression and idealization, condensed in a moment of sound and image. Isabelle stands facing the window, showing her ass to M. Personne. In an ironic comment, she asks, *"Vous admirez le paysage?"* Later in the same scene when she is playing the daughter in the imaginary family (a scene which is in some ways a response to the [forbidden, sexual, familial] desire expressed earlier by Paul in relation to Cécile at the soccer field and at the dinner table), M. Personne asks Isabelle to show her "belle forêt" to "Maman," at which point we see an image of some trees in autumn. These images and sounds work on the level of a play on words, visual puns where rather common metaphors for the feminine body are taken apart through juxtaposition. But, as in the example above ("Le Commerce")—remembering the images of Denise on her bicycle in the country (in the section called "L'Imaginaire") and how that image represents feminine difference in the logic of this film—an image of the landscape standing for the feminine body in the context of this humiliating little scene (no matter how impervious Isabelle may seem) appears to be a privileged moment belonging to the logic of ambivalence, aggression and idealization which characterizes this film.

What is at the beginning held out to us as the possibility of difference turns into an impossibility in this no-win logic of ambivalence, where difference can exist only at the price of lived sexual relations. By the end of the film, looking back on those images at the beginning of Denise on her bicycle, at her window writing, talking with Isabelle in the car, the possibility of difference that they seemed to represent looks more like a women's world, a mythical retreat from the aggressiveness of sexual relations, finally, as impossible as the idealized other represented in the appropriation of Duras to stand for women's desire. *La passion, c'est pas ça.*

Jacques Dutronc

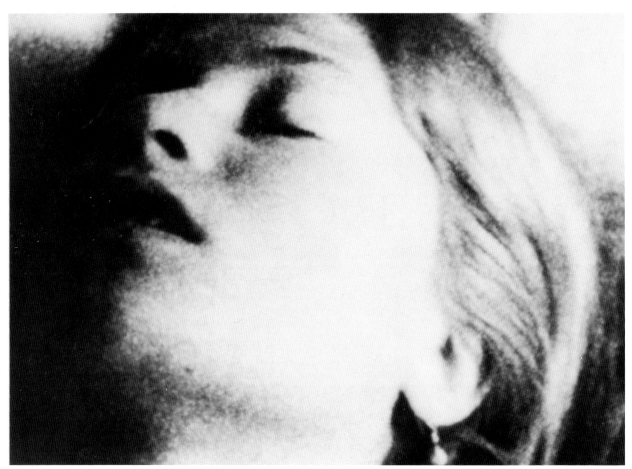

Isabelle Huppert

Pornography, Eroticism
CONSTANCE PENLEY

Near the beginning of *Sauve qui peut (la vie)*, in a scene that has been singled out for accusations of pornography (specifically, pedophilia), "Paul Godard" drops by a sports field to pick up his twelve-year-old daughter, Cécile. He asks the coach, who has just remarked that he has a daughter the same age as Cécile, if he ever "feels like caressing her tits or fucking her up the ass?" This scene and others like it that mention or depict homosexual propositioning, bestiality, prostitution, masturbation, sadism, masochism, sodomy and voyeurism, do indeed afford the spectator a wide-ranging iconography of the pornographic. But is the film pornographic?

In pornography, a fantasy of control and mastery realizes itself through the spectator's visual negotiation of the scene (sadomasochism, of course, implying a very complex notion of mastery). But in this film, in several ways, our version of this scene is incomplete, ambiguous; the fantasy of the full subject necessary to the pornographic scene cannot take hold here. For example, we don't actually see the verbal exchange between Paul Godard and the coach, as it occurs over Cécile's saccadic stop-action image (a close-up of her catching and throwing a ball), only cutting to Paul Godard's face before and after he speaks. Without the typical shot/reverse-shot dynamic, welding character and dialogue, Paul's speech tends to "float," and we can even ask if it is *his* speech (spoken in diegetic reality), or an incestuous wish (the speech of the unconscious). At the very least, "Do you ever feel like caressing her tits . . . ?" is not unambiguously assignable to him as a character, but is, also, a question asked by and in the general fiction of the film (at the level of the enunciation).

In the sports field scene (preceded by the title "Fear"), the spectator is referred several times to an "outside" of the film, and this also works against the narrow fiction, the closed world of the typical pornographic scene. Paul Godard is a fictional character, but he is also meant to be *Godard*. The joke about Castro that he tells the coach ("Have you heard the latest about Castro? . . . He complains that Cubans don't work as hard as Americans") cites something exterior to this scene that is both social (Castro, now) and reflexively filmic (Godard's earlier "political" films where Castro was a frequent image). A further social reference in this supposed pedophilic scene gives the lie to that reading: following the coach's reply ("No"), Paul complains that it's not fair that mothers can touch their children more easily than fathers. By thus framing Paul's question, the film suggests not that men want to touch their daughters because they have per-verse desires, but that they have perverse desires because there are taboos against touching them.

As for Cécile's image, it does not make itself available to any simple voyeuristic pleasure or easy visual mastery, both because of its "startling physics and strange mechanics" (as Jean Epstein described the use of slow and accelerated motion), and what it shares with other, similar moments in the film where a woman's image is the site of an ambivalence expressed as an idealization/aggression in relation to that image. These various images of women are, in fact, more or less unsecurable by any subjecting male gaze: the woman at the train station who gets slapped but still refuses to choose between two men, the prostitute Marilyn-Nicole who recites to her clients a litany of pejoratives used for medieval women. And Isabelle, at the moment when she is presented exactly as the inevitable icon of the pornographic lovemaking scene, the close-up of the moaning woman's face serving as the guarantee of pleasure, is heard thinking about the errands she has to run. For all of its pornographic "images," the film is, rather, about the refusal or failure of a controlling male gaze, that gaze designated here as a pornographic one.

"Startling physics and strange mechanics" also crop up in the bodily comportment and sexual gestures of the characters throughout the film, and the *ridiculousness* of their movements tends to deflect any pornographic interest. Disobedient prostitutes are usually beaten up by their pimps; here they are spanked. Bestiality is rendered by an extremely rapid shot of a woman presenting her rear to a cow for a lick. People move into an embrace and, irresistibly, begin hitting each other. Orgasm is blatantly faked. The four-way sex scene with Isabelle, the prostitute Marilyn-Nicole and the two businessmen turns into a Rube Goldberg machine. The rhetoric of pornography does not allow such absurd and incongruous gestures.

Important to an understanding of the sports field scene, as well as others marked with the icons of the pornographic, is its larger narrative frame. *Sauve qui peut (la vie)*'s fictional origin of enunciation is quite possibly Denise, from whose novel-essay-diary we hear extracts throughout the film. (*Isabelle*: "Is your project a book?" *Denise*: "No, but it may be part of one.") The problem that the film sets itself, then, is the relation of these pornographic "images" to a possible origin of enunciation that is a woman's narrative. The reference to Duras, who is diegetically present (she is spoken to, we hear her voice) although we never see her, and the instructions given the students watching her film by Paul Godard to think about "woman's speech" (*parole de femme*) whenever they see a truck passing (as we do

Jacques Dutronc

Cécile Tanner

several times in the film—a reference to Duras's *Le Camion*) also suggest that the question here is not simply one of "images"—pornographic or not—but of the very possibility of women speaking and writing, and of what they might have to say. In another way, too, it is not a question of "images" but of the metaphorical propositions to which they contribute. Godard has adopted a long series of metaphors to designate both the position of the filmmaker in relation to culture and the film industry, and the common workings of sexuality and money: consumerism (*Une femme mariée*), tourism (*Pierrot le fou*), prostitution (*Vivre sa vie, Deux ou trois choses que je sais d'elle*), and, now, pornography. Pornography is one of his most successful metaphors: the filmmaker as pornographer, sex and cinema (in our society) as pornographic. Like prostitution, pornography presents a configuration where sexuality cannot be seen apart from the selling of it. But pornography as a metaphor has an important advantage over prostitution insofar as it cannot be romanticized. "Filmmaker as prostitute" has an air of proud martyrdom about it that "filmmaker as pornographer" does not. Prostitutes as individuals can be romanticized, as Godard has done repeatedly in his films, but, in pornography, as a business and as a fictional form, there are no martyrs or heroines.

Frequently works that are accused of being pornographic are redeemed by assigning them to the category of the erotic. *Sauve qui peut (la vie)*, if it were pornographic, could never find such redemption because it is deeply anti-erotic. In the erotic formula, masculine and feminine, male and female, are absolute opposites. The fantasy of eroticism is that these two opposites are complementary (to reverse Lacan—"There *is* a sexual relation"). It is because of this wish that death is so important to eroticism: if the sexes can be complementary, and can, together, achieve a sort of unity, then there is nothing left to be desired, and the end of desire is death. The sexes never come together in *Sauve qui peut (la vie)* (and thus the death at the end does not have to be experienced as a genuine death). Everyone is moving at different speeds. They can't kiss, really. They can't touch, really. The film is the antithesis of eroticism.

If a criticism is to be made of this film it cannot be along the lines of an alleged pornographic debasement of women. The point of disturbance, the site of possible objection, lies, rather, in the film's specific *privileging* of women. The men in this film can't move, Godard has said, only the women. The women are, for the most part, complex and powerful, although uncertain as to where or how to move; but Paul Godard is truly morbid and only comes to life (here, to self-consciousness) in his "death scene." In the masochistic fantasy of this film Paul Godard is destroyed by the women, or at least by his passivity in relation to their greater readiness to seek change. In the final scene he lies dying in the street while the women in his life walk away indifferently. We do see scenes in this film of women being debased and humiliated; the women are, however, shown to have a sharp awareness of their situation. Isabelle explains to her sister that the client is primarily interested in humiliating the prostitute; the prostitute Marilyn-Nicole recites all the pejorative names given to women in the Middle Ages while she is servicing the businessmen. The film leaves you with the impression that women are more interesting and forceful than men, fascinating, and, ultimately, destructive.

Godard, when discussing the work that he had done in *France/tour/détour/deux/enfants* and *Sauve qui peut (la vie)* on changing the temporalities and rhythms of film through the use of a kind of half-accelerated, half-slow-motion image, remarked on the far greater degree of fascination to be found in looking at the image of a woman or a little girl treated to this variation of rhythms than that of a little boy:

Jacques Dutronc

I concluded that when one changes the rhythms, when one analyzes a woman's movements, even ones as simple as buying a loaf of bread, for example, one notices that there are so many different worlds inside the woman's movement. Whereas slowing down the little boy's movements was a lot less interesting; every time the image was stopped the same thing was always going on. But with the little girl, even when she was doing something completely banal, one could suddenly see a look of extreme sadness and then a third of a second later a look of joy: *c'était des monstres. . . .* As I am scientific and know certain theories, I had the impression that I was watching different bodies and worlds, galaxies transforming one into another with a series of explosions, whereas the little boy was much less graceful and interesting plastically . . . ("Propos rompus," *Cahiers du Cinéma*, no. 316 [Oct. 1980]).

Here, it is clear that women are seen as more engrossing than men; they are *naturally* enigmatic (further, Godard suggests, this interest is something to be investigated— "As I am scientific and know certain theories . . .").

Seizing on the pornographic as the problem of *Sauve qui peut (la vie)* makes it hard to discern a deeper and more problematic logic located not in individual images (women being slapped, spanked, wrestled to the floor, variously humiliated) or bits of dialogue ("Did you ever feel like caressing her tits . . . ?") but in an idea about sexual difference that this film ceaselessly proposes. Although the fictional work of the film takes up sexual difference as a theoretical problem (the possibility in narrative of a feminine origin of enunciation) and as a problem or difficulty in people's lives (Paul's inability, for example, to feel himself as anything but *excluded* from the world of women, from femininity), it

constructs this difference as essential, absolute and irreconcilable to the point of violence. Unlike in classical film, the women here are linked to activity and the man to passivity; in this reversal, femininity becomes the primary term of sexual difference and masculinity its other. Women, then, in this schema, acquire a certain superiority, but it is at the price of a difference defined as essential (in their nature) and as necessarily bound to extinguish its opposite. The film offers a strikingly different narrative repartition of the terms of masculinity and femininity, but because it leaves unquestioned what it sees as the natural fascination of women, these terms sort themselves out, finally, according to a logic of male masochism as the response to a failed aggression against these idealized women. *Sauve qui peut (la vie)* begins with a celebration of femininity in its essential difference—Denise in stop-action riding her bicycle in the country, her body, face and movements "like galaxies transforming one into another with a series of explosions"—and ends with the imagined consequences of this difference for men—Paul dying in the street.

ALPHAVILLE
1965
Anna Karina

Violence and Enunciation
JANET BERGSTROM

I was struck by the violence of the film *Sauve qui peut (la vie)*, how it repeatedly stages the impossibility of living sexual difference as anything but an absolute dichotomy (masculine/feminine). This is so, at the least, diegetically, but I think that a large part of the sense of frustration and loss generated by the film comes from the way it extends beyond the usual boundaries of fiction. Godard is surely meant to be closely identified with his protagonist, Paul Godard, and the function of quotation here (the Duras episode, for example) is only a more pointed use of this *extending* strategy very familiar from Godard's earlier films. From such a description, the film may sound like another rendition of a theme-song dear to Godard (cinephile, pessimist, Romantic—his hero dies at the end, bereft of love), but it seems to me that *Sauve qui peut (la vie)*, almost *necessarily* through violence, gives us something for the future with respect to the figuration of sexual difference in "experimental"-narrative film in the way that the film manages to introduce a split into the overall logic of the enunciation. While we follow mainly Paul's story, we are also given several important women characters with their own narrative trajectories who provide us with an array of examples of resistance to male narrative logic at the level of characters, as well as moments given over to a woman alone (Denise at the window-seat with her notebook) or women together (Denise and Isabelle in the car) that are significantly different from scenes to which they might be compared from earlier Godard films. In part, this is because of the way they are inaccessible to the male protagonist, even via the overlay of Romanticism and idealization that has characterized the position of the desired woman within the logic of the enunciation in most of Godard's films.

By violence, I mean first and foremost the violence of the cut, that is, violence engineered on the level of film technique, through editing. It is no accident that the incidents of most extreme violence combine eroticism and aggression on the level of the characters with stop-action, modulated editing effects. What we see, quite literally, is the production of ambivalence, aesthetically stunning, yet horrific in its implications because the editing reduplicates formally—generates—both violence and eroticism through the cut. We have a film that binds an elementary psychological fact of sexual attraction, ambivalence, to a basic element of filmic construction.

The stop-action sequences are enumerated by Raymond Bellour in "I Am an Image" (*Camera Obscura*, no. 8-9-10); he suggests that they fall into two groups, tending either to idealize or express aggression against the woman. Here I would like to show, by taking a few examples of the latter, the associative logic of violence, that is, how violence on one level (physical contact) is transferred to another (psychological) and how, by means of a system of witnesses incorporated by cross-cutting point-of-view shots into the scene, the film's labyrinthine narrative-symbolic structure is connected. Editing is therefore essential to the effect of the sequences themselves (a sense of *violation* emphasized by a recurring percussive theme in a minor key); editing also often specifies a character's view that makes a narrative connection to otherwise non-aligned spaces and gives an immediate metaphorical reading to the violence witnessed. For example, it is obviously important that it is Denise at the train station who sees a girl brutally slapped by two bikers, trying to force her to choose between them. (A close-up of the girl's face is knocked from one side of the screen to the other in staggered movements, stubborn, in pain, refusing.) When Paul lunges over the kitchen table at Denise, we see erotic-violent contact registered as pain (physical and emotional) on Denise's face as Paul's weight carries her to the hard floor. It makes a difference that it is Isabelle watching rather than a male character or no one. Paul's usual containment of emotion, his frustrated attempts throughout the film to keep Denise, the resulting aggression, might then have appeared in a more sympathetic light. In this case, what we see is complicated by prior and subsequent connections with Isabelle. On the one hand, we will see Denise and Isabelle in a car together later, talking about what they want to do with a kind of relaxed attention never possible in the interactions between Paul and any of the women characters, including an earlier scene with Isabelle as his prostitute, her thoughts elsewhere. On the other hand, Isabelle shares with Paul a typecast lack of expressiveness that goes hand in hand with her imperviousness as a prostitute in the *combinatoire* scene in the businessman's office and her matter-of-fact initiation of her sister into prostitution, setting herself up as pimp (her questions, appraising her sister's breasts, the 50/50 financial contract). Thus Isabelle could be seen as a pivotal character in the attempt at a split enunciation, an idea to which we will return.

Less obviously violent, but for me even more chilling, by far exceeding the ambivalences of the prostitution scenes, are those played out exclusively on the level of cinematic representation, images stopping others, again according to the logic of masculine/slash/feminine. These scenes are linked to those where we see Cécile, Paul's twelve-year-old daughter, which focus on her identity (from Paul's narrative point of view) as an unknowable being coming into social and physiological existence—feminine, her breasts are beginning to develop. The point is that we learn this from the voice-off questions and answers between Paul and another father as we watch Cécile's face in close-up, in stop-action, as she turns to catch a ball on the playing field. If anything, she is an image of androgyny or pre-sexual definition, if it were not for the commentary. But the questions and answers do violence to Cécile's image insofar as we can see in microcosm the process of internalization/defense against an identity projected onto her as exclusively sexual. Thus, within the logic of the film, she is represented as being *categorically* different from Paul, who is no longer defined primarily as a father but now masculine as opposed to her, feminine—in this film, *another* feminine opponent. So from his point of view, she is just coming into the system of sexual ambivalence: desire/aggression. That his desire for her is markedly unrealizable doesn't obviate it on the level of fantasy (which the other father naturally disavows, asked baldly if he ever feels like fucking his daughter). This confusion and repression, absolutely in line with the logic of sexuality elsewhere in the film, registers itself more directly against Cécile later as aggression (the T-shirt episode).

The examples I have in mind that are linked to the representation of Cécile show us the violence of ambivalence in more subtle ways that are not tied to character motivation but operate on the level of the enunciation generally. There is the otherwise innocuous scene in which Isabelle picks up Paul while he is standing in line for a movie. It doesn't even look like prostitution; the violence comes in at the level of representation, since as Paul turns his back to us to face Isabelle, again in stop-action, he moves with respect to the camera angle just so that the final cut comes as he has obliterated all of her image from the screen except for one of her eyes, following him, disembodied. Likewise, we have a cut from Isabelle looking out Monsieur Personne's hotel room window to the street, where we see (passing to the visual point of view of the enunciation) a chance encounter between a man and woman, a show of pleasure and recognition, yet again the man moving so as to block the woman's image from the screen. Even more painful is the moment when Paul approaches Cécile to kiss her, another meeting by chance. The stop-action editing not only makes the father's attempt at contact immeasurably more difficult (countless impediments to movement), but we get a rear view of Paul so that we focus instead on Cécile's apprehensive look as his head approaches hers.

To make this connection more general, one can recall an example already made infamous that demon-

strates a relationship between sexual ambivalence and editing from *Number Two*. The husband bends his wife forward over a washing machine, forcing her to comply sexually with a desire that is not hers. The interpretation of violence comes not from the "story" alone, but much more so from the lateral wipe that edits into this sexual image the unseen face of their daughter watching. Thus, not only are we given an example of video-specific editing technique (transferred to film), a virtuoso equivalent of the film-specific shot/reverse shot simultaneously, but semantically the video edit electronically mixes the child's face in a diagonal movement into this image of her parents: Freud's primal scene (sexual intercourse between the parents experienced by the child as violence against the mother) is anything but banal here because we witness a virtually unreadable face (the little girl's) in the process of being imprinted, literally, electronically, as well as in social/psychological terms which sexuality inevitably intermeshes.

One can see why editing presents an inherently interesting—in fact, inescapable—challenge to the filmmaker involved with redefinitions of the positioning of masculine/feminine within a cinematic narrative, since editing is where the physical aspect of film as a medium can be perceived most dramatically (violently, erotically) to engender imaginary cinematic effects. The transfer between levels (physical, imaginary) is literally invisible to the spectator in the theater; the cuts cannot be seen, only the realignment of space and/or time witnessed, and necessarily by a process of internalization. (The scene has already changed.)

In *Sauve qui peut (la vie)*, not only are we given an extremely elliptical editing style, both within sequences and joining them to each other (the single-shot sequence only arguably retaining its status as such, testimony to the strength of classic narrative conventions), but we are treated to the "new" stop-action sequences, conceptually related, but where the modulation of time and space is designed to be noticed. These montage techniques might risk seeming high-tech (flashy) in their conceptualization and execution if abstracted too much from their narrative and structural function. But the stylish editing shouldn't obscure the experimental and tentative features of the narrative that it gives shape to, where we experience a manner of "storytelling" that splits the logic of the enunciation along the lines of sexual difference.

On the one hand, the narrative gives the effect of condensation to the point of being very difficult to piece together completely at first viewing. Subsequent viewings, however, prove how logical the narrative is, as an argument can be elegant in its logic, since a high degree of narrative, visual and aural information is used with an uncommonly low incidence of redundancy to move the story forward. On the other hand, a paradox presents itself in that, although tightly constructed, the narrative goes off in more than one direction. The important thing about this divergence from what one might see as an imagined destination (think of the prominence given to means of transportation in this film, which obviously carry a metaphorical dimension) is that another logic of desire is represented than that of the male protagonist, Paul Godard, with whom we are more or less familiar from many of Godard's earlier films.

First of all, it must be realized how Godard's films have always reversed the symbolic dynamics of the classical Hollywood cinema insofar as it is not his "own" identity that he is eager to bolster by reducing the female protagonists to his shadows or mirrors. (I am speaking now both of his male protagonists and of an explicitly defined male logic of enunciation, as dramatized at the beginning of *Number Two* where we see Godard at the video control panel.) It is just the opposite, because Godard's heroes want to identify with the woman, or with the feminine. And the woman, insofar as she is desirable, is by definition in his films unknowable; the omnipresent theme of communication in Godard is used precisely to state that communication, much less commutation, is not possible between masculine/feminine. Therefore we see an endless replay of the fantasy of the masochistic male protagonist-narrator, who is imagined as literate, Romantic (as in both Romanticism and "romantic love"), analytical of the social uses of power, images and sexuality, but incapable of escaping his own position within this constellation. This ambivalent stance toward the position of knowledge, hence power, he sometimes turns back on himself, as does the implicitly self-accusing narrator (literally the voice of Godard) in *Two or Three Things I Know About Her* or *Vivre sa vie*, albeit in the guise of revealing social and media stereotypes in the better interest of women. This is a side-effect, perhaps, of the big analogies constantly redrawn—we are all media-defined, we are all prostitutes. Or else his ambivalence is expressed as idealization in all the instances where he saves the romantic image for the enunciator/narrator, or, one might even say, for the camera. (This slippage of terms is undoubtedly too easy in the case of Godard to leave unanalyzed, but for the moment let it be left at that.) Anna Karina's photograph functions this way in virtually every instance: she is always present to us as a series of stills, so carefully does the camera frame her, even when she dances. A memorable shot, often reproduced, comes from *Alphaville*, where we see her

through a window, absorbed in thought, holding (to be seen) *Capitale de la douleur*. There are dozens of similar moments that could be cited that have a place both inside and beyond Godard's narratives. One could imagine a beautiful book of photos of women posed in variations on this attitude from all of Godard's films, excepting the "kill the Romantic" phase with Gorin and the Dziga Vertov Group.

The space/time of contemplation is never, in Godard, that of men. Even if they waste time, so to speak, by expressing a non-linear confusion, they are still noisily active. Belmondo, in *Breathless*, is always on the move, talking, gesturing, trying to make connections, exteriorizing. In contrast, our eyes can linger over these inward-looking women the way we are asked to give our attention to painting or classical music or literature, art forms to which their images are often juxtaposed (conforming to Barthes's definition of beauty in *S/Z*: the beautiful can only be described by comparison). But we look, with Godard, at (not into) an interior state that cannot possibly be reached; in fact, it is in the moment of erotic and, for Godard, aestheticized desire that the cut-off of absolute difference is most strongly experienced. However, in *Sauve qui peut (la vie)* Godard attempts to go beyond this. His attempt, in the spirit of the essay form that has always guided his view of innovation (*essayer*, to try), cannot be seen in the figure of Paul Godard, who remains within the logic of the dominant system of male protagonists, albeit the masochistic version. One must look to the general logic of the enunciation of the film, which has Paul's story, although dominant in terms of screen time and in terms of interconnecting characters, framed and interrupted by figures of resistance to his thus paradoxical superiority (the luxury hotel, the public recognition factor, his skills in reasoning, even as a storyteller). Thus in retrospect we may reinterpret the apparently idyllic shot that we see of Denise riding her bicycle in the country near the beginning of the film, away from "us," in stop-action. Its function appears differently when we realize that it is more or less repeated as the last shot before the scene of Paul's parallel rejection by Cécile's (unnamed) mother through an aggressive-defensive indifference, and then his look at Cécile (or at both of them?) as he backs into the Mercedes that "kills" him. Whether his death is real or symbolic is obviously not the point, since there is no longer a way, even an ambivalent one, for him to imagine his identity through these women who have been defined by the film as his main points of reference.

The effort made to represent female characters on the screen who are attempting to carry through on their own desire, even if ill-defined, even if conceived of in terms of direction rather than goals accomplished, can be seen most consistently in the case of Denise. She is both weak and strong, vulnerable and resilient. We can see the qualitative difference she is allowed by this narrative both from the contemplative women of Godard's earlier films, and from her exchange with Paul as opposed to her conversation with Isabelle or the times she is shown alone. As a means of comparison, we can remember the references to Denise and writing. She is almost always seen carrying her notebook, and she often writes in it, although we never see what it is that she puts down. Several characters in the film ask her what she is writing—is it a book, a novel? She doesn't know—that is what she always answers. But Paul asks in order to challenge her, to prove that she doesn't know what she is doing *in general*, which he immediately extends to an argument, based on her indefiniteness, against her leaving the city, her job, leaving him. When Isabelle asks her the same question when they are in the car talking over the exchange (Isabelle will rent Denise's apartment), the tone and tempo of the conversation are noticeably different. Denise isn't put to the test about a lack of specific objectives because Isabelle too wants to change her life, to take a new direction that is not yet altogether known. Similarly, when we see Denise writing, sitting on the window-seat in her new room in the country, she appears no less lovely than other women photographed earlier as stills by Godard, but her seriousness in writing, as an activity, as a direction, is at the least equally evident. Therefore, we have a woman character who is unreachable to the male protagonist, but not to us, since we are given other views of her that show a separate logic of desire being pursued in the face of difficulties, uncertainty, fragility.

Isabelle, on the other hand, has a presence that never seems vulnerable. This is most evident in the *combinatoire* scene where she is contrasted to the starkly naked Nicole, who wants not only to be called Marilyn, to have a name that is a disguise, but clearly to project the working disinterest of an Isabelle. (As Isabelle has explained to her sister, what they want is to humiliate you.) Nicole's physical stance, particularly at the beginning of the scene, as well as her facial expression and her attempts not to look at her "employers," indicate to us well enough how difficult that is, while Isabelle is one of Godard's typical prostitute heroines, who vary in attitude from lovely, uncertain, sad, tragic, etc., but never appear as ill at ease or abused as an image as Nicole. I think the relationship of Nicole to Isabelle in many ways replicates that of Denise to Paul, although with more sadism in the way we can see Nicole fighting against the weakness of being vulnera-

ble. The entire office scene is in the end the kind of joke that serves as an attempt to displace the anxiety of a sexual threat onto inadequate substitutes, even if it is momentarily funny as a mild pastiche of de Sade's more elaborate combinations and somewhat interesting as another of Godard's metaphors linking cinema and prostitution. This kind of attempted displacement characterizes most of the humor in the film.

However, aside from the question of abuse to Nicole's image, resulting in our discomfort as well as hers, in an audience's laughter, there is an important reason for Isabelle's identical composure in all circumstances, and for the fact that she isn't subjected to the same kind of verbal-visual-psychological violence in the office scene as Nicole. This is because she is tied very closely to the general logic of the enunciation in the film (and that particular strength/weakness thereby implied), given more time with a separate story than any other character but Paul or Denise. And, as I suggested before, I believe that she is the mediating link between them, not only as characters—she comes into both their "stories"—but as divergent expressions of desire as imagined by Godard and Miéville here, masculine/feminine. (Anne-Marie Miéville's exact contribution cannot be determined; we know that she collaborated on the conception, writing and shooting of the film with Godard.)

And so one might speculate that it is Isabelle who represents, within the fiction, both sides of the enunciation at once. In this respect, her imperviousness is perhaps analogous to that of Duras, who can be present, yet absent in this film. That is, the presence of Duras is felt strongly in the classroom scene, when she is in fact "there," but not in the room: she wishes to remain outside the door, as one of the students incredulously exits and reenters to verify. Her words, however, are read aloud, quoted by Paul, who is at this point identified as closely as possible with the filmmaker, Godard, since he reads Duras's often cited statement about why she makes films and then adds that her reason is also his. ("I make films because I don't have the strength to do nothing.") Moreover, afterwards we hear her easily recognizable voice as she is presumably in the car with Paul and Cécile, but her image is never seen. In other words, the demand for the presence of Duras "in person" is not only not met, it is denied three times over—to the students, to Denise, to us.

That Duras and her film are left out of the on-screen narrative (one could infer that *Le Camion* has been shown) conforms exactly to the logic of the sharp cut that, paradoxically, unifies *Sauve qui peut (la vie)* through a system of violent breaks, analogous to the characters meeting and breaking apart. One scene is

**SAUVE QUI PEUT
(LA VIE)**
1979
Nathalie Baye

almost tangibly sliced off, like a hot knife through but-
ter (the violence and eroticism of the cut), to expose the
next, usually via radical ellipses that do not allow (that
try to prevent) a post-rationalization of the relationship
from scene to scene of time and space. However, the
cuts that deny us the visual presence of either Duras or
her work can hardly be thought of as doing violence in
any sense to either. The effect of her "present absence"
is a tour de force for both Godard and Duras, within
the film and extending beyond it to the work of these
filmmakers we know from elsewhere, since her absence
is represented as the effect of her desire. She is "pic-
tured," in this film, as holding the position of greatest
strength insofar as she is identified with the principle
or logic of the enunciation, indirectly, through the cinematic use of imaginary space and time. In hommage,
but also as she represents another example of a woman
living out a *direction* in the film, Duras is elevated to
the position of absolute decisiveness, lack of confusion,
certainty of movement in her work (filmmaking, exploration of "*parole de femme*"), as well as knowing and
insisting on her immediate desire (not coming into the
classroom, taking an early plane). If Duras is thus represented as another feminine figure of identification for
Paul, and another who moves out of his life, her words,

her work, remain. And the impassiveness that links her
with both Isabelle and Paul is also different, because
Duras only takes up the outer vestiges of what has been
defined in the film as the male position. It is specifically
through her mode of enunciation, which has a tempo-
rality and a texture of its own, which has a remembered
past, that she is defined. This allies her with the feminine as the direction of her work but puts her beyond
the particular system of sexual ambivalence (aggres-
sion/eroticism) that is *this* film's motivating anxiety.

Note

* These three articles on *Sauve qui peut (la vie)*, reprinted with
revisions, were written by the editors of *Camera Obscura* as an
introduction to a special issue on Godard, no. 8-9-10 (Fall
1982).

JE VOUS SALUE MARIE
1985
Myriem Roussel

THE OTHER SIDE OF THE BOUQUET

ALAIN BERGALA

At the very heart of the cinematographic act, there always comes a moment when the desire for the shot, whatever it is, has to take form in a concrete, terribly definitive, exclusive shot, where this desire, inevitably, both inscribes itself, and yet fails to materialize. This is where the pleasure and anxiety of shooting a film come into play together, the point where the ideal, imaginary film happens in and through the reality of gestures and decisions made during the shoot. It's where the meeting of the absolute of desire and the surprises of the contingent create what Godard referred to in the sixties as a "definitive by chance." This particular moment has become more than ever a moment of profound solitude, since, in the cinema of our time, as "Monsieur Coutard" says to the troubled director in *Passion* (1982), there are really no more rules, and no more Law to respect or transgress. Godard's entire work of the eighties could be said to bear in various ways a mourning and nostalgia for that time when "there were rich people and poor people, when there were fortresses to capture, ranks to scale, desirable things defended well enough to preserve their allure," as he says often in *Nouvelle Vague* (1990). For Godard, such was the time of the Nouvelle Vague in the early sixties. Back then, French cinema—in the hands of academic filmmakers—was still a well-defended, corporatist fortress that Godard and his *Cahiers* friends tried to take by storm by shooting their first films against the gray norm of "French films of quality," and under the banner of the great filmmakers they had elected as Masters.

When Hitchcock died in April of 1980, Godard went to Cannes with *Sauve qui peut (la vie)* (1979) under his arm, the film that marked his return to "cinema cinema" after a long absence. He was far from being the conquering hero; he stated with bitterness: "The death of Hitchcock marks the passage from one era to another. . . . I believe we are entering an era defined by the suspension of the visual, or, more exactly, by the ebbing of the visual. Our age represses the visual. . . . Moreover, I found the cinema very dislocated. . . . I felt as if I were making my first film, but at the same time, it's all sort of discouraging. I don't think we'll have the strength to make cinema much longer."[1] Then, at the beginning of the

eighties, it was for Godard a question of rediscovering the desire to make cinema, in a time when the Masters were all dead, the fortress had crumbled on its own, eroded from within by the televisual virus, and the Law in cinema had become weak and obscure at best. And for him, much more than for any other filmmaker, this desire to make a film is focused imperatively through the desire to compose a shot. Filmmakers rarely speak of this strange thing: the desire or lack of desire to compose a shot. Not the desire to make a film, which is another thing altogether, but simply the desire to film a particular shot—something that is never obvious across an entire film, which is made up of hundreds of them.

In the construction and filming of any shot, there occur two related mental operations that can't always be disentangled in the actual chronology of the shoot: arrangement and attack. When a fiction filmmaker prepares to film a shot (and never mind for the moment which of the two hats he wears), he always needs to arrange his figures in space, and decide how he wants to attack that space and the motif—in other words, from what angle, and at what focal length and what distance. In most films, where the authors try to efface themselves beneath the story they're telling, the attack always takes cues from the composition. This common-sense approach determines the vector of the shot's readability, and affirms the good-faith contract with the spectator. One of the filmmaker's pleasures, however—a pleasure unknown to the theater director—is that his art, like the painter's, permits him to treat composition and attack separately. If we're to believe Robert Bresson, who has magisterially practiced this perverse pleasure throughout his career, Auguste Renoir declared one day to Matisse: "I often paint bouquets from the side I haven't arranged."[2] In the cinema, similarly, Godard can arrange in the same space a young woman, a table, and a bouquet of flowers on the table, and at the last moment attack his shot in such a way that the bouquet of flowers masks part of the woman's face. This drive to *not* attack the shot, or the scene, from the point of view from which it has been composed, and this propensity to increasingly disjoint composition from attack, are, even if Godard never mentions it, what informed the Godardian *cinématographique* of the eighties most insistently, sometimes secretly, sometimes openly. But these tendencies have a history.

In the sixties, when Godard made his entrance into the world of cinema, there was still a Law with its own guardians. Conscientious critics explained to him upon seeing *A bout de souffle* (1960) that there is good and bad continuity, that there are screenwriting rules to be respected, and that in a film, dialogue must always be audible, while the actor's face must never be obscured while he or she is talking onscreen. Accordingly, Godard wisely played his character of enfant terrible of the new cinema and opened *Vivre sa vie* (1962) with a long take (a sequence in and of itself) in which he impeccably attacks his two actors from the back, and drowns their dialogue in the noise of the bartender washing dishes. This was how, at the time, he affirmed himself against the Law, by leaning on it firmly, not really perverting it, but simply doing the opposite of what others were doing, or what was considered forbidden. But his style of masking—there are many other examples in *Vivre sa vie*—is just as frank as that of his preferred frontal attacks; the one is just the reverse accomplice of the other.

By the beginning of the eighties, when Godard returned to the cinema, the fine innocence of the old days had been lost forever. He no longer found any Law to speak of, let alone one he could lean on: now, all styles coexisted in a slack permissiveness. Even the great prohibition on representing the sexual act had been hypocritically lifted in the ghetto of X-rated cinema. Criticism, moreover, had renounced any truly critical function, in the face of the explosive power of publicity, while great filmmakers who might provide some yardstick for others were now few and far between. Still, Godard was convinced, like Orson Welles, that "there can be no experimentation if there is no tradition to lean on, nor can there be any desire to experiment."[3] With the Law faltering to such a degree, the very desire to shoot had become threatened. Godard would thus have to do all the work himself: simultaneously construct a semblance of a Law to transgress, and invent its transgression. It's the price he would pay (wholly evident when it's the actual subject of certain scenes in *Passion* or *Je vous salue Marie* [1985]) to preserve on his own account that basic desire without which cinema is only ever its own simulation: the desire to create a shot, to film anew, as if it were the first time, a motif already filmed so many times, by so many others and by himself: a woman's face, a car, and a bouquet of flowers.

Sauve qui peut (la vie) wasn't just the film that reopened the doors of cinema to Godard; it also bore the germ of a future trilogy: *Passion*, *Prénom Carmen* (1983), and *Je vous salue Marie*. Before returning to work, Godard began by taking stock of the field, noting the uncertainties of the Law and of desire at the beginning of the eighties. At the time, with this first film, it was still just a matter of theme: the filmmaker had detected in his experience of the outside world a turbulence he would incorporate into his script. But very quickly, we would see Godard test this changing world in the heart of his work, in the very act of making a shot, and in the context of the contradiction between composition and attack. This is how he has most often registered the changes taking place around him, with a clear advance over other filmmakers: Godard risks experimenting with them at the center of his filmmaking practice, putting them to work, instead of just making a work about them.

Paul Godard, the man at the point of all the intersections in *Sauve qui peut (la vie)*, is caught between two women, Denise and Isabelle. Denise has chosen to affirm what she believes to be her true desire, which drives her to move and speak, and she's always ready to fight to defend it. Isabelle lets herself be tossed about in silence, at the will of events and encounters, and with an ambiguous smile that contains her true desire. This structure will provide a matrix for the three films to follow: a man caught between the desires of two women, "one open, the other closed," as Jerzy says in *Passion*. Caught, in other words, between one who actively manifests her desire in the world's face, and another who buries hers like an unutterable secret. We have the hysteric and the virgin, right up through the end of *Je vous salue Marie*, the film that closes the trilogy and this cycle of preoccupations; both come together in the image of the Virgin on her bed of suffering as she reinvents the convulsive arch of the hysteric. In *Passion*, Jerzy will be caught between Hanna and Isabelle; Joseph, in *Prénom Carmen*, will be caught between Carmen and Claire; and Joseph again, in *Je vous salue Marie*, between Marie and Juliette. Godard had to invent this last triangle, which is completely unlikely within the tradition of the Marian myth, in order to complete a seamless tapestry of his triptych. In all three cases, it's the gap between the desires of two women (at least in the expression of desire they present to him) that throws a man into uncertainty and the oscillations of his own desire. If only there hadn't been between Denise and Isabelle, whose names inevitably invite a longing for a single "Denisabelle," this hyphen uniting them, this *is*-thmus that connects them and condemns the man either to just miss or just be missed by them. Nevertheless, this gap between composition and attack, which Godard will explore more and more

SAUVE QUI PEUT (LA VIE)
1979

in the films to follow, remains the basis for rekindling what little desire he still feels for one or the other of these two women.

In a strange scene witnessed by Denise while waiting on a train platform, a scene apparently unconnected to the main plot, a young woman is commanded by two boys, both motorcyclists, to choose between them. She absolutely refuses to do so, even when they beat her, resisting to the end the injunction of the Law of the father, here incarnated in the sons, who, indistinguishable in their helmets, insist with the untroubled, obtuse conscience of proxies. Even though she rejects the Law of the father, it still rules in this scene, supported by the sons. Godard shoots the defrocking with an absurd figure to whom he dedicates an entire interstitial shot: a train station employee decked out in a strange, overly large costume, full of pockets and pleats, like one of Kafka's innumerable figures of the Law.

In the next scene, apparently unrelated to the first, a concrete, contemporary father appears: Paul Godard looking for his twelve-year-old daughter on a playing field. While the other Godard, the filmmaker, is decomposing the movements of the young girl, Paul is talking with the coach, who has a daughter the same age, and drawing him into his desire and confusion: "Haven't you ever wanted to caress her, fuck her up the ass, or, I don't know, whatever. . . . Sometimes I think it's unfair that a mom can touch her daughter, her daughter or son, more easily than the father can." The forbidden, even if it is, for Paul in this scene, more trivially social than really symbolic, manages nonetheless to evoke a double desire: that of the incestuous fondling acknowledged by the father, and that of Godard de-composing the gestures of the young girl—in other words, attacking the movement in the purity of action, devoting it to the pure pleasure of an attack that owes nothing more to its finality. This play with incest, in which Godard sets up at the same time a simulation of the Law ("You will be his daughter, he will be your father") and its imaginary transgression, will culminate three films later in the desire to attack the very subject of the Virgin. Since Myriem Roussel didn't want to make a film about incest with Godard as father,[4] their compromise was to make a film together on the Virgin, thus drawing up a tacit contract between them: "You will be the Virgin, and I will be both Joseph and God the Father; thus, you will be at the same time my wife, my daughter, and my mother." (If she is his mother, he must be Jesus "also," a role Godard probably somewhat enjoys, given how readily he mocks his overdeveloped real-life propensity to dramatize himself as a crucified Christ.)

Later in the same film, in the now-famous sequence of the prostitution chain, Godard installs at the center

Cécile Tanner

Isabelle Huppert and Roland Amstutz

of his film and at the threshold of the new decade an allegorical figure of the desire of the Master with his imposing statue of "the man with the ivory face." The statue organizes under our eyes and to our ears the long, meticulous, laborious scene that alone enables him to achieve once again, perhaps, not pleasure, which is visibly excluded, but orgasm. Through this somber figure of perversity drained of affect, Godard observes with a flourish that the era has ended when pleasure could happen simply with the turn of a shot, through the grace of an actress or a camera movement; all we can hope for today from the cinematographic act is a hard-won, painstakingly tracked climax. At the center of the scene, delicately disconnected from the business at hand, is a sumptuous bouquet of flowers. It is around this bouquet that Godard organizes more than one attack of shots between Isabelle and the ivory-faced man, like their secret link, simultaneously a hiding place and a medium, a bit of beauty and communication before or beyond the terror.

In this film, where Godard begins attentively to film the landscapes around him, the question of attack begins to loom before him autonomously, faced as he is with landscapes whose arrangement is nature's affair, with no invention required: "The problems I set for myself in this film with respect to the landscape are: what if I wanted to film a landscape from the back, a problem painters are familiar with. . . ."[5] Of course, in this film, the style is still classically frontal, compared to his earlier shooting style, in both composition and attack, doubtless because he was rediscovering with a certain innocence the pleasure of shooting cinema.

By the time he began to make *Passion*, just after taking stock of the field, Godard had come to think of himself, within the cinema surrounding him, as one of the last dinosaurs, a strange specimen, the sole survivor of his species. For someone who has always been stimulated by envy—which has nothing to do with competitiveness—there are no longer many filmmakers to measure

himself against, be jealous of, or to steal an actor or a scene from. The fathers were dead, the peers had been challenged, and the amnesiac sons had not relieved them: there was no one on the horizon who could have unexpectedly reawakened his desire. Some time later, *Grandeur et décadence d'un petit commerce de cinéma* (1986) recited mournfully the litany of deaths on cinema's field of honor, while *Histoire(s) du cinéma* (1989–) wallowed in the twilight feeling of being the last bastion of the faded splendor of an irredeemably lost art; he flashed a few suspended images of that art before us anonymously, one last time before the descent into oblivion. "Night has fallen," goes a very beautiful text read in each of the first two episodes, "another world rises, hard, cynical, illiterate, amnesiac, turning aimlessly, spread out and flattened, as if perspective, the vanishing point, had been suppressed. The strangest thing is that the living dead of this world are made in the image of the preceding world: their reflections, their sensations are from before."

Thus, for *Passion*, Godard had to search outside cinema for Masters to measure himself against, and for Great Classics to lean on and pervert. First, he chose certain great painters, becoming an almost respectful disciple, and, effortfully, humbly, re-created in-studio some of their more famous paintings, taking as meticulous care in the choice of colors, fabrics, and sets as the ivory-faced man took in choosing and arranging the figures in the erotic scene according to the rigorous protocol of his fantasy. But for once Godard doesn't

Rembrandt van Rijn
THE NIGHT WATCH
  1642
  Oil on canvas, 12' 1/4" x 14' 5 1/2"
  Rijksmuseum, Amsterdam

PASSION
  1982
  "The Night Watch"

Francisco Goya
THE THIRD OF MAY, 1808
1814–15
Oil on canvas, 8' 9" x 13' 4"
The Prado, Madrid

PASSION
1982
"The Third of May, 1808"

have to invent the composition—it's imposed; it's enough to look at the paintings, abide by their law, and faithfully copy their mise-en-scène. Liberated by this constraint, so to speak, there remain to him only the pleasures and anxieties, for once absolutely pure, of an attack radically dissociated from its habitual corollary, composition. Completely happy with this windfall, Godard discovered something he perhaps hadn't expected. Invention, for him as for Rossellini, has never been a matter of program: he often begins with the act of discovery, between chance and necessity, always rooted in the concreteness of creation, and it's only later that he derives the lessons of his discovery, extending them in another scene or weaving them into another film. The naked eye can follow the trail of this precious discovery in the shooting of the great tableaux vivants that mark out *Passion*. When he shot *The Night Watch* by Rembrandt, the mystery of a tiny, "overexposed" character, a dwarf, became the object of his investigation and consumed all his attention. Godard made several attempts at filming her, not without a certain stiffness, as in certain educational films. He began by respectfully presenting us with his rather faithful re-creation of the painting in an establishing shot. In a first shot of the dwarf, he attacked her frontally, at ninety degrees, like a pure reframing effected within the painting itself, in her "place" between the man in red with the rifle and the captain in black with the ruff. In the second shot, we have the first deviation in the attack: Godard displaced his point of view slightly to the right, obliquely attacking the plane of the painting, let's say at fifty degrees, so that the little woman is now glimpsed briefly between the captain with the ruff (who in the image now switches from her right to her left) and the man with the white hat. Three shots later, Godard returned one last time to his motif and displaced his point of view even more laterally to the right and toward the plane of the painting, so as to attack the figures in the first row almost in profile, the dwarf appearing this time on the right of the man with the white hat. In this last shot, even though the axis of his camera flirts very close to the plane of the painting (something like a ten-degree angle) while Jerzy and Coutard speak offscreen about cinema and the Law, Godard never crosses *behind* the imaginary window that separates the space of the viewer from that of the painting, where his camera could see from the back what the painter portrayed from the front. He had just discovered the pleasures of flirting with the transgression of separating bit by bit the attack from the composition, but still obeyed the greatest taboo, that against passing to the other side of the window, into the space inhabited by the figures.

This was exactly what he did, however, with Goya's *The Third of May, 1808*. Here the camera practically buries itself in the canvas and thrusts itself between the executioners and the victims (arranged in profile in the painting), to capture in the very real time of a shot–reverse shot their terrible face-off, whose unbearable pain the painter had sought to suspend forever. Here, it's quite visibly the subject itself of the painting that seems to have awakened the desire to shoot, rather than one figure in detail. Still, the emotion in the framing of a young, frightened girl, an image that recurs across the film in different forms, tells us that Godard's desire to shoot, even when the "subject" of the scene is of the greatest importance, depended upon another desire, one relative to an object, or, in this case, a posture. Such a desire is by nature always errant, erratic, and more or less disconnected from the more induced desire for the scene. Of all filmmakers now working, and regardless of what he says, Godard is undeniably the most incapable of shooting a scene only for its given subject, no matter how dear to him, without something else, unrelated to the content of the scene, triggering his desire to shoot. It's doubtless because of this happy crack in his then-extreme moralism that the militant films of 1969 to 1972, even those made under the influence of and crushed by the most punishing political superego, are still films by Godard, and we can see often, in the twist of a shot, the fresh resurgence of an absolutely individual desire to shoot, deaf to all doctrine. When he shot (in *Passion*) *The Entry of the Crusaders into Constantinople*, which was easy to re-create, another figure grabbed his attention and supported his desire to shoot—that of the two women in the lower right of the composition, and especially the "powerful nude back" of one. It is this woman's back, according to the script, that is the focal point for the "totality of cries, tears, and sounds of armor and horses."[6] But this time, unlike with *The Night Watch*, Godard did not change the axis: he respected the frontality of the attack for the entire length of the camera movement that runs along the surface of the tableau vivant like a gaze. With the artifice of machinery, he staged the imaginary moment of pictorial creation when, arranging a last figure on the rectangle of the canvas, the painter is done and finishes his composition. Though this was the last figure to be arranged on his canvas (Godard filmed this metaphor quite literally: a crane places the two young women within the frame of the camera), it was nonetheless, in his interpretation, the cause of the painter's desire.

This is exactly what Godard tries to film, the supposed desire of the Master, a desire that infects him, unless it's Godard's that infects the painting, which

"The Entry of the Crusaders into Constantinople," after Delacroix

"The Virgin of the
Immaculate Conception,"
after El Greco

"The Virgin of the
Immaculate Conception,"
after El Greco

amounts to the same thing. The young woman who appears in that character for the first time in one of his films will become "his" Virgin. Thus, he doesn't have to distinguish himself from the painter with an attack of his own. If the woman's back signals his desire to shoot, it comes precisely from the axis and posture of her back in the painting itself—two elements that Hitchcock, judging by his fine collection of perverse shots of women's backs and shoulders, would have appreciated.

In three tableaux vivants, Godard discovered and explored, without ever repeating himself, all possibilities opened up by what was for him a new situation: a given composition that imposed its law. Like all discoveries, his was timid at first. In the first tableau, Godard slightly displaced the axis of his attack in relation to the painter's. Then, like a child tentatively exploring forbidden territory, he grew bolder and strayed further, barely reaching the boundary, but stopped nonetheless at the threshold of the forbidden. In the second tableau, he threw himself into the transgression and brutally broke across the demarcation line of the forbidden, not with any great pleasure, but deliberately, just to see what would happen. In the third tableau, as if he'd gone too far, or perhaps to remember how it was before he began his exploration, when the Law reigned unchallenged, he returned to a strict respect for the attack prescribed by the painter.

It is only then, after crossing all the stages that he had to pass, that he became truly free. In the shooting of the last tableau of the film, from El Greco's *Immaculate Conception*, there is no longer anything reactive, nothing more that could still obey the advance–retreat dialectic of exploration in unknown territory. Now he can play with the Law without the slightest rigidity, indeed, with a staggering grace, turning about the wings of the angel, finding his own way in the movement of elevation that organizes these figures as an ensemble, attempting it

twice, without the second try either completing or negating the first, and redescending finally along the bouquet of figures "with a movement in which weight plays no part," to use Simone Weil's definition of grace.[7] In these sensual brushes with the forbidden, the act of passing to the other side of the figures frustrates the weight of the Law, without ever truly forgetting or denying it. Godard has found the happy medium of his desire to film, and these three shots rank among the most sublime and inspired of the film.

But while Godard for his part is advancing by leaps and bounds from tableau vivant to tableau vivant, Jerzy, his filmmaker character and alter ego in the fiction, is stuck, faced with a law he hurls himself against and that causes him to suffer: the obligation everyone saddles him with to tell a story. Although since the beginning of the film he has given up explaining himself on the subject to the financiers, producers, and other film professionals, he still wants his desire to be recognized by at least one of the two women he oscillates between, which would help him come out of his affective indecision and creative impasse. But he won't manage it, he'll give up finishing his film and run off finally with a third woman, a girl in the kitchen, because she at least agreed to believe that a car can be a flying carpet. His dream film will remain a deep, dark secret, and he will only be able to iterate the impasse: "It's not going very well!" It's that he no longer expects the validation of his work from a human law but, in a totally Rossellinian way, from an external, necessarily nonhuman source, a sign from the light that he hopes will deliver him from the anxiety and the uncertainty, and give him access at last to a complete aesthetic climax, one that Godard, we may be quite sure, must have experienced in filming El Greco's painting.

Between the discoveries of *Passion* and their sublime and painful culmination in *Je vous salue Marie* comes *Prénom Carmen*. This film strikes me as a work of latency, one in which all the questions that haunt Godard at the beginning of the eighties, even if they are constitutive of his work, remain mostly rhetorical, a bit too serious, at the level of a still too-visible program in the finished film. It's as if the concrete realization of the film had neither really transformed nor reanimated these questions, which is all the stranger since we know that Godard, after some days of filming, had to switch actresses and trade Isabelle Adjani for Maruschka Detmers!

In *Prénom Carmen*, Joseph is a bank security guard, a little guardian of the law who's supposed to watch over the riches that guarantee the social order. He falls brutally in love with the beautiful Carmen as she aims her gun at the bank he's supposed to be protecting. In order to flee with her without attracting attention, he proposes handcuffing himself to her, as if she were his prisoner. This chimera of a mixed figure, the Law chained to desire (an image Godard borrowed from Hitchcock), brings to the surface the vagaries of a Law that is confused about its compromises with desire. But, if desire has always been the Law's linked counterpart, it's not to be chained to it, but to lean on it. Joseph will bear out the sad experience of this for, believing he might otherwise lose Carmen's desire, he will estrange her more surely and irreparably by chaining himself to her.

The play on incest, which reared its head in *Sauve qui peut (la vie)*, proceeds clandestinely in this film, with Carmen's allusion to her adolescent relations with Uncle Jean: "I lived here. It's the house of one of my uncles. I must have been thirteen or fourteen. Over there was the living room; this is where his bedroom was . . . [she adopts a serious and pensive pose during a long silence] . . . his bedroom." The uncle is nearly the father, but is not really the father, and the allusion to what might have happened in the room is so suspensive—in the uncle's as well as the niece's formulation—as to cause the spectator to perceive it as nostalgia for something that did not take place, but that crossed the mind of each at the time, and reoccurs to them when they meet again, with the particular smiling tenderness that one may feel toward the evocation of something that did not take place and will remain forever in the realm of reverie. But this uncle who also recalls their past, in the same hesitant, suspensive rhythms ("It was a long time ago. The last school vacation was . . . a long time ago"), is Godard himself. He thus displaces onto Carmen–Maruschka Detmers (without really believing it, as she is much too wholesomely sensual) his dream of a film about incest with Claire–Myriem Roussel, who remains discreetly on hold, on the horizon of this film, as the absolute Other woman, the potential Virgin she will soon become.

The question of attack in *Prénom Carmen* becomes the subject of a long sequence in which Godard, as is his habit, lets himself be carried away by words, stringing together metaphors and mounting a parallelism between the "attack on a bank" and "attack on a piece of music"—not Bizet, as it happens, but Beethoven, the late quartets. The latency of the thought process is such that, even in this transition film, Godard attempts to understand what's happening at the mysterious moment of the attack, and so he observes how the bow attacks the strings, how four musicians in rehearsal attack a notoriously difficult piece of music. How does he himself attack the filming of this music that is coming into being? Here again the composition is in a certain way given: the musicians must face each other in pairs, in order for each to follow the movements of the other three. The attack on such a scene, if you want to film one of the characters "legibly," with no constraints or masking, is more or less prescribed by a "card party" composition: you place the axis of the camera at forty-five degrees, between the character opposite and the one to the right or left. Or yet again, still in classical fashion, you shoot one character straight-on, and show part of the back of the one facing him or her. Godard chose an axis between the two, neither really one nor the other, and a lower attack. Thus, the image of the musician shot straight-on is masked intermittently (as is the film by the Maltese cross) by the elbow and bow of the musician with his back to the camera, each time he "draws" his bow. This intrusion of an image from the back into the frontal image is governed by the technical parameters of the musical instruments, and by the score itself; yet, it feels like a random movement in relation to the organization of the visible, like an unforeseen blinking, which Godard organizes, but doesn't determine. This must have accounted in large part for his pleasure in filming it from such an unusual angle. The intrusion of this visual beating of wings functions simultaneously as a visual nuisance (the masking, the blur) and as a return of seeing, a little as if you were seeing the same gesture palpitating simultaneously from the front and the back, superimposed.

In *Je vous salue Marie*, which closes the trilogy, Godard's very choice of subject places him from the outset

PRENOM CARMEN
1983
Myriem Roussel

JE VOUS SALUE MARIE
1985
Myriem Roussel

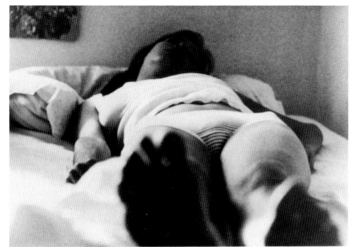

between desire and the forbidden. It is common knowledge that this film on the Virgin came about in lieu of two films he dreamed of making with the same actress: one on father–daughter incest, the other on Freud and Dora, two films that were never made. But this story of the Virgin as interpreted by Godard is clearly both a film on the temptation of incest and a film on another forbidden relation, that between analyst and patient. When Godard, raised and educated a Protestant, decided to tell the story of the Virgin through images, he had to confront a double resistance in himself: first, the theological rejection of the cult of the Virgin by the Reformation; and second, a defiant Protestant reaction to the Catholic love of ornament and imagery, which has encouraged the figuration of the Virgin everywhere, and in all her states. Godard devoted himself to filming the sacred through the figure that is, to him, a priori, as a Protestant, the most forbidden, and certainly the most dangerous. He has less of a right than others to take up the representation of the Virgin, and he has volunteered that during the filming, he felt more than once, quite physically, the manifest presence of this interdiction, as if it were coming from the Virgin herself: "There were days when we were punished, punished for having wanted to do it: 'That's not true, that mustn't be shown, thou shalt not show my face and belly like that.'"[8] Orthodox Catholics, as we've seen, would agree with the Virgin.

Going against all tradition, Godard attacked his subject from a decentered point of view, focusing on the character of Joseph and his sufferings. While Mary accepts very quickly the miracle of her election, Joseph is caught squarely between his love and his desire. His love for her tells him he must believe her and renounce his own desire, which she is now obligated to refuse. He is caught also in the dread of uncertainty over the question of the Name-of-the-Father: his fiancée is going to have a child that is not his and asks him to believe that it is also not another's. In a scene at the farm immediately following the birth of the child, Mary's father puts his finger on this crucial point of the Symbolic, on the very foundation of the Law: "So, is he going to call Joseph Daddy? How are you going to work it out?" Joseph's entire ordeal, which occupies a good part of the first half of the film, will be to overcome his desire and distress before the loss of his symbolic reference points. But, because he is fighting the wrong battle, when he tries to submit to the forbidden, against his desire (which perforce becomes all the stronger, to the point of exasperation, like that of Joseph in *Prénom Carmen*), he will meet with defeat after defeat. His calvary will end only when Mary, initiating a final battle with the angel, makes him understand clearly that it's not a question of stamping his foot and sacrificing himself at the foot of the forbidden, but of totally renouncing his disbelief, his doubt, and accepting the "taboo that spares the sacrifice": Mary has another Master, not a rival, not an equal, but an absolute Other to whom Joseph, too, must submit. Then, and only then, will there be no more sin or interdiction, and Joseph will be authorized to touch Mary's belly. Up to this point, Godard has been content to accompany poor Joseph on his path and in his pain at seeing Mary's body; he's undergone the same trials and will succeed, finally, after a thousand difficulties, in getting a pure shot of Mary's belly, a shot uncontaminated by other images. At exactly this point in the film, Godard effects an ingenious reversal. He dismisses Joseph: his work is done, and he's helped Godard finish a part of his. Now, in the long and very beautiful scene in the room, Godard can finally be alone with Mary. With no further need of a proxy within the image, he will himself occupy, offscreen, the silent place of the Master and of God the Father. And this is the supreme test: Godard expects his actress to give him the truth she contains like a secret, but to which she does not herself possess the key. Faced with this terribly unspoken demand, this exasperating patience (Godard has all the time in the world), she will twist this body that harbors its inexpressible secret, and respond in her own uncontrollable way, before the camera, with all manner of painful and ecstatic postures, including the hysterical arch and catatonia, to what she assumes to be the request of the Master. The stake has never been so clearly the disjunction, the gulf between the composition (the postures that the actress offers him and hides from him) and the attack, which Godard attempts repeatedly, from all sides, at different distances, from all angles. More than ever the essential question has become that of the attack in and on the shot, of the body of the film reduced here to its simplest and most naked expression, that of the actress' body simultaneously offered and refused.

From the moment of her election, Mary has been excluded from the community of women, for Godard, good disciple of Rossellini that he is, and from personal experience, knows this truth, which tortures him: election equals exclusion. In a quick, discrete shot, we have already seen Mary hesitate before a supermarket display of lipsticks, torn between desire and the forbidden. Earlier, she had quickly given up this token of femininity that she coveted with nostalgia, but that she no longer had the right to wear. At the end of the shot, she gestures with a sad little smile (no, thank you, she was only looking) to an invisible person offscreen; whether it's the angel reminding her of her mission, or an obliging saleswoman, doesn't matter. At the very end of the film, when Mary has accomplished her mission, she can reenter the community of women, freed at last from the prohibitions linked to her election. She is returned into circulation among other women, reintegrated into the circuit of this normal humanity that Godard continually tries to figure out how to join. He films this metaphor literally. Up to the end of the film, he stubbornly shoots Mary's face or body, with the difficulties we have seen. Then, out of the blue, he radically changes his attack and shoots at a high angle, lively, easy, painless shots clearly lifted from Jacques Tati's *Trafic*—for example, Mary's legs visible below an elegant dress, strolling in medium heels along segments of streets traced with various arrows and other signs, and followed by a man who looks as if he might want to pick her up—further proof that she's turned back into an ordinary woman, walking through the middle of the community of men and consigned to their lust. In fact, the man following her is the Angel of the Annunciation, but she no longer recognizes him. He takes leave of his mission, and frees her of her own, disappearing after a last, utterly trivial "Hail, Mary!" We then see Mary in close-up, with her wavy hair, seated in a car and lighting the first cigarette of her new life. Godard chose the classical camera position for shooting someone at the steering wheel of a stopped car: through the open window of the car. In the following shot, a bit closer but with the camera still on the same axis, she timidly lifts a bright, shining tube of lipstick to her pale lips. This will be the ultimate proof and test of her reintegration, the sign that she is once again available to her own desire. But the interdiction under whose law she has suffered continues to weigh upon her, even if she is formally released from it. Breathlessly, Godard shot this moment of hesitation, her desire mixed with fear, as she brings the lipstick toward and away from her lips, just as he himself hesitated to enter with his camera into the space of the tableaux vivants in *Passion*.

At the ultimate and decisive moment when the lipstick is about to touch her lips, when she will cease to be "alone among all women" to become again a woman among and like others, Godard does not turn Mary's eyes away. With this gesture, she recoups the right to sexual pleasure, and regains at the same time her mortal state. The two shots where this annunciation in reverse takes place, however, are strangely unsettling; it's as if Godard had felt at that moment the imperious need to decenter the filming of this scene with an absolutely unexpected attack, so as to confront its obscenity with an even more violent filmic act: a shot in profile, quite surprising because of its atypical focus, sharp on the curls in the foreground, and frankly blurred on the lip-

stick reaching for her lips. This is the last shot of the film: a close-up on that blood-red, toothless, gaping mouth, opened onto a black hole, deframed, open wide in a silent cry of orgasm and death.

Ten years of Godardian images after Hitchcock's death, we are perhaps in a better position to understand what he meant in 1980 when he declared that this was an era of the "ebbing of the visual," at a moment when images seemed more than ever given over to a galloping inflation. What did he mean exactly by the "visual" that he decreed "repressed" in and by most of these images? In the global stock of images (both documentary and fiction), the shots he set aside for his *Histoire(s) du cinéma* with a surgical—and enormously confident—precision are all the more precious for approaching Godard's notion of the "visual" in that they represent a minute selection, which owes nothing to the established cultural hierarchy, but everything to a sudden intuition of "recognition" of the images that concern him. Our first observation, according to the evidence, might then be: the "visual" for Godard is an entirely special quality of the visible that happens only in very rare images, and has nothing to do with a simple capacity to capture or reproduce things. Nor is it a question of a vulgar marking of the gaze in the image, which designates too often the look at the expense of the thing looked at. The "visual" is a stamp whose imprint is much more unpredictable, and impossible to reproduce, and whose presence largely eludes the willful efforts of the filmmaker. It can be obtained in all innocence, just as it can refuse itself to whoever tries to trap it. From this point of view, Hitchcock was a "visual" filmmaker, but not always for the good reasons he gave in his interview with Truffaut. The Hitchcockian look is sometimes allowed to ignore the Master's main concern, for the "spectators' direction," and reveal what his obsession with a perfect economy of readability forced itself precisely to repress: his relation to the body of the actress, for example, whenever she took precedence, in the drive to shoot, over the function of the shot in the scene. These Hitchcockian skids have given us some of his visually most unforgettable shots.

The "visual," according to Godard, might well be the name of this unexpected unveiling of the look that seizes us suddenly, once every ten thousand shots, when a shot changes course, with a double emotion: that of a rediscovered freshness and acuity of vision, and that of a fragile and moving hyperpresence of the beings and things on the screen. The viewer is caught unawares, by virtue of an unexpected attack that makes mysteriously present what was until then merely visible. At such moments, that actor, that tree, that sky, are no

JE VOUS SALUE MARIE
1985
Myriem Roussel

JE VOUS
SALUE MARIE
1985

longer a celluloid actor, tree, and sky, but things that once really lived and breathed on this earth, for a few very real seconds, and with their wave of still living emotion are miraculously able to reach us. They become removed temporarily from the fiction, restored for the duration of a shot to this planet and this species that are temporarily ours.

The shots devoted to women in *Histoire(s) du cinéma* are particularly evocative of this kind of emotion, which is all the stronger when they're removed from all dramatic context. The places where this imprinting of the visual plays itself out are too many to name, but it has nothing to do with being photogenic. On the contrary, the photogenic qualities of a Greta Garbo, for example, would actually be a deficit of the visual as we've understood it so far. Nor has it anything to do with the actress' ability to act. This mysterious designation seems to take place somewhere between posture (the disposition of the body, the way in which it appears to offer itself to the gaze) and attack, in the way the filmmaker, suddenly inspired, forgets old habits, becomes oblivious to codes, and finds in that instant a new, previously unimagined relation between the two—a bizarre, slightly twisted, and yet very fresh relation, like pure spring water, something never pre-

scribed, in any case, from the program that lurks in any shot scheme.

Most shots in most films only take concrete shape as the result of a series of deductions, which both programs them and progressively diminishes opportunities for the visual along the way. The scene is deduced from its function in the script, the shot is deduced from its function in the scene, the composition is deduced from its function in the shot, and the attack is more often than not deduced from the readability of the composition. Ten years after his prophecy on the ebbing of the visual, it's enough to look at any scene at random in *Nouvelle Vague* to realize that Godard, even when he forces himself with earnestness and conviction to tell a story, remains unshakably refractory in the face of this logic of deduction; at the moment of filming, he refuses to give in, to submit the visible to it, like a horse that balks before a fence. He then starts to search (this search can be just waiting) within the visible, and, more often than anyone else, finds in it a reason to shoot that's no longer either a reason or a program, just something that rekindles in a flash his desire to shoot *that* particular shot. It's an injunction that happens at the crossroads of reality itself and of a more unpredictable drive that has nothing to do with the script, an inner drive that's always deviant, yet always on the alert, looking out for the unpredictable burst of the visual within or against the visible—a quality of light, a posture, a movement, a masking, a sign that suddenly beckons him imperiously.

For the Godard of the eighties, this quest for the visual more than once took the path of resistance—resistance not only to the readable, but to the visible itself, as if he were secretly obeying an internal dictum, not unlike Valéry's axiom that in art "you must create the need, the aim, the means, and *even the obstacles*." [9] Godard's *Histoire(s) du cinéma* began with another axiom of resistance to the visible, this one borrowed from Bresson: "Don't go showing every side of everything." [10] The gap between composition and attack created in Godard's work over the course of the decade one of those subterranean contradictions that secretly mark all creative advances, and that flicker occasionally on the surface of a film or a sequence, before plunging just as quickly back into that obscure zone where the work of negativity is as vital to the progress of the work as that which gives the superficial illusion of moving toward its accomplishment. I know of few cases as exemplary of this negativity at work in all acts of true creation, which Blanchot speaks of, as this refusal to submit on the part of the act of filming, which alone can make a true act of it, to the natural inclination of the visible.

Notes

1 "Alfred Hitchcock est mort," interview with Serge July, *Libération*, May 2, 1980. Reprinted in Alain Bergala, ed., *Jean-Luc Godard par Jean-Luc Godard* (Paris: Cahiers du Cinéma, 1985), p. 416.

2 Cited in a footnote by Robert Bresson in *Notes sur le cinématographe* (Paris: Gallimard, 1975), p. 39.

3 "Orson Welles," interview with Alain Bergala and Jean Narboni in *Orson Welles*, special edition of *Cahiers du Cinéma*. Cited in "Le Chemin vers la parole," interview with Jean-Luc Godard, *Cahiers du Cinéma*, no. 336 (May 1982). Reprinted in *Jean-Luc Godard par Jean-Luc Godard*, p. 504.

4 "I had moved away from the father and daughter idea; then it became a variation on Freud and Dora. . . . The actress I wanted to have relations with—both personal and professional—either became afraid, necessarily, or else remained human. . . . Then it occurred to me: God the Father and his daughter. . . ." Remarks by Jean-Luc Godard in the *Interview* with Philippe Sollers filmed by Jean-Paul Fargier.

5 "Propos rompus," *Cahiers du Cinéma*, no. 316 (October 1980). Reprinted in *Jean-Luc Godard par Jean-Luc Godard*, p. 465.

6 "*Passion*, introduction à un scénario," in *Jean-Luc Godard par Jean-Luc Godard*, p. 493.

7 Simone Weil, *La Pesanteur et la grâce* (Paris: Plon, 1988), second edition, p. 10.

8 "La Curiosité du sujet," interview with Jean-Luc Godard by Dominique Païni and Guy Scarpetta, special "Godard" issue of *Art Press* (February 1985), p. 18.

9 Cited in Maurice Blanchot, "La Mort possible," in *L'Espace littéraire* (Paris: Gallimard, 1955). Emphasis added.

10 *Notes sur le cinématographe*, p. 107. In fact, Bresson writes: "Don't show every side of everything. [Leave a] margin of the undefined."

PRENOM CARMEN

1983

Jacques Bonaffé and Maruschka Detmers

THE HOLE AND THE ZERO

The Janus Face of the Feminine in Godard

Laura Mulvey

When I last wrote about Godard, in 1979, my argument ended with an appraisal of the adverse effects of his sexualized, surface images of woman, as against the positive effects of his radical exploration of cinema itself. I said, "Sandrine's body [in *Numéro deux* (1975)] is shown without questioning traditional uses of female beauty and sexual allure prevalent in dominant image production. Yet the film rigorously undercuts itself by refusing to use imagery that simply holds the spectator's gaze."[1] Now, over ten years later, I want to try to find a critical approach that does more than use images of women as a litmus test of a film's critical worth. Godard, in the 1960s, was daringly innovative with cinema, and his work during the late 1960s and early 1970s influenced all the important debates taking place about politics and the avant-garde. His 1980s cinema is still innovative and experimental, but the experimental instinct and innovative rationale have changed. I want to see if it is possible to chart these changes through the changing spectrum of the roles and representations of women in his films.

These roles and representations bear witness to a bruised but obstinate engagement with sex and sexual difference that has painfully traced a zigzag track through many of Godard's films. They also often function as a kind of channel or crossroad at which different strands of ideas, quite unconnected with sexuality, crisscross to suggest links or interconnections that would not otherwise have appeared. In both these models, woman functions as a signifier of more than herself, but the significance of the "more" varies according to the shifts in Godard's own political and aesthetic trajectory. Concentrating particularly on the changing configurations in late Godard, but taking earlier work into account, I want to argue that the feminine is a weak link in the chain, or rather a symptomatic site that offers a point of departure for decoding and deciphering the web of other meanings (political, aesthetic, psychosexual) that then themselves reflect back onto and inflect the significance of the feminine.

The metaphors I have been using (crisscross, configuration, channel, web, weak link in the chain) are meant to imply that processes of metonymy and displacement may be at work here. However, the feminine in Godard also sets up another kind of spatial figuration, one that corresponds to his fascination with women as mystery and enigma. Here, the metaphors that come to mind are more likely to be those of unmasking, unveiling, and bringing to visibility a hidden interior concealed behind a separate, conceptually polarized exterior. Paradoxically, it is in this figuration, deeply imbricated with fantasies of sexual difference and the female body, that the psychoanalytic comes to the fore. Following Freud, who compared the primary processes to the hieroglyph and the rebus (which contain the clues to their decipherment in their formal structure and cannot be reduced to the metaphor of veiling), I see the interior/exterior figuration, far from providing a model for analysis, as itself a rebus needing to be analyzed. It cannot be understood in the simple terms of discovery that, desiring and dreading, it attempts to offer. The interior/exterior opposition corresponds to a fantasy of woman as artificially "made up" to attract by a surface representation of difference that distracts from the hidden, secret, anxiety-provoking sign of difference.

In Godard's cinema, although this figuration is rooted in the psychosexual, its topography links it to other thematic strands. For instance, while Carmen shares its telltale iconography, seductive on the surface, secretly destructive and castrating, Marie represents the opposition between body and soul, the opposition between materiality and the idea, and the carnal and the spiritual. The interior/exterior opposition links, through the female body, into other meanings, and the figure of the feminine enigma allows Godard to present other enigmas. During the 1960s, the themes of his films begin to revolve around art, politics, sex; these in turn are articulated specifically into the characteristic, inextricably intertwined Godardian triad: cinema, factory, and body. This move into materialism marks Godard's middle period, and it is the sphere of politics/the factory that gradually gets written out of his films by the time he reaches *Prénom Carmen* (1983) and *Je vous salue Marie* (1985). Although cinema and the body/sexuality are still central, their meaning and their imbrication have changed. The tension between surface and secret, the visible and the invisible, shift from a materialist curiosity to a sense of the inevitability of mystery.

A screen is a surface that displays pictures and yet can hint that something is concealed behind it. It is an emblem of ambivalence about what can be seen and not seen, what is spectacularly fascinating and what is fascinatingly secret, what is pleasurable and what is fearful, what is conventionally acceptable and what is repressed. As a projection of images onto a screen, cinema attracts the metaphoric connotations of "a screen," expanding the simple white rectangle that receives the image into further spatial dimensions. Metaphors of surface and concealment arouse our curiosity, our desire to see and to know something that is hidden and illicit. In *Les Carabiniers* (1963), Michel-Ange sees a film for the first time and goes through the stock responses that tradition has attributed to people's first encounter with the illusion of cinema.[2] When a girl in a bath comes on the screen, he tries to climb up, to see *inside* the screen, which falls on top of him, a victim of the well-known guarantee of illusion and fascination supplied by the cinema machine in alliance with the eroticized female body. There is nothing *behind* the screen, but the cinema can open up its own *behind* by breaking its collusion with the screen's surface, its illusion and fascination, to reveal its mechanics of production. There is, built in, the potential for the disappointment that accompanied, for instance, demystification of the Wizard of Oz. Godard's response to the problem of the screen illusion was not limited to the materiality of mechanisms of cinema. Why, he asks while showing the camera and acknowledging the audience, these sounds and these images?

I have argued recently that the concept of female spectatorship should be theorized to include the drive of curiosity as a critical response to the lure of voyeurism.[3] The image on the screen becomes an enigma to decipher: why these sounds and these images? In *Je vous salue Marie,* Marie visits her family doctor. Before he examines her and verifies her virgin pregnancy, he goes behind a screen to wash his hands, meanwhile making a remark that she cannot hear. The camera is in long shot, composed around Marie, sitting in her underwear on the examining table. She asks him to repeat his remark, and the camera is repositioned in medium shot on the doctor, as he says, seemingly for the benefit of the audience rather than Marie: "I've always wondered what we can know about a woman, and then I discovered that all you can know is what men knew already: there is a mystery there." Faced with the Virgin Mary, of course, mystery becomes Mystery. It is as though Godard had struggled for so long

to get behind the surface, that, in this film, he has taken a step back to examine it with awe and with irony. However, in doing so, he installs a fetishized concept of beauty, smooth and complete, in cinema, in the body, and in nature.

This triad produces a very different aesthetic from that of his political phase. In the midsixties, in what could be called his Debord phase (notably with *Une Femme mariée* [1964] and *Deux ou Trois Choses que je sais d'elle* [1966]), the society of the spectacle and spectacle of consumerism made up a third theoretical strand, alongside the body and cinema;[4] and in his Marxist phase (for instance with *British Sounds* [1969] and *Tout va bien* [1972]) he looked behind the façade of consumerism at the process of the commodity's production in the factory. These three elements (cinema, the body, and the commodity) are all connected through the concept of fetishism. Before going on to consider Godard's later work, I want to collect some themes that relate to the idea of fetishism, and his strategies for opposing it, in order to see how the elements that contributed to his enormous theoretical influence in the 1960s and 1970s emerge in a different mix in the early 1980s with *Passion* (1982), *Prénom Carmen*, and *Je vous salue Marie. Passion* is a watershed film, a point at which Godard's changing aesthetic and political priorities attain visibility. *Carmen* is a transitional film, a film of crisis that marks the distance that lies between *Passion* and *Je vous salue Marie.* Finally, I will juxtapose "Carmen" and "Marie" to form a diptych, in order to consider the significance of the male/female sexual relations in both films, in which the two female characters are apparently polarized but indicate a single anxiety posed by the female body. First, I will introduce *Passion* through Isabelle Huppert's characters in that film and in *Sauve qui peut (la vie)* (1979), the film that immediately preceded it.

The last traces of analytical, politically radical Godard, mainly personified in Isabelle Huppert's character in both films, drained away somewhere between *Sauve qui peut* and *Passion.* In *Sauve qui peut,* she plays a prostitute. Not a victim, like Nana in *Vivre sa vie* (1962), nor a working-class housewife, like Juliette in *Deux ou Trois Choses,* but still within the tradition of Godard's preoccupation with prostitution. For Godard, the links between prostitution and capitalist society are both figurative and real. The housewife in *Deux ou Trois Choses* becomes a prostitute to gain financial access to consumer goods for herself and her home and her family: she uses herself as sexual commodity to acquire commodities. The woman's attribute, saleable sex, her exchange and circulation, is analogous to the commodity and its exchange and circulation. Both have to produce a desirable surface, a masquerade of availability, an appearance of self-sufficiency, an erasure or emptying of history. While Marx saw commodity fetishism as originating in labor power's invisibility in the expression of a commodity's value, *disavowal* of the origin of value was achieved only by generalized exchange. Money/gold circulates the commodities, guarantees their autonomous value, and conceals their contaminated origin on the production line. The question of visibility emerges here. Juliette's opaque, placid, passive exterior as sexual object is juxtaposed to her inner thoughts, conveyed, on the sound track, to the audience but not to the characters on the screen, while Godard's own whispering voice also mediates, commenting on the action on the screen and questioning its spontaneity and its autonomy.

Godard's citation of Brecht, in Marina Vlady's introduction to *Deux ou Trois Choses*, had a strong influence on the development of avant-garde theory at the time. The citation also created a bridge between a Brechtian dismantling of the "plenitude" of the spectacle, cinema's function as commodity to be consumed, and the structure and function of commodity fetishism in late capitalist society. Although the mediation is enabled through the figure of the prostitute and movie star, spectacle and commodity in herself, theorization of fetishistic aspects of cinema concentrated, at first, on the apparatus. If the shiny, glossy surface fascination of the screen could be unmasked, to reveal the process of production concealed behind it, the film would be stripped of its fetishistic aspects. In Godard, this desire to free cinema into the complex space and time of intertextual reference, direct address, self-reflexivity, material specificity, and so on, parallels the Marxist desire to defetishize the commodity, by making visible, through political analysis, the specificity of its process of production. In this way, the materialism of a modernist aesthetics meets the materialism of Marxism in Brecht and through to Godard.

In two complementary scenes, Godard uses the figure of the prostitute to forge further chains of reference between two different aspects of capitalism and sexuality. In *Deux ou Trois Choses*, the two prostitutes are called to an American businessman's hotel suite. Their client asks them to walk in front of him, one wearing a Pan Am flight bag over her head, the other a TWA flight bag, while he photographs them. The American's erotic investment in his powerful and expensive camera, and the girls' masking by the two great logos, turn the prostitute/client relationship into a ritual, grotesquely celebrating both the dependence of American consumer capitalism on the representation of its phallic power for sexual pleasure and the imbrication of the commodity with sexuality. In the second

scene, in *Sauve qui peut* (which has since drawn a great deal of interesting comment from critics), the prostitute and other subordinate employees create a Rube Goldberg sex machine of cold, impersonal, Taylorized erotic gestures under the management of their boss for his profit and satisfaction. While the first scene revolves around images of consumption, the second mimics the production line. While the first explores the fetishism of the commodity, the second caricatures capitalism's relations of production, which fetishism conceals.

However, the sex machine is itself, obviously, at one and the same time, deeply fetishistic. It uses the mechanical, synchronized movements of the robot, through which the process of production, otherwise dangerously close to exposing the labor theory of value, can conceal its secrets. Robert Stam describes it in the following manner: "Like a filmmaker [the boss] assigns precise movements to his actors. . . . The orgy participants, like assembly line workers, are reduced to well-defined jerks, twists, moans and quivers."[5] Raymond Bellour and Pascal Bonitzer have similarly drawn attention to the analogy. Bellour has pointed out that the stop-motion frames privilege particular moments in *Sauve qui peut* and "make impossible the imaginary pause that the image needs in order to satisfy its false plenitude," and that they allow "the rebirth of the image, this movie toward a writing-painting freed from the deceptive imaginary plenitude described by the forward movement of the machine. . . ." This, he says, takes place between two gazes: the daughter's gaze at the death of her father, and the sight of the prostitute's ass gazing back at the camera.[6] There is also a sense of terminal loss suggesting that Godard, this time, is not engaged so much in the deconstruction of the cinema machine, or its liberation, but rather in recording the blockage of these processes. The imbrication of cinema, the factory, and the body is there, visibly in motion, but it no longer signifies more than just that.

Factory-body-cinema. In *Passion*, these three grand themes that preoccupied Godard for so long come to occupy three distinct spaces that overflow into one another through the intertwined strands of the narrative. Work-sex-sound/image. The factory sphere is represented by Isabelle Huppert as worker and Michel Piccoli as boss. Piccoli's character is reminiscent of the boss/client in the *Sauve qui peut* sex-machine scene; Isabelle's character is only connected to that scene through the presence of the actress and the fact that her character is, at the opening of the film, within the sphere of the factory/machine and subject to the power of the boss. The sphere of cinema is represented by the

Jean-Luc Godard

Myriem Roussel

director, his cast and crew, and the studio ("the most expensive in Europe") where they are making a movie, itself called *Passion*. The factory/cinema analogy continues, and there are numerous overlaps between these two spheres. Piccoli's presence, although here on the side of the factory, provides a ghostly trace of his role as the scriptwriter in *Le Mépris* (1963), rewriting the *Odyssey*, rather as, in this film, the director tries to re-create Old Master paintings. In their behavior and social gestures, the dramatis personae of the film crew echo the factory hierarchy and division of labor. Jerzy, the director, is authoritarian and peremptory on the set. Sophie, the production assistant, behaves very much like a factory manager; she insists on the rules, the importance of productivity, and the place of narrative in cinema. Patrick, the assistant director, behaves very much like a foreman; he bullies and exhorts the extras to "work," rounding them up and overseeing the management of the set, literally chasing the girls. The sphere of sex/the body is represented by Hanna Schygulla, Piccoli's wife, who owns the hotel where the cast and crew stay and the film world overlaps with that of the factory next door. Jerzy spends time with Hanna when he should be directing the film, making her watch a video of her face, in close-up, recorded under the sway of strong emotion, as he tries to persuade her to move into the world of cinema and play a part in the tableau after Rubens.

Isabelle, the factory worker, is sacked at the beginning of *Passion*. Her narrative concentrates primarily on her struggle for reinstatement or compensation, and is thus arguably in keeping with Godard's earlier commitment to working-class struggle. Her character is physically and emotionally vulnerable; her slight stammer conveys a lack of mastery over language and the discourses of culture that isolates her from the world of film. Toward the end of the movie, Piccoli capitulates and pays her off, too exhausted by his racking cough to continue the fight. She is suddenly transformed from worker into a free agent, a potential entrepreneur, able to choose her future, as though the narrative had decided to move away from the signifier of the working class and its struggle, in a gesture toward one kind of production, and that one artistic, rather than political. Cinema thus stays as a central point for investigation and inquiry, but the "how" is now decidedly directed more toward the creative process, although the economic and technical are still present.

The relationship between Jerzy and Isabelle points to parallels between her struggle with the factory boss and his struggle to reconcile the industrial demands of production and distribution with creative autonomy. On another level, there is a parallel between Isabelle's

stammer, her struggle for articulate speech, and the director's loss of direction in his film project. Both characters are trying to find a flowing form of expression and find themselves blocked. The director has to find a way through his film without having recourse to a story, as required by the investors, Sophie, and general expectation; nor can he master the lighting on the set. He is attempting to re-create in tableaux, and then film in three dimensions, some of the great and famous paintings of Western art. Created on a flat surface by the painter, with the illusion of depth and movement frozen for one split second, these images have to move from the trompe l'oeil of the canvas surface into the trompe l'oeil of the screen surface. In the process, the director, like Michel-Ange in *Les Carabiniers*, is attempting to penetrate *inside* the space implied by these familiar paintings, transforming them into the round for the camera's participation and exploration. The stunningly beautiful tableaux are re-created on huge sets like labyrinths, channeling and then blocking the flowing movement of the camera. A technician with video camera and cables, or other external, interloping elements, may break up the magical trompe l'oeil by presenting, in the image on the screen, the processes of its production. However, while the earlier metaphor of "unveiling" evoked the surface/secret dichotomy of the fetish, the appropriate metaphor here is penetration, not behind but into the surface. The surface now possesses a channel to its own behind.

The initial identification between Isabelle and Jerzy is like a last remaining trace of a theoretical condensation of the process of production, in capitalism and in art, that characterized Godard's deconstructive, Brechtian aesthetics. In *Passion* Godard's priorities seem to change direction. It is as though he were describing the shift of emphasis in his work, away from materialist modernism, into an exploration of art and the problems of creativity themselves. Isabelle, from this perspective, would (until her victory) represent the past of Godard's own shifting political trajectory and the changing climate of the 1980s, which said, in André Gorz's words, "Farewell to the working class." Jerzy describes himself as searching for a solution to his problems with cinema in between the two women, as different as day from night. The problem of cinema is imbricated with the female body, in a strange reversal of the 1960s preoccupation with the politics of the society of the spectacle and its relation to sexual politics. Now, the female body begins to be reconstituted as the prop of cinema. At the end of the film, Godard seems to signal a move out of the everyday into the world of fiction and fantasy. A young girl, a dancer and acrobat who works as a maid at the hotel, provides the film with an ending.

Jerzy is her "prince," and she accepts a lift in his car when he tells her, his "princess," that it is not a car but a magic carpet that will transport them back to Poland. The film ends with an escape from the space of the film and the space of the factory, but the space of the body, signified by the feminine, has been taken over by the fantasy escape of a fairy story.

After *Passion*, Godard made two films in succession that both deal directly with myths of feminine "mystery" and the "enigma" of the female body. The two myths are, on the face of it, diametrically opposed to each other. One, *Prénom Carmen*, reworks, in its main narrative strand, Prosper Mérimée's 1845 story, whose heroine, due to the success of Bizet's 1875 opera, quickly became an icon of feminine seductiveness and infidelity, and of rampant, independent sexuality. The other, *Je vous salue Marie*, daringly retells the myth of the Annunciation and the Virgin Birth and the story of Mary, the Christian culture's icon of feminine chastity, submission to the will of God, and spirituality. The two films polarize femininity into a binary opposition, the carnal and the spiritual. But the simple fact of polarization always links, as well as opposes, and the attributes that separate Carmen and Marie only superficially conceal the underlying "fit" between them. Both myths symbolize a zero point for Godard, at which the mystery of the feminine, profoundly destructive on one level, becomes a threshold to and signifier of other, *more profound* mysteries. There is a complex conflation between the enigmatic properties of femininity and the mystery of origins, particularly the origins of creativity, whether the creation of life or the creative processes of art. In both films the forces of nature have a presence unprecedented in Godard's cinema. Although landscape has often played its part, alongside quotations and works of art, in his montaged images (the journey through France in *Pierrot le fou* [1965], the Mediterranean in *Le Mépris*, Denise's bicycle ride in *Sauve qui peut*, the sky in *Passion*), in these two films, landscape has evolved into nature, and in both films is associated with the feminine.

I described *Passion*, earlier, as a watershed in Godard's work. The spheres of narrative space, separated out into thematic strands, replaced the chapter structure that Godard had used in *Sauve qui peut* and often in his earlier films. In *Prénom Carmen* the film is divided into different spaces according to formal strands rather than narrative or theme. It is as though the elements of film that are usually wound together in a hierarchical organization have been unraveled, so that sound acquires image track and image is used to generate sound track. The music is taken from Beethoven's late string quartets. A string quartet is intended for informal performance, and a "chamber" space, in which the members of the quartet practice, materializes alongside the space of the story to give an image to the music on the sound track.[7] Godard, in an interview, describes the sound in this film as "sculpted."

The only character from the sphere of the music to have contact with the narrative is Claire (Myriem Roussel, who will play Marie in the next film), although the quartet is present, as indeed is the whole rest of the cast, in the final scene in the hotel. While the sky and the countryside will have an important place in *Je vous salue Marie*, in *Prénom Carmen* the sea creates both sound and image tracks, creating a counterpoint to the Beethoven (and Claire), and acting as a metaphoric extension of Carmen. Equally, the strand of narration, or the desire for cinema, is personified by the director's presence on the screen, a kind of limbo, occasionally overlapping with the space of the story itself, dominated by Carmen. The narrator's participation in the narrative is true to Mérimée's original story, but Godard's presence is also like a materialization of his whispered voice, so familiar from previous sound tracks, and also, again, a reversal of his earlier, deconstructive appearances as part of the process of production.

In *Prénom Carmen* Godard plays the film director who has taken refuge in a nursing home (for the physically ill and the mentally ill) because he cannot make films. He is not literally ill. On the contrary, the fever that he needs in order to stay in the hospital seems to be also the fever that he lacks in order to make films. For the director, Godard implies, the cinema is a necessary object without which the world cannot be borne; although his special camera is there with him, like a fetish object, in his hospital room, it cannot, alone, conjure up cinema. When the nurse comes to take his temperature, gently encouraging his hopes for a fever, he says, "If I put my finger up your ass and counted to thirty-three, do you think I would get a fever?" In the next scene Carmen appears. Unlike the nurse, who seems to function more as a channel to desire, Carmen represents the feminine as "to be looked at." This investment in her seductiveness creates the sense of surface, of sheen and gloss, that the theoreticians of the 1960s and 1970s associated with the fetishism of both commodity and cinema. Carmen is the director's niece, whom he has desired since she was a little girl. She appears to ask her Uncle Jean's help for a film she is making with some friends and she marks both the onset of desire and the onset of the fiction, the adventure, the fantasy. Like the tower that starts to crash at the beginning of *Le Sang d'un poète* and then crumbles on the ground at the end, bracketing all the action in between as subjective, outside space and time, so the

nurse appears to bracket the narrative action in *Prénom Carmen*. When Uncle Jean needs his coat mended during a production meeting, the nurse reappears as the wardrobe mistress, and then remains his constant, inseparable companion, performing (in the sense of acting a part, with appropriate gestures and phrases) the role of production assistant, a trace of the Sophie part in *Passion*. At the end of the film Uncle Jean says to her, "That was a long thirty-three seconds."

Godard's performance is ironic, sad, and harshly self-parodic, as though to preempt the accusations that his late cinema is likely to draw, from, say, feminist or political quarters. He depicts the film director's dilemma as hopelessly fetishistic, his obsession with cinema and the female body as helplessly dependent, masochistic, exploitative. Cinema and sexuality merge into a condensation that is unashamedly masculine, while also being apologetically impotent. The director's fever is roused by and through the female body, as though, at the zero moment of creativity, Godard confronts bedrock and finds nothing left except the desire for desire. The cinema that slowly materializes, like a genie masturbated out of its bottle, is therefore a distillation, almost an abstraction or a reverie on the very limits of the filmmaker's fantasy. And the genie appears in the form of a femme fatale, also summoning up, generically, Godard's first great passion: film noir.

When I first saw *Prénom Carmen*, I was very moved. It was not the film, its story, or the plight of the director that moved me. It was, probably, the film's situation in Godard's own history, its lapse out of self-referentiality into nostalgia. The final title, "In Memoriam small movies," brought back the memory of the dedication to Monogram Pictures in *A bout de souffle* (1960). There is, thus, a double palimpsest, one layer tracing his own early work and, deeper still, the traces of the Hollywood cinema that had been his point of departure. The bridge that links the past to the present also inscribes the presence of what is crossed. Just as Godard represents the greatest of sixties radical cinema, so, also, his work is bound to raise the question of what happens after innovation, how the political filmmaker, working within the ethos of a particular historical conjuncture, has to deal directly with time, its passing, and its propensity to wash over a radical movement, an avant-garde, leaving its members stranded above the tide line. The theme and imagery of "strand-ed-ness" is central to *Prénom Carmen*, for instance, in the repeated shots of the sea, and the director's sense of being abandoned by cinema is dramatically replayed when Joseph is ultimately abandoned by Carmen. Cinema itself is only made use of, by the young people, as a masquerade to cover their attempted kidnapping.

Myriem Roussel

Philippe Lacoste

If, as it seemed to me, *Prénom Carmen* marks a moment of crisis in Godard's history, it also reveals the bare constitutive elements of his late cinema, all that remains when everything else is stripped away. The return to zero is a return to the origins of the director's own primal desire for cinema, rather than to the point zero that investigates the social circulation and significance of images, as, for instance, in *Le Gai Savoir* (1968). His struggle is now to represent what makes the making of cinema possible, its obsessive, romantic, delusory hold over the director, rather than a modernist, Brechtian struggle to represent the process of production of cinema and the process of production of meaning. Although there is an obstinate courage in Godard's "self-portrait" as the director who sees cinema slipping through his fingers, and a poetic heroism in his ability to turn even such an intimation of loss into new "sounds and images," the question persists: why, at the moment of crisis, should he return to these particular sounds and these particular images? And, above all, what is the significance of the juxtaposition between Carmen and Claire/Marie as two polarized icons of the feminine?

My sudden rush of nostalgia after seeing *Prénom Carmen* was focused above all on *Pierrot le fou. Pierrot le fou* was already a version of the Carmen story. That is, a story of *amour fou*, in which an essentially respectable and law-abiding hero is seduced by an irresistible, unfaithful woman into a descent into an underworld and a life of crime, on the run from the police. The end is death: Don José kills Carmen, who prefers death to losing her freedom, and, in Mérimée's original, as well as *Prénom Carmen*, Don José/Joseph gives himself willingly up to the police. The Carmen story arises from a separation between the hero's settled, everyday life and the other, nether world of passion, violence, and adventure. The gap that separates the two is bridged by the spell cast over Ferdinand by Marianne, over Joseph/Don José by Carmen.

Carmen returns to *Pierrot* not only with almost subliminal references such as a whistled phrase of "Au clair de la lune" and Joseph's repeated refusal to be called "Joe" (*"Je m'appelle Ferdinand/Joseph"*), but with a return to the kind of cinema defined toward the beginning of *Pierrot le fou* by Sam Fuller, appearing as himself: "A film is a battleground. Love. Hate. Action. Violence. Death. In one word . . . emotion." The bank robbery that Carmen stages shifts Joe from the side of the law to that of the criminal, just as Marianne's confrontation with the gunrunners shifts respectable Ferdinand from the bourgeoisie to the underworld. In both cases, *amour fou* leads to violence and a journey of crime, pursuit, and death ("Une saison en enfer"). The "emotion" is also

motion, the moving pictures, the movement of the narrative, the adventure that takes over the hero, and the fascination exerted by the heroine that binds together all the other levels of movement. Both Joe and Ferdinand are abandoned by the story when they are no longer desired by the heroine; Joe has no "role" in the final heist, and his sexual impotence is compounded by his narrative impotence.

For both Josephs (the Don and the Saint), sexual desire is an emasculating enslavement to the feminine, leading to abasement, whether with reconciled exaltation, in Marie, or with antagonized aggression, in Carmen. Both men confront, in narrative, the mythic condensation between the feminine and the enigma, both of which are described as "taboo" (the reference in *Prénom Carmen* is derived from the lines in *Carmen Jones*: "You go for me, an' I'm taboo/But if you're hard to get/I'll go for you, an' if I do/Then you are through/'Cos, if I love you, that's the end of you!"; in *Je vous salue Marie*, the angel explains to Joseph that "the taboo outweighs the sacrifice"), and both the men have to endure extremes of jealousy. Carmen wants to find out "what a woman can do with a man," Marie has to teach a man to relate to her body without sexuality. In each film the iconography of the central female character contrasts with the iconography of a secondary female character. While Claire, in *Prénom Carmen*, prefigures Marie, and is detached from the carnal world of Carmen by the spiritual abstraction of music, Eve, in *Je vous salue Marie*, is a presence of sexuality. She is a student taking classes on the origins of the universe with an exiled Czech professor with whom she falls in love. Eve is first shown sitting in the sunlight trying to solve the puzzle of Rubik's Cube. She represents the curiosity of her namesake, but, at the same time, the puzzle reflects the overall theme of mystery and enigma that runs through the film. In juxtaposition to the ultimate enigma, Marie's virgin pregnancy and birth, the mystery of the origins of life is discussed by the students. The professor holds the view that the beginnings of life were "organized and desired by a resolute intelligence," which interacted with chance at a certain moment to overdetermine the course of nature. To prove his point, Eve stands behind Pascal, covering his eyes, and guides him step by step through Rubik's Cube. Her directions, "Oui . . . non . . . non . . . oui . . . oui . . . oui," are repeated by Marie as she guides Joseph's hand to her stomach, teaching him to approach her body without touching it and accept the mystery that has befallen her.

While Carmen is linked to the restless movement of the sea, waves on the shore, and the tide, Marie is linked to the moon and the still surfaces of water, sometimes broken by ripples. The moon and water are ancient symbols of the feminine (as opposed to the sun and the earth) and the moon and the tide coexist in a cyclical time of repetition and return, which breaks radically with the linear time of, for instance, history and its utopian aspiration toward progress. Godard associates the cyclical with the sacred and the feminine. The roundness of the moon is reduplicated by Marie's other iconographical attribute, the basketball she takes with her to team practice and that Joseph hits from her hand whenever he challenges her chastity. The ball is round and complete, the circle of the feminine once again, but impenetrable, with *no hole*. In this sense, the ball functions as an object of disavowal, not in the classic scenario of fetishism that denies and finds a substitute for the absence of the mother's penis, but, rather, a denial of the wound, the open vagina, the hole. In one of the most complex and beautifully orchestrated shots in *Passion*, the camera moves between the film crew's space and the space of the set, contrasting the work involved in producing the image with the "finish" of the image itself. In this case, the image consists of a beautiful young and naked girl, who, at the director's request, floats in an Oriental pool and spreads her arms and legs into the shape of a star. As the camera moves slowly across the surface of the water, it seems opaque with the reflection of tiny points of light, like the reflected stars rippling at the opening of *Je vous salue Marie*. As the camera moves closer to the director, his friend asks him what he is looking at. He answers, "The wound of the world," and then turns away to try to perfect the lighting on the set. The theme returns in *Prénom Carmen*, when, after making love to Carmen for the first time, Joseph says, "Now I understand why prison is called 'The Hole.'" Marie's body, on the other hand, in its virginity, is perfect. The angel interrogates Joseph at one point in their stormy, aggressive relationship, asking, "What is the common denominator between the zero and Marie?" And answers himself, "Marie's body, idiot." The zero, the magical point of return for a new departure, the perfect circle, the space of the womb, that inside of the female body that is not the hole/vulva/wound. When the wardrobe mistress sews up the hole in his jacket in *Prénom Carmen*, Godard seems to suggest an affinity between the function of suture in cinema (the element considered most responsible, during the deconstructive seventies, for the false cohesion of conventional cinema and the subject it produced) and fear of the gaping hole, the wound. The fetishism of the smooth cinematic surface, and of the perfect surface of the female body, reassures, but only so far as "I know. . . . But all the same . . ."

Marie separates female sexuality, the female genitalia that represent the world, from reproduction, the space of the womb. The most frequently reproduced still from the film has itself acquired something like fetish status. Joseph's hand reaches toward Marie's stomach, which is stretched into the shape of a curve and framed, cut off precisely at groin and shoulder height. Joseph accepts the mystery, in relation to and through Marie's body, so that the enigmas of femininity and female sexuality are solved and sanitized, in polar opposition to Carmen's sexualized body, which has to remain ultimately uncertain and unknowable.

In *Sauve qui peut* the prostitute, Isabelle, acts sex with her client, Paul, while her interior monologue can be heard on the sound track. Constance Penley comments: "Isabelle, at the moment when she is presented exactly as the inevitable icon of the pornographic lovemaking scene, the close-up of the moaning woman's face serving as the guarantee of pleasure, is heard thinking about the errands she has to run."[8] Godard is illustrating a gap between the visible and the invisible, an external artifice that engages belief and an interiority that demands knowledge. This gap in men's knowledge of women's sexual pleasure reinforces the castration anxiety provoked by the female genitals, separated, as they are, from female reproductive organs, lacking any visible "sign" of pleasure. Gayatri Spivak discusses the problem, for men, presented by female sexuality as unknowable. She quotes Nietzsche: "Finally—if one loved them . . . what comes of it inevitably? That they 'give themselves.' The female is so artistic." And she comments, "Or: women impersonate themselves as having an orgasm even at the time of orgasm. Within the historical understanding of women as incapable of orgasm, Nietzsche is arguing that impersonation is woman's only sexual pleasure. At the time of greatest self-possession-cum-ecstasy, the woman is self-possessed enough to organise a self-(re)presentation without an actual presence of sexual pleasure to (re)present."[9] It is easy to see the phrase "women are so artistic" in Godard's mind's eye. At what point does art turn into artifice and vice versa? The woman's simulation, like cinema's, is spectacle, and what can only be seen as a surface still conceals its secrets; whatever the spectator *wants* to see, he may still suspect . . .

At the very end of *Je vous salue Marie*, Marie sits alone in a car, her face in close-up. She takes some lipstick from her bag and, as she applies it to her lips, the camera moves in to fill the frame with the shape of her mouth, which becomes dark and cavernous, surrounded by her bright, newly painted lips. She lights a cigarette. The cycle is complete: the Virgin turns into a whore, the hole returns to break the perfection of the zero.

Although Godard's cinema becomes more and more absorbed into the surface, it is not a return to a cinema

of plenitude and cohesion. It rigorously splits open the components of sound and image and narrative. His films are seen to be films, especially through the sound track's relation to the image, but they no longer articulate contradiction or struggle for change. And Godard's long-standing political concern with work and with the relationship of production to contemporary capitalist society is replaced, in *Je vous salue Marie*, by concern with creativity and with the relationship of the spiritual to the origins of being. And these mysteries, particularly nature and woman, cannot be penetrated except by God. The myths, clichés, and fantasies surrounding both Carmen and Marie constitute, not a mystery, but a rebus for a feminist criticism of Godard; yet as Godard retells these stories he shows, not only that they are Janus-faced, but how particularly *telling* they are for our culture. While trying to decode a deep-seated but interesting misogyny, I came to think that Godard's cinema knows its own entrapment, and that it is still probing, struggling to give sounds and images to mythologies that haunt our culture. For feminist curiosity, it is still a gold mine.

Notes

1   Laura Mulvey, "Images of Women; Images of Sexuality" (co-written with Colin MacCabe), in *Godard: Images, Sounds, Politics* (London: Macmillan, 1980).

2   I am indebted to Raymond Bellour's first lecture of his series at the National Film Theatre, London, February 1991.

3   Questionnaire on female spectatorship, *Camera Obscura*, no. 20-21 (May–September 1989), pp. 248–52. Also see the introduction to *Visual and Other Pleasures*: "Like voyeurism, curiosity is active and thus, in Freud's terms, masculine, but it can confuse the binary male/female active/passive opposition that I associated [with visual pleasure in 'Visual Pleasure and Narrative Cinema']. In the myths of Eve and Pandora, curiosity lay behind the first woman's desire to penetrate a forbidden secret that precipitated the fall of man. These myths associate female curiosity with an active narrative function." Also see my paper "Pandora: The Mask and Curiosity," in Beatriz Colomina, ed., *Sexuality and Space* (Princeton: Princeton Architectural Press, 1992).

4   Links between the spectacle and commodity fetishism had been made by Guy Debord in his pamphlet "The Society of the Spectacle," which in the late sixties, culminating in May 1968, had widespread influence. He says: "The spectacle is the moment when the commodity has attained total occupation in social life." In *Une Femme mariée* and *Deux ou Trois Choses*

Godard shows the female body to be the signifier of commodity fetishism, linking it to the society of the spectacle through the discourse of sexuality in advertising.

5   Robert Stam, "Jean-Luc Godard's *Sauve Qui Peut (la Vie),*" *Millennium Film Journal,* nos. 10/11 (Fall/Winter 1981–82).

6   Raymond Bellour, "I Am an Image," *Camera Obscura,* no. 8-9-10 (Fall 1982), pp. 120–21.

7   I would like to thank Michael Channon for confirming and developing this point for me.

8   Constance Penley, "Pornography, Eroticism," *Camera Obscura,* no. 8-9-10 (Fall 1982), p. 15 and reprinted in this volume as part of "Sexual Difference and *Sauve qui peut (la vie).*"

9   Gayatri Chakravorty Spivak, "Displacement and the Discourse of Woman," *Displacement: Derrida and After,* Mark Krupnick, ed. (Bloomington: Indiana University Press, 1983).

PLATES

LE PETIT SOLDAT
1960
Michel Subor, Anna Karina

SIX FOIS DEUX/
SUR ET SOUS LA COMMUNICATION

co-director: Anne-Marie Miéville

1976

"Photo et cie"

NUMERO
DEUX

NUMERO DEUX

1975

- à mon avis, papa c'est une
  usine.
- à mon avis, maman c'est un
  paysage.

NUMERO
DEUX

- c'est mon cul, c'est ma
  cuisine, c'est mes enfants,
  tu vois Pierrot, il y en
  a trop et en même temps
  c'est pas assez.

**NUMERO
DEUX**

- en guise de récompense, il
  lui colla cinq balles dans le
  buffet !

- et pourtant, il l'aimait, quelle
  drôle d'époque.

**FRANCE/TOUR/
DETOUR/
DEUX/ENFANTS**
co-director:
Anne-Marie Miéville
1977–78

Nathalie Baye

SAUVE QUI PEUT (LA VIE)

1979

Isabelle Huppert

Cécile Tanner

"The Virgin of the Immaculate Conception," after El Greco

Jerzy Radziwilowicz

"The Bather," after Ingres

Isabelle Huppert

PRENOM CARMEN

1983

Maruschka Detmers, Jacques Bonnaffé

Anne Gauthier

Myriem Roussel

Thierry Rode, Philippe Lacoste, Myriem Roussel

Thierry Rode, Myriem Roussel, Malachi Jara Kohan

Jean-Pierre Léaud

Nathalie Baye

Jean-Luc Godard

Philippe Rouleau

Jean-Luc Godard, Peter Sellars

Molly Ringwald

Alain Delon

Domiziana Giordano, Alain Delon

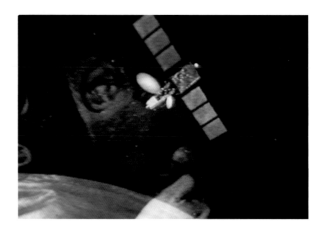

JLGFILMS

Anne-Marie Miéville
Jean-Luc Godard

Histoire(s) du cinéma

Puissance de la parole

Les français entendus par

Le rapport Darty

Dans une prison de Moscou,Jean-Victor Poncelet,officier de
l'armée de Napoléon,reconstruit sans l'aide d'aucune notes
les connaissances géométriques qu'il avait apprises   dans
les cours de Monge et de Carnot. Le <u>Traité des propriétés
projectives des figures</u> , publié en 1822,érige en méthode
générale le principe de projection utilisé par   Désargue
pour étendre les propriétés du cercle aux coniques et mis
en oeuvre par Pascal dans sa démonstration sur l' hexagram-
me mystique.

Il a donc fallu un prisonnier qui tourne en rond en face
d'un mur pour que l'application mécanique de l'idée et de
l'envie de projeter des figures sur un écran prenne prati-
quement son envol avec l'invention de la projection cinématographique. Notons également que le mur de départ était
rectangulaire.

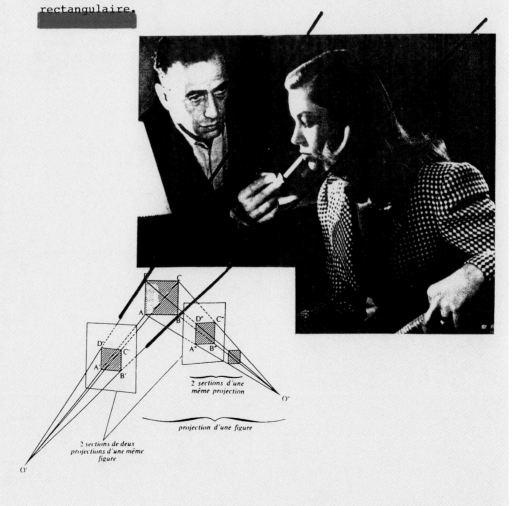

2 sections d'une
même projection

projection d'une figure

2 sections de deux
projections d'une même
figure

HISTOIRE (S) DU CINEMA
1A
TOUTES LES HISTOIRES

Production:Gaumont/JLG Films/La Sept/FR 3/Télévision Romande

HISTOIRE (S) DU CINEMA
1B
UNE HISTOIRE SEULE

Production: Gaumont/JLG Films/La Sept/FR 3/Télévision Romande

PUISSANCE DE LA PAROLE
FRANCE TELECOM

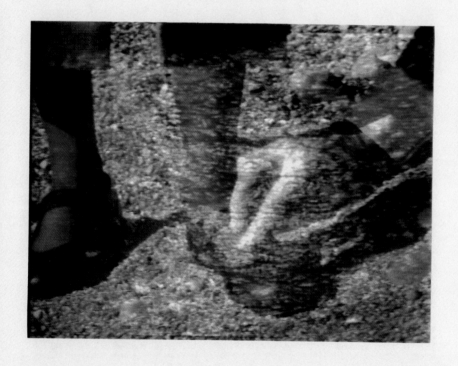

Production : Gaumont / JLG Films

LES FRANCAIS ENTENDUS PAR
LE DERNIER MOT

Production : Erato Films / JLG Films

JLGFILMS

HISTOIRE(S)

DU

CINEMA

AVEC UN "S"
ET
PARFOIS
DES "SS"

JLG**FILMS**

HISTOIRE(S) DU CINEM
(PRODUCTION)

_____

LA SEPT
FR 3
GAUMONT
JLG FILMS
CENTRE NATIONAL DE LA CINEMATOGRAPHIE
RADIO TELEVISION SUISSE ROMANDE
VEGA FILMS

pour les chapitres 1A et 1B diffusés d'abord par CANAL PLUS

_____

LA SEPT
JLG FILMS
FR 3

pour les chapitre 2 A et 2 B

_____ _____

JLG FILMS
FEMIS

pour les chapitres
3 A et 3 B
4 A et 4 B
5 A et 5 B

_____

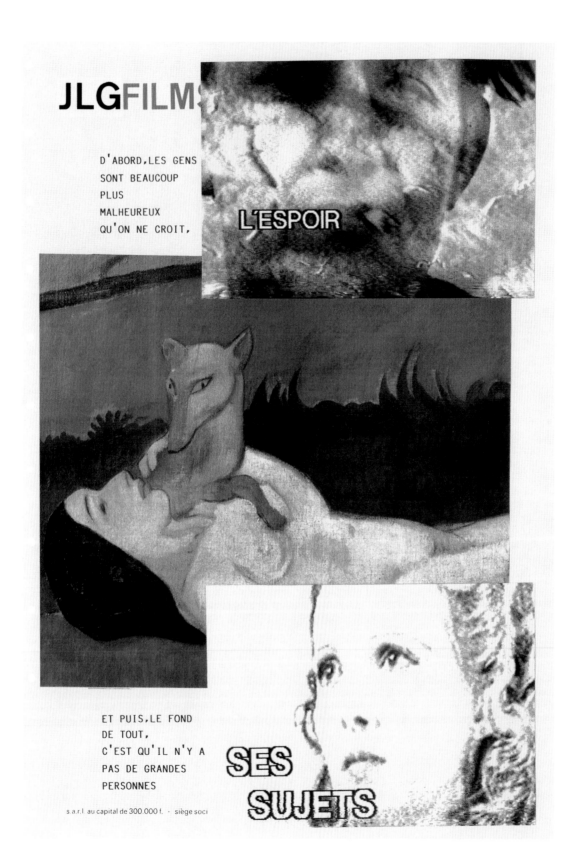

JLGFILMS

D'ABORD, LES GENS
SONT BEAUCOUP
PLUS
MALHEUREUX
QU'ON NE CROIT,

L'ESPOIR

ET PUIS, LE FOND
DE TOUT,
C'EST QU'IL N'Y A
PAS DE GRANDES
PERSONNES

s.a.r.l. au capital de 300.000 f. - siège soci

SES
SUJETS

JLGFILMS

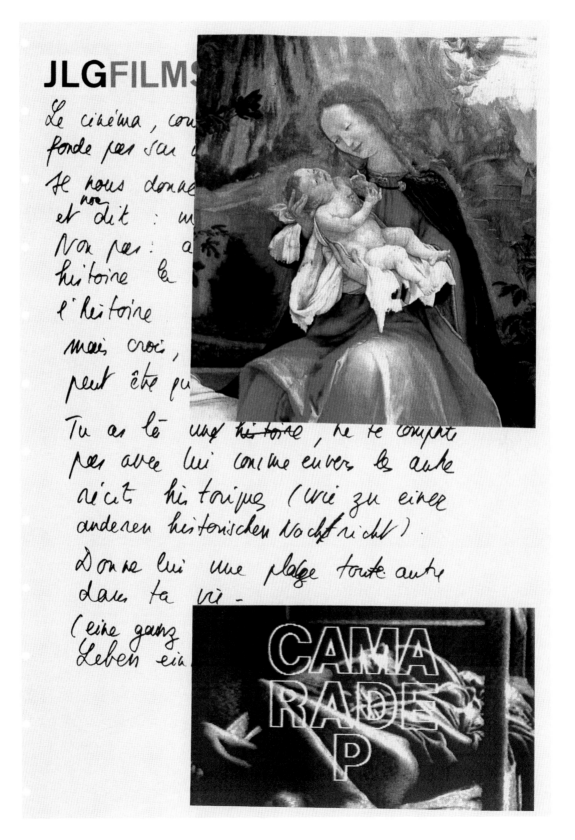

Le cinéma, co[...]
fonde par sa [...]
Je nous donne[...]
et dit : [...] *non*
Non pas : a[...]
histoire la [...]
l'histoire [...]
mais croi, [...]
peut être pu[...]

Tu as là une ~~histoire~~, ne te compare
pas avec lui comme envers les autre
récits historiques (wie zu einer
anderen historischen Nachricht).
Donne lui une place toute autre
dans ta vie.
(eine ganz [...]
Leben ein[...]

JLGFILMS

Parceque voilà ce qui s'est pas

La photographie aurait pu être inventée en couleurs.
Elles existaient . ————————
Mais voilà .
Au petit matin du 20ème siècle
de reproduire la vie .
On inventa donc la photographie
Mais comme la morale était enco
se préparait à retirer à la vie

on porta le deuil de cette mise

Et c'est avec les couleurs du de
blanc , que la photo se mit à e

Pas à cause de la gravure .

Le premier bouquet de fleurs de
une lithographie de Doré , il l

Et très vite , pour masquer le
Technicolors prendront les même
les couronnes mortuaires .

Et Scarlett O'Hara se dira une
y pensera demain .

       A quoi ?
       Au bonheur .

JLGFILMS

Excerpts from a document written and assembled by
Jean-Luc Godard alongside *Histoire(s) du cinéma*:
"Toutes les histoires" and "Une Histoire seule"

COMMUNISM WORE ITSELF OUT
DREAMING FACTORIES LIKE THESE.

CINEMA HAS ALWAYS BEEN THE ACT OF WHITE
BOYS SHOWING OFF FOR OTHER WHITE BOYS.

OR TELL THE STORY OF HOWARD HUGHES: BRAVER THAN MERMOZ AND
RICHER THAN ROCKEFELLER, PRODUCER OF "CITIZEN KANE" AND HEAD
OF TWA.
IT'S AS IF MELIES HAD RUN GALLIMARD AND THE FRENCH RAILWAY
SYSTEM AT THE SAME TIME.
AND DEAD AS DANIEL DEFOE DIDN'T DARE MAKE ROBINSON DIE.

TO SAY THIS: THE POWER OF HOLLYWOOD.

1940, GENEVA, MAX
OPHULS. HE FALLS
UPON MADELEINE
OZERAY'S ASS JUST
AS THE GERMAN
ARMY TAKES THE
FRENCH ARMY FROM
BEHIND.

HAPPINESS IS NO
LAUGHING MATTER.

BUT THOUGH THE MYTH BEGINS WITH FANTOMAS,
IT ENDS WITH CHRIST.

WAR IS THERE AS PROOF . . .

AND YET, FROM "SIEGFRIED" TO "M," AND FROM "THE DICTATOR" TO LUBITSCH, FILMS DID GET MADE, DIDN'T THEY?

AND IT'S THE POOR CINEMA OF THE NEWSREELS THAT HAS TO WASH
ALL SUSPICION FROM THE BLOOD AND TEARS, JUST AS THE SIDEWALK
GETS CLEANED WHEN IT'S TOO LATE AND THE ARMY HAS ALREADY
FIRED ON THE CROWD.

NO CLOSE-UPS, EVER. SUFFERING IS NOT A MOVIE STAR; NEITHER IS
THE BURNED-DOWN CHURCH NOR THE DEVASTATED COUNTRYSIDE.

AND SO, FOR ALMOST FIFTY YEARS, THE PEOPLE OF THE CAMERA OBSCURA, OF THE DARKENED ROOMS, HAVE BURNED THE IMAGINARY TO WARM UP SOME REALITY. NOW REALITY IS TAKING REVENGE, DEMANDING REAL TEARS AND REAL BLOOD.

AND IF GEORGE STEVENS HADN'T USED THE FIRST 16MM COLOR FILM AT AUSCHWITZ AND RAVENSBRUCK, ELIZABETH TAYLOR'S SMILE WOULD CERTAINLY NEVER HAVE FOUND A PLACE IN THE SUN.

THE BIRTH OF TELEVISION RUINED ALL THE CINEMAS OF EUROPE.

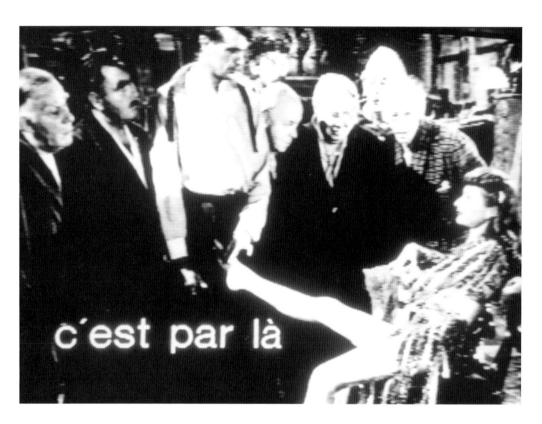

THAT'S CINEMA'S ROUTE BACK TO SPECTACLE.

BUT WHEN IT INHERITED THIS HISTORY, CINEMA INHERITED NOT ONLY ITS RIGHTS TO REPRODUCE A PART OF REALITY, BUT, ABOVE ALL, ITS DUTIES. AND THOUGH IT INHERITED ZOLA, FOR EXAMPLE, IT WASN'T THE ZOLA OF "L'ASSOMMOIR" OR "LA BETE HUMAINE."

DON'T GO SHOWING EVERY SIDE OF EVERYTHING,

LEAVE YOURSELF A MARGIN OF THE UNDEFINED.

IMAGES AND SOUNDS,

LIKE PEOPLE WHO MEET EN ROUTE AND CAN NO LONGER PART.

AND THOUGH TELEVISION HAS REALIZED LEON GAUMONT'S DREAM—
TO BRING THE SPECTACLES OF THE WHOLE WORLD INTO THE MOST
WRETCHEDLY POOR OF BEDROOMS—IT HAS DONE SO BY REDUCING
THE SHEPHERDS' GIGANTIC SKY TO TOM THUMB'S SIZE.

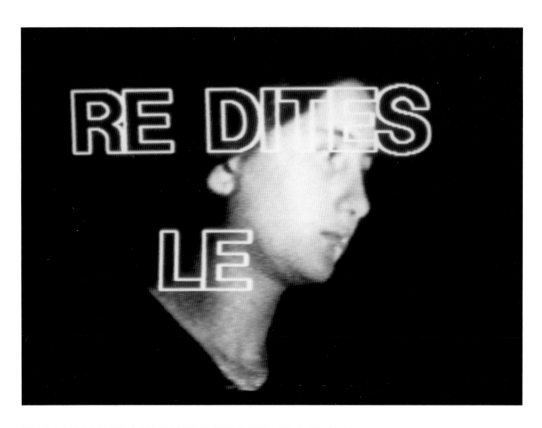

THE LONELY PLACE WHERE MEMORY IS A SLAVE.

CINEMA PROJECTED, AND MEN SAW THAT THE WORLD WAS THERE.

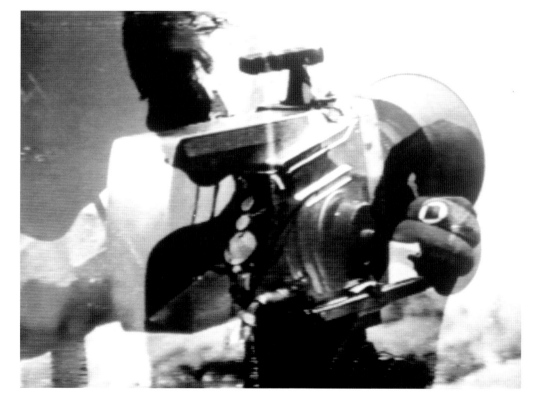

GIVE THIS STORY AN ENTIRELY DIFFERENT PLACE IN YOUR LIFE.

THE TWO GREAT STORIES HAVE BEEN SEX AND DEATH.

IT IS TIME

FOR LIFE

TO GIVE BACK TO CINEMA

WHAT IT STOLE FROM IT

(LOUIS DELLUC)

WHICH OPENED THE GATES OF DREAMS TO THE YOUNG FREUD.

IT WILL ONLY TAKE ONE OR TWO WORLD WARS TO PERVERT THIS
STATE OF CHILDHOOD AND FOR TELEVISION TO BECOME THIS SAD,
HALF-WITTED ADULT.

CINEMA

authorizes Orpheus to look back without causing
Eurydice's death.

EACH ART HAS ITS VERB.

In the creation of art, the verb is there to authenticate the
subject with the same name.

To paint is the act of painting. To have fun, that is, to compose and sing, is the act of music. To write becomes the act of
writing and of the writer. To film, that is, to record a sight and
project it, is the act of cinema and of the makers of films. It's
always freedom speaking.

Only television has no creative act or verb to authenticate it.
That's because the act of television both falls short of communication and goes beyond it. It doesn't create any goods, in fact,
what is worse, it distributes them without their ever having
been created. To program is the only verb of television. That
implies suffering rather than release.

(Illustrations selected and captioned by Godard)

GODARD MAKES [HI]STORIES
Interview with Serge Daney*

In 1989, French television viewers will see the first two parts of Jean-Luc Godard's series *Histoire(s) du cinéma*. The idea for the series is not new—it dates back to when Godard taught film courses in Montreal. It took shape when the television station Canal + (with a four-million-franc budget) signed an agreement with Godard, soon after it began broadcasting. After a period of development, the project has become a reality. In Rolle, Switzerland, Godard is face-to-face with his memories, his idées fixes, and the material he has patiently gathered. Downstairs is the video equipment he will use to render his "(hi)stories" visible, and to enable himself to improvise from a single word, connecting, reconnecting, and disconnecting the strands of his obsession. Upstairs, there are the printed material, the books, the film journals, and especially the famous yellow notebooks in which Godard tirelessly catalogues the photos he looks for and those he finds by chance. The filmmaker is recounting how it has been with his beloved cinema. Less a history of the cinema than history through cinema, Godard's fundamental premise hasn't changed: the cinema has always sought only one thing—montage—something twentieth-century man has desperately needed. This history will not be told verbally, instead it will be constructed using cinema's own materials: the image (still or moving), music, words and wordplay. Alone at last with the century's mementos, Godard looks more like an athlete or dancer in training than like an artist above the fray. If we were in the Middle Ages, he would be a Renaissance man, between art and science.   S.D.

This interview took place December 3, 1988, in Rolle, Switzerland. It was an ongoing interview, filmed in order to serve eventually as an educational supplement to the series *Histoire(s) du cinéma*. What is printed in bold type summarizes passages of our conversation; the quotes that follow are moments we selected in which Godard best defined his work as a historian.

The interviewer began by saying that he wasn't surprised that Godard was asked to do the *Histoire(s)*. There are many good reasons for choosing him, and it could only have been done by someone from the Nouvelle Vague generation, which was situated simultaneously in midcentury and midcinema—neither too early nor too late. This was the only generation that had the opportunity to think of itself "historically."

It's the *only* way to do history, that's what I would say. I think this was the only way for me to realize that, while I had a personal history as an individual, had it not been for cinema, I wouldn't have known that I had a history of my own. It was the only way, and I owe it to the cinema.

The greatest history is the history of the cinema. It's a nineteenth-century concern resolved in the twentieth. It's greater than the others because it projects, whereas others reduce themselves. When Foucault wrote *Madness and Civilization*, he reduced insanity to this [Godard points to a book]. When Langlois projected *Nosferatu* and in the small village where Nosferatu lived you already saw the ruins of Berlin in 1944, a projection took place. So, to put it simply, I say that it's the greatest history because it can project. Other histories can only reduce themselves.

My goal, then, alas [laughter], is like that little poem by Brecht: "I examine my project carefully: it's unrealizable." Because it can only be done on TV, which reduces. Or which projects you, the viewer, but then you lose consciousness, you're rejected. Whereas in cinema, the viewer was attracted. But we can make a memento of this projectable history. It's the only history that projects, and it's all we can do. But it's the greatest history and it's never been told.

With the triumph of the audiovisual media, "cinematic" films are beginning to all look alike. Yet, contrary to what must have been the case for the Nouvelle Vague, it's more and more difficult today to organize this impressive mass of films into a linear history. The feeling of time—with a before and after—has changed.

I only came to this idea of coming before or after very late. When Rohmer, who was a professor at the time, used to talk about Flaubert, he knew that, logically, Flaubert came after Homer or Saint Thomas Aquinas. But when he saw Nicholas Ray's *Bigger than Life* and a film by Murnau, I'm not sure that he talked about them with the clear notion that Ray came after Murnau.

The cinema was a place, a territory. What I remember most about the screenings at avénue Messine is that it was a place without history, and I think that must be what completely overwhelmed us. It wasn't even the discovery of a new continent.... There was an unknown feeling, in the strict sense of the term. We had never seen anything like it. A world with no history, but that spent all its time telling stories.

What was very powerful was that this had nothing to do with reading. This saved us, because we had all wanted to write a first novel (we were of our time). I admired Astruc tremendously because he had done it, and Rohmer and Gégauff too.... But what we felt in front of projected films—that there was nothing more to write—saved us. And writing was terrifying. How could you expect to write better than Joyce or Rilke? In the cinema, though, it was allowed. We could do things with no "class," with nothing, with neither head nor tail. Just the fact that they were made that way meant something, whereas in literature and even in painting, there were norms, and judges who judged. I think there was this feeling of freedom. A man and a woman in a car—once I'd seen *Journey to Italy*, I knew that even if I never actually made films, I could. It wasn't that this made me equal to the greats. It was more that the fact of just being able to led to a certain sense of dignity or whatever.

The interviewer insists. We can no longer experience things that way, and, at the same time, cinema's heritage now seems crushing. Is doing the history of it today a matter of passing along a toolbox in anticipation of a new questioning (that other—younger—people will carry out)? Or are we satisfied to say: Here's what's been seen, what was visible, and here's what I was the last possible witness to?

It would probably be more along the lines of your second point.... I believe in man as long as he creates things. Men have to be respected because they create things, whether it's an ashtray, a zapper, a car, a film, or a painting. From that standpoint, I'm not at all a humanist. François [Truffaut] spoke of "auteur politics." Today, all that is left is the term "auteur," but what was interesting was the term "politics." Auteurs aren't important. Today, we supposedly respect man so much that we no longer respect the work and in the end we can only respect man with words, and we don't even respect the words. Except for serious people, like Dolto or others who are less well known. The only people I know who respect the work as much as the man tend to be women. Because for them, due to the fact that they produce children, there's parity between the man and the work, an equilibrium, a democracy. For a man, there is none, except by a continual back-and-forth. I believe in the works, in art, in nature, and I believe that a work of art has an independent purpose that man is there to foster and to participate in.

So I would say, rather, look, there's something that existed and that was relatively unique—cinema. Things like that must have happened four hundred million years ago (give or take two or three thousand years), when Mycenae disappeared or a certain kind of animal or vegetation. And there was something then, an image, an image that was only a movement. And that image was telling us something that we didn't want to hear. So we preferred to talk over it instead. From this point of view, if you will, the work, for me, is the child and the person is the adult, the parent. And something happened—the child showed his parents who they were, and talked about himself at the same time! And the parents didn't want to hear about it and got frightened. It was the only time in the last four hundred million years that a certain way of telling stories was "history."

But to see this, you have to display it, do what Lévi-Strauss, Einstein, and Copernicus did. If you say that around 1540 Copernicus introduced the idea that the Sun no longer revolved around the Earth, and if you say that a few years later, Vesalius published *De corporis humanis fabrica*, which shows the inside of the human body, the skeleton, and écorchés, well, then, you have Copernicus in one book and Vesalius in another.... And then four hundred years later, you have François Jacob who says, "The same year, Copernicus and Vesalius...," well, Jacob isn't doing biology anymore, he's doing cinema. And that's all history really is.

Just as when Cocteau said, "If Rimbaud had lived, he would have died the same year as Marshal Pétain." You see the portrait of the young Rimbaud, you see Pétain's portrait of 1948, and you put the two together, and there you have a story, you have "history." That's cinema. The only thing I would want to say to someone is, "Cinema alone...." In fact, I begin with a chapter entitled "All the (Hi)stories," then I continue with "Only One (Hi)story/One Lonely (Hi)story." Then "Cinema Alone," which means "Cinema alone has done that," but, also, "Cinema was very alone, so alone that..."

Once again, it's art and science. Can we integrate them so easily?

Wait, we'll discuss that later. But first, there's this superambitious idea I have, a theory, a theory not even Michelet had when he wrote his *History of France*! My idea is that history is alone, it's far from man, that's it. And that there's something that stays strictly within the cinema, and that's montage. My idea as a practitioner, a gardener, of the cinema, was that one of cinema's goals was to invent montage, as I just described in a simplified way with Copernicus and Vesalius. That's montage. For example, what's the difference between the current president of the French Republic, François Mitterrand, and General de Gaulle? Personally, I would say that if cinema, as a scientific tool, wanted to show the difference, it would say this: It's about two Frenchmen who had a territory, and there was a war and invaders. At one point, one of them was taken prisoner, and began his rise to power by escaping and returning to France. The other one, on the other hand, escaped France and went abroad. That's the real difference. What was called cinema had always been looking for things like that.

The word "montage" has been used a lot. Today we say, "Eisenstein's use of montage, Welles's, Bergman's, or else the absence of montage in Rossellini's films. . . . But the cinema never found montage. Something disappeared when the talkies came in and language, words, took over. . . .

It's obvious when you watch an anchorwoman speak about Afghanistan and the commuter-train strike and things like that. If the cinema had been able to grow up and become an adult—instead of remaining a child managed by adults—she would talk about them as if they were Copernicus and Vesalius, and that would be clearer.

What's left of the cinema, then, isn't even a great idea like that of montage, but a movement toward montage?

That *was looking* for montage. In fact, I'll demonstrate this, since it can be shown with its own elements. When Griffith invented the close-up, he wasn't trying to get next to an actress, as legend maintains. He was trying to find a way to bring together something close and something far away. As for Eisenstein, he discovered the angle shot. When you look at his best-known films, at the famous shots of the three lions in *October*—well, if the three lions create an effect of montage, it's because there are three angles, not because of the editing. The Germans, who didn't use montage, worked from more distant elements—sets, a world-view, lighting. . . . But they were looking for

something, we can't say what that was today, but it was something that hadn't existed anywhere else, and that went without "saying," so to speak. That was the tremendous power of silent films.

My idea is to say: There, that's what cinema was. The fact that we see it, that we can still project it, it's like when Schliemann discovered some ruins and said: "Well, Troy must have happened there." That's the way it is.

The history of a failure, or a failure so grand that it's still worth telling, even though everything's been buried?

Language, speech, and the press came along. And with them came what happens when we "say" something and we're not cured of language yet (except when we say it because we're very sick and we have to see an analyst and the analyst is a good doctor). There's a great battle being waged between the eyes and the tongue. Only Freud, or people like that, whom we tend to ridicule these days, tried to see it differently.

The fact that my father was a doctor probably unconsciously led me to this. Because language says right away: It's sinusitis, it's montage. With the cinema, there was a sign that something was possible if we took the trouble to call things by their name. That it was a new way—that no one had ever seen before—of calling things by their names and that was also broad and popular because it needed a public immediately.

Faced with all these medical metaphors, the interviewer returns to the charge. Ought we to compare art and science to this extent?

Cinema is an art, as science is an art. But then something else happened, along with communications, with technique. Technique in an operational, not an artistic, sense. Not the movement of a watch made by a little Juras craftsman, but one hundred twenty million Swatches. The Télécoms and semaphores, they were born at the same time as foolishness, as *Madame Bovary*. Flaubert described it.

Science is like art, it's the same thing. And at a particular moment in the nineteenth century, science—not art—became what then became known as "culture"—because the word didn't exist before then. And when that happened, science became something else. Little by little, cinema, which was a popular art, and perhaps because of this popularity, but especially because of science, which had developed in the meantime, gave birth to television. But television isn't art, it's culture, commerce, and broadcasting.

Can we say that cinema is the compunction of the audiovisual media?

Yes. But who called cinema "art" anyway? Only Westerners. It's interesting to approach the history of cinema as the last chapter of the history of art, which itself is the last chapter of a certain kind of Indo-European civilization. The other civilizations didn't have art. Not that there weren't potters in China, or novels in Japan and Mexico, that's not what I mean. It's that the *idea* of art is European. It's no surprise that people are talking about Europe today, since it's about to disappear.

So, cinema is art. We used to oppose art and business when some people were turning this art into a business. But our argument with Hollywood has always been more along the lines of: Gentlemen, you should behave more as Durand-Ruel and Ambroise Vollard did toward Cézanne, or the way Théo van Gogh did toward his brother. You shouldn't act from a purely commercial point of view, because as soon as you commercialize art it becomes something else—culture.

We—the Nouvelle Vague—were the only ones who said that American cinema was art. It was hated sometimes. Bazin conceded that *Shadow of a Doubt* was a good Hitchcock film, but not *Notorious*. As a true social democrat, and deeply secular, he found it utterly despicable that such a wonderful mise-en-scène could be done for such a "worthless" subject. But only the Nouvelle Vague was able to say that there is art in certain things that are diverted from their object (or subject) by the big corporations. And then there came a time when the big corporations—like the great feudal lords—commanded the great poets. As if Thalberg had spoken to Stroheim the same way Julius II spoke to Michelangelo: No, paint this angel's wing like this, not like that!

No, only the West had that idea. It's given it up, maybe out of masochism, I don't know. Cinema was even a movement toward other civilizations: when you see a Lubitsch film, what does it tell you? It tells you something that you'd find in *The 1001 Arabian Nights*. Other art forms didn't do this. They were strictly European, but at a certain moment, under the influence of cinema, they changed. Picasso's African period happened at a time when there was cinema. Not because of colonialism, but because of cinema. Colonialism already existed in Delacroix's time, but he didn't paint paintings influenced by Arabian art.

Cinema is a visual medium that, I think, was never allowed to find its own language. It would have developed its own language based on some process or another, but not on something like . . . *L'Evénement du jeudi*! And Mallarmé, who wrote about the blank page, surely he thought of that just after seeing one of Feuillade's seri-

als. If there were an inquiry into what Mallarmé did the day he wrote about the blank page, well, I say we'd find out that he'd come out of a Feuillade film. I could even tell you which episode—"Tragic Error"!

A certain feeling of belonging to the world has vanished. Cinema had adopted us, it took care of us, rather as if we were foster children. But television divides us into factions, or else speaks to us as if we were powerless adults.

But cinema didn't fail, its parents did (if we think of cinema as childhood). That's why it was so popular. Everyone can like a van Gogh, but then someone invented a way to spread van Gogh's crows everywhere (albeit in a somewhat less terrifying form), so that everyone loved them and felt close to them.

Cinema was like the earth. Then came television, which was the invention of the plow. If you don't know how to use it, the plow is a bad thing. If you don't know how to till the earth or grow this or that kind of wheat. But television became a whole other thing. I believe the cardinal points have been lost. Cinema had done East and West, from Moscow to Hollywood, with Central Europe in between (because that's where cinema comes from, only from there). There's a great axis—like this.

Cinema is made to spread out, to flatten. I always compare it to the court system: you open a file, that's cinema [Godard opens a file]. And then you weigh it. . . . It's like a novel, because the pages are consecutive. But because it's visual, there's the weight of a page and the weight of the next page. . . . And then there's something else: its direction, that is to say, its cardinal points. Now, television falls back on East–West, and doesn't go North–South; yet, it was up to television to do North–South. That was what cinema couldn't do, hadn't to do.

Television, on the other hand, has to have its day, however stupidly. The other day I was watching a documentary made by a pretty good producer—Marin Karmitz—about Françoise Dolto. She was interviewing children, and there wasn't even a whole question, nor the child's whole gaze, nor the child listening. And this was Dolto! The government won't subsidize even fifty of her centers, but it will give her fifty medals of the Legion of Honor. When that happens, Dolto's written message can no longer get through, because language has become something else. If you publish Dolto in *L'Express*, she doesn't come across, something else does. On the other hand, the child stays sick.

Do we want the child to stay sick? I think so. The Nouvelle Vague was actually exceptional because it believed—because it followed Langlois and others before him—it believed what it saw. That's all.

CINEMA

The Nouvelle Vague is the only generation that saw the encroachment of television upon cinema (and vice versa). But in the beginning, there was a kind of happy incest. The great filmmakers (Rossellini, Renoir, Welles, Hitchcock) weren't against television, on the contrary. It wasn't until later that things went bad.

You shouldn't confuse the soil and the tool. Television isn't soil, it's a tool. When the tool becomes the soil, the result is AIDS. Personally, I think we will eventually cure cancer, but that we don't really want to. It hasn't been proven that we wanted to, nor that we know how to see. When François Jacob examines lymphocytes, antigens, antibodies—whatever—and he isn't doing what he did when he related Copernicus and Vesalius. . . . When he doesn't open to a page of Chandler, John Le Carré, or Peter Cheyney's early novels (the ones where you really see how cells, spies, and codes work—you see, they're even the same words). . . . All I can say is that's where you have to look. And you, François Jacob, with your own individual genius, you should say other things—that's where you'll find the vaccine, or the start of a vaccine. If you don't do that, you won't find it. Do cinema! But when he goes to the movies, what he likes is *That Murderous Summer*, so . . . [laughter].

Television gives us little news about the world, and even that is from a narrow, provincial point of view . . . which was less true of cinema.

For me, this became clearer when I noticed, after a certain number of years, that they hadn't shown the concentration camps. That they had talked about them, generally, but not shown them. I became interested, undoubtedly because of what you were saying, because of my guilt, my social class, etc. But the camps, they were the first thing that should have been shown, the same way Marey showed how man walks with his chronophotographic gun, or something like that. They didn't want to see them. And that's where it stopped and I thought, the Nouvelle Vague wasn't a beginning but an end.

Cinematic language has always developed in wartime, but after 1945, after the first great "private" spectacles, the camps, cinema no longer developed.

Italian neorealism was the last twitch, and the Nouvelle Vague, which came from Italian neorealism, was the twitch of a twitch. Then there was Fassbinder, who I feel stood alone. Like Anthaeus, who was big and strong, and tried it in his own patch, in his own garden. . . . And when Fassbinder died, the elders pretty

much did, too, Rossellini, Hitchcock. . . . But they died "in their art," if you will. I hope to study that in a chapter entitled *"L'Industrie de la mort,"* which is the story of the death of one of the greatest creators of forms of the modern world: Hitchcock. When you see a car, a tram, a man entering, or a chase in *Topaz* or in *Frenzy*, and you watch the beginnings of all that in *The Thirty-Nine Steps*, you see a world that has "turned." This is the world that I think Fassbinder was trying . . . in an extremely voluntaristic way [wrings his hands] . . . with a very correct purpose, which was to make films about Germany, because he was German. He died of a kind of overdose of creative obligations. And after, came what we know today.

Cinema looks at the world less, but it's been focusing on the world's "signs" for a long time.

Cinema has always looked at the world less than it has looked at the world looking at it. And when television came along, it quickly replaced the world and didn't look at it anymore. And when you watch television, you don't see that television is watching you. But when Ingrid Bergman hides a key in her hand, that key looks at you. And that happened at a time when we didn't want to see the world in the state in which the camps had left it.

Cinema disappeared at that moment. It disappeared because it had foretold the camps. Chaplin, who was a unique case, known as no one has been known, Chaplin, whom everyone believed, well, when he made *The Great Dictator*, they didn't believe him. They could have believed him at least a little. And when Lubitsch dared to say, "So they call me Concentration Camp Ehrhardt," people said: What are you talking about? Give him the hook! Even though he was Jewish, an immigrant, and if anyone had ever proved himself in comedy, it was him. All of a sudden, people didn't laugh anymore. Something happened there.

Retrospectively, that's when I told myself that as a director, a maker of films, I'm in occupied territory. I'm in the Resistance. I do it more or less well. I'm probably like René Hardy or Trepper, like in those novels I like so much, where you work for all sides, without really knowing which anymore. We're in occupied territory. In my opinion, when Lelouch is successful, he's an Otto Abetz to a *résistant* in France. And Tavernier is a Vichyist, in my opinion. It was from this point of view that I wrote to Malraux—and God knows I admired Malraux, and still do—about *La Religieuse*. I wrote, "I am writing you from a faraway place—Free France."

But because, in spite of it all, this isn't a real occupation, we're a little marginal and broken-down. That's why sometimes we have to say: Let's try again. We always question ourselves at the end, well, at the dawn of the twilight of our lives. That's when we ask ourselves to which [hi]story do we belong. . . .

Fear. It's a word that comes up a lot, as often as the medical metaphors. Fear of seeing, fear of not seeing, fear of seeing what others have seen, and the desire to see it, etc.

Personally, I'd say that seeing can only be peaceful. When a child is first able to see something in focus, there's something peaceful about it. The same goes for speaking. On the other hand, *saying* is not the same thing. I would compare looking and saying, and seeing and speaking (or singing). The desire is there. It's peaceful, but at times a struggle, for example, a suffering like what a mountain climber feels when he's climbing, a diver, or a lover leaving. I'd say that's what rights are, and in rights there's the notion of duty, like the line dividing two parts of an iceberg. . . . It's the duty to say in the course of a patient's treatment, the duty to look into the recovery that is extremely painful. Even though I'm the son of a doctor, it's hard for me to go to the doctor because then you have to say and look, and you have to confront that with seeing and speaking. (In a way, my problem is that I use my duties too much and my rights not enough.)

Cinema started out silent, and was very successful. Sound, just like color, had always been an option. They had their own processes, even if they weren't technically perfect—which they still aren't. . . . But they didn't want sound. Mitry and Sadoul described how Edison came to demonstrate his talking cinema, but it was already under way at the Grand Café. First, there were twelve disciples, then thirty, forty, then four hundred million. It wasn't until *later* that we wanted talkies, which is, moreover, fairly well explained by social circumstances. Talkies came at a historical moment, when Roosevelt spoke up, democracy spoke up and said: New Deal. And after a few stock market crashes, Fascism spoke up, and Hitler said what he said. It's "saying," but a *wrong* saying that took over. It wasn't Freud who took over in Germany, it was Hitler (yet, they were neighbors and lived only a few streets apart).

Despite the Spanish Inquisition, the Napoleonic Wars, despite everything, there had been some not insignificant humanistic achievements. And in order to preserve them—despite the absolute horror of the concentration camps—what had to happen was that, for once, *seeing and saying become one* and that then other goals be redefined. And only cinema could do it. Yet literature had done it. There were absolutely fantastic books that are quite forgotten today, like David Rous-

set's. But it must've been my filmmaker's unconscious that led me to search in this direction, since my personal history, in terms of class, religion, childhood, had absolutely nothing to do with it.

Do you think that because cinema didn't know how to bear witness when the times called for it, that it will wither away?

It's not a matter of bearing witness. It's because it was the only instrument—no microscope, no telescope, only cinema. I've always found something touching in the work of a director I only sort of like, George Stevens. In *A Place in the Sun*, there's a deep feeling of happiness that I've rarely encountered in other films, even much better ones. It's a simple, secular feeling of happiness, one moment with Elizabeth Taylor. And when I found out that Stevens had filmed the camps and that for the occasion Kodak had given him their first rolls of 16mm color film, that explained to me how he could then do that close-up of Elizabeth Taylor that radiated a kind of shadowed happiness. . . .

Since we've been talking about the problematics of "need," what would an "image need" be like today?

There is a desire for images, as the only things that have satisfied that notion of *identity* that became so fundamental toward the end of the nineteenth century. Today, even a believer who goes to pray still feels like an individual and not like the people Malraux spoke of and who used to listen to Saint Bernard. I think there's a need for identity, a need to be *recognized*. For example, if I see an image of you, I don't say it's an image of Toubiana, and in the fact of "recognizing" there are both the point of view of the scout on an exploratory mission—like Davy Crockett in John Ford's films— and a feeling of recognition, in the sense of gratitude. We are grateful to the world for recognizing us and for allowing us to recognize ourselves, and I think that, until the camps, cinema was the identity of nations and of peoples (who were more or less organized into nations) and that after the camps, it sort of disappeared. I deal with this in a program, program 3B, *"La Réponse des ténèbres,"* which talks about war films and says, more or less, that cinema is primarily a Western art form, made by white guys. And when I talk with Anne-Marie [Miéville], whose family wouldn't let her watch films, except for Westerns, which she hated . . . still does today, even John Ford's, she has trouble with all those men on horses, all those guys. . . .

And all of this to say: Why was there no cinema of the Resistance in 1940–1945? Not that there weren't some Resistance films, on the Right and the Left, here

TELEVISION

and there, but the only fiction film of the Resistance that resisted America's occupation of cinema or a certain standardized way of making films was an Italian film. Italy, the country that had fought the least, that had suffered a great deal, that lost its identity, and that took off again after *Open City*. But that's the only time. The Russians made propaganda films or films about martyrs, Americans made advertisement films, the English did their usual thing, Germany didn't know how to make Resistance films, and the French only made prisoner-of-war films. The Polish are the only ones who tried twice in a row to make films about the camps: Munk's *Passenger* (which was never finished), and Wanda Jakubowska's *The Last Stage*.

Well, for a long time, cinema represented the possibility of being part of a nation, yet remaining itself within that nation. All that has disappeared. If people still like cinema today, it's more the way the Greeks liked the stories about Zeus. If they like Belmondo's films—not mine or Straub's, because they're not shown—if they still like the idea of films on television, even if, or especially when, they've been cut, it's because there is a faint memory. . . . We don't have our identity anymore, but when we turn on the television, there's a vague little signal that tells us that maybe we do have one. And then films will disappear from television.

We talk more and more about "images," but we know less and less what we mean by this expression.

We use the word "image" even though that's not what they are anymore. One image leads to another, an image is never alone, contrary to what we call "images" today, which are sets of solitudes connected by speech that, at worst, is Hitler's, but that will never be Dolto's, Freud's, or Wittgenstein's. Americans are more accurate, more pragmatic: they say "pictures," which is also the term for photos. And for film they say "movie."

Let's get down to specifics. How did Godard organize his {Hi}stories? To begin with, what's his game plan?

My [hi]story of cinema begins with a chapter called *"Toutes les histoires,"* lots of short [hi]stories where you can see signs. It goes on to say that this [hi]story stands alone, the only [hi]story there has ever been. So—you know how unbounded my ambition is—I say it's not only alone, but also the only one there ever will be or that there ever was (later, it won't be a [hi]story, but something else). It's my mission to tell it. It's my preacher side coming out, if you will; this is what I preach.

And then there are instead some specific studies cut in. There's one I called *"Fatale Beauté,"* in remembrance of a film by Siodmak with Ava Gardner, called *The*

Great Sinner, an adaptation of Dostoyevsky's *The Gambler*. The idea is that, for the most part, it's been men that have filmed women, and that's proved equally fatal to this [hi]story. . . .

Then, there's a more practical study that I've always wanted to do and that can be done with video. I call it, inspired by Malraux, *"La Monnaie de l'absolu."* It's an attempt to do a visual critical study. I once did it in a program using the war as an example. I was saying: This is how a great filmmaker like Kubrick showed the Vietnam war and this is how a Cuban documentary filmmaker showed the same war. You judge; you look. And then I derive some ideas. For example, I took René Clair's *Quatorze juillet*, then I read three lines of yours about the film, and then I asked: How could he say this? Is that right: While Pola Illery is doing this and Annabella is doing that? Can this really be described like that? No. So, I say that Serge was stricken for a split second by the ultimate evil.

One segment, which I've mentioned before, is called *"La Réponse des ténèbres."* It examines why Italy made the only Resistance film. Then there's another about montage called *"Montage, mon beau souci,"* which comes from an article that I had written in all innocence but that I don't understand very well today. The idea is that, just as painting succeeded in reproducing perspective, cinema should have succeeded in something, too, but was unable to, due to the application of the invention of sound. But there are traces of it. . . .

Then, there's a last chapter called *"Les Signes parmi nous,"* which I mentioned before, and that says if you film a traffic jam in the streets of Paris and if you know how to see it (not just me, but François Jacob and I) we discover—if we know how to see—a vaccine for AIDS. *"Les Signes parmi nous"* is a novel by Ramuz that I've always wanted to do: a peddler arrives in a little village above Vevey and announces the end of the world. There's a terrible storm for five days, then the sun comes out, and the peddler is kicked out. The peddler is cinema!

Note

* This interview was originally published as "Godard fait des Histoires," in *Libération*, December 26, 1988. The illustration on page 158 is from Carl Theodor Dreyer, *The Bride of Glomdale*, 1925–26 (Einar Sissener and Tove Tellback), that on page 163, from George Sidney, *Bye Bye Birdie*, 1963 (Janet Leigh).

SCENARIO DU FILM PASSION

1982
Jean-Luc Godard

VIDEO THINKS WHAT CINEMA CREATES
Notes on Jean-Luc Godard's Work in Video and Television

PHILIPPE DUBOIS

There is surely no filmmaker in our time who has explored so persistently, and with so much depth and diversity, the question of the **transformation of images** as has Jean-Luc Godard. In the field of contemporary media, where cinema no longer enjoys the arrogant certainty of total, monopolistic power, Godard has long been a leader. In the sixties, he and his Nouvelle Vague colleagues had already reflected critically on cinema, but in ways and with means that were still completely cinematographic. Since 1974—since *Ici et ailleurs*, a watershed film—he has broadened his questioning, most notably by experimenting with new, electronic systems of sound and image that redefine representation in relation to space, time, bodies, and speech, and bring responses, satisfying or not, to questions that cinema can't not ask itself. To take risks, to attempt failure: this is Godard as fundamentally an essayist, attempting [*essayant*] *in order to see*, "to see not this or that, but only to see if there's something to see."[1] The appearance and immediate incorporation of video into his work, its systematic and varied use over the last fifteen years, along with the will to appropriate totally this medium for himself, to the point of having equipment installed "at home" (from the first *Sonimage* base at Grenoble in 1973, to his current studio at Rolle on the banks of Lac Leman), all show to what extent video has become for Godard a vital, indispensable, and everyday tool, the very site and means of his existential relation to cinema.

Since 1974, Godard has produced more video works than films, statistically speaking. The cinema films number 3 + 8: the three essay films of 1974 to 1976, already marked by complex and organic relations to video, and the eight well-known fiction feature films that followed one another after 1979, and that account for the filmmaker's public profile. During that same time, Godard has made more than fifteen videotapes— with different statuses, forms, and issues—that have appeared at regular intervals over the last fifteen years. So, for Godard, video is not a mere moment in his itinerary. This isn't a "period" ("the video years"), but rather a way of being in general, a form of looking and thinking that functions continuously and as if live with

regard to everything. Far more than an object (a work, a product) or a technique (electronic signals, a medium), video is for him a permanent **state**, as in a state of matter. It's a way of breathing through images, of being intimately joined with them, a way of posing questions and attempting answers. It's video as *always there*, within reach of hand and eye, as a way of **reflecting** (on) cinema, in all its forms and states: video in film (*Ici et ailleurs*, *Numéro deux* [1975], *Comment ça va* [1976]), video in TV (*Six fois deux* [1976], *France/tour/détour/deux/ enfants* [1977–78]), video before film (the "scenarios," or "scripts," of *Sauve qui peut (la vie)* [1979], *Passion* [1982], and *Je vous salue Marie* [1985]), video after film (*Scénario du film Passion* [1982]), video instead of film (*Grandeur et décadence d'un petit commerce de cinéma . . .* [1986]), video about film, or cinema, or images in general (*Soft and Hard* [1986], *Puissance de la parole* [1988], *On s'est tous défilé* [1988], *Histoire(s) du cinéma* [1989–], *Le Rapport Darty* [1989]).

Questions clearly arise: in what way is this videographic "other being" connected to his cinema? could we say that, starting in 1974, there is something like a general "video state" of the Godardian cinema, which in the beginning formed a material and integral part of the films, then progressively separated itself out to exist more and more independently? what then would be the modes of existence of this "independent video state"? and, further, how would it affect the films themselves? To approach these questions, I propose a journey that is both historical and theoretical, where I will distinguish, in a necessarily schematic way, four main, successive postures and, above all, a series of figures of writing that will try to encompass this web of questions. Before beginning, let me note that it may be significant that the appearance of video in Godard's work corresponds fairly precisely to the appearance of Anne-Marie Miéville in his life and work.

1 • The uniqueness of *Numéro deux* is that it's a film conceived by television, but clothed by cinema. It's a uniqueness and a great misfortune, because the clothes don't fit the child. The television that conceived this film does not exist enough, while the cinema exists too much. Everyone knows that TV doesn't allow originality, and that cinema only permits received ideas. To take on the contradiction.... For me, as a filmmaker, admitting that you're stammering, that you're half blind, that you can read but not write, is, in our everyday framework, to respond more honestly to this famous question of communication.

—*Jean-Luc Godard*[2]

The first phase is that of the three "essay films" of 1974 to 1976. We know that *Ici et ailleurs*, *Numéro deux*, and *Comment ça va* are the films that mark the last expressions of Godard's strictly political inquiries, and at the same time are "experimental" works in all senses of the term, where the political questions are displaced and replayed through the technical and formal apparatus of film itself, through the body-language of cinema. This was the end of his collaboration with Jean-Pierre Gorin (the end of the Dziga Vertov Group), and the beginning of his coproductions with Anne-Marie Miéville (the beginning of *Sonimage*). Godard, realist that he is, posited the following observations: television had won the war of images, the media no longer communicated anything, information was no longer getting through, meaning had been lost, reading a newspaper had become a matter of lies and amnesia, and looking at an image had become a mechanical operation, a blind person's gesture ("The hands are doing the work of the eyes and that's what's wrong").[3] How? Why? What is one to do? All of Godard's work during this period asks these kinds of questions. And video, which he discovers and appropriates at this time, appears to him the only possibility of **fighting back in kind**, that is, responding *in images and sounds* to the set of questions that address why we no longer know how to communicate, speak, see, and think, and how we can still try to speak and create with images and sounds. The electronic tool is the very instrument that allows Godard to formulate this double questioning, and to propose some hypotheses.

The three films, all made at the Grenoble base, are essays, not only because of their sociocritical purpose, but also because they're marked by literal attempts at mixing the mediums, by the organic imbrication of film and video images. These are attempts both old and new: the old comes out of the political period, and means to take apart, deconstruct, and critically analyze certain mechanisms (the video-scalpel as tool of de-composition); the new, which opens up the future, aims to invent a new form of writing, to work positively, starting from brand-new figures, and to give birth to a new body of images (with the video mixer as instrument of recomposition). Video is the exact point of intersection between these two parts, the medium

of these experiences of de-composition–recomposition.

When we look at these essay films together, we already notice three essential figures that cut across the films and continue to crop up in infinite variety:

1 • The mise-en-scène of direct address

In each film, and in different forms, the "explanatory," discursive function of the essay is embodied explicitly in specific enunciative apparatuses. In general, the "I" always speaks to a "you," according to different formulas: it's **the letter** of the father to the son that furnishes the enunciative structure of *Comment ça va*; in *Numéro deux*, it's the **interpellating speech** directed at the spectator in the prologue and epilogue by Jeannot, a gadget among his machines, who reestablishes contact (he's there, we see him, he speaks to us, he explains, he tells his stories); it's also, of course, almost everywhere, **the voice-over**, the famous voice of (Godardian) pedagogy, the voice of the "theorized/terrorized" that Serge Daney has described so well;[4] or yet again, it's **conversation**, two voices in dialogue, as it takes two to speak, to "have relations" (the three films are made up of dualities at every level); it is, finally, the use of the **screen as a page** or a painting: a site for writing live, for inscribing messages the spectator can not only read but see, see them make and unmake themselves by a touch on a keyboard, transform, repeat, short-circuit themselves, in real time, like an electronic message ("a film between the active and the passive, between the actor and the spectator," says one of the inscriptions in *Ici et ailleurs*).

All of these forms of videographic mise-en-scène of speech lead back to a single great trait of enunciation: **direct address**, direct between everything—between the author-narrator and the spectator, between the sound (off-screen) and the image (onscreen), between two characters, between the spectator and the screen-apparatus, and so on. Direct in all these cases means *interaction*—immediate feedback, a perpetual back and forth, reciprocal self-modulation—and *interconnection*—the short circuit, the encounter, the changeover, the knot. Direct—live—is here the very figure of the essay, of experimentation, of working without a safety net.

2 • The electronic treatment of the image

When the films of 1974 to 1976 incorporated video images organically, in consistently exemplary sequences that are all strong beats in each of the three films, it was always in the form of an electronic *mixing* of images, whether collage, wipes, keying, or superimposition. Godard prefers to call it a **linking** of images. This describes the two sequences of electronic collage of photos in *Ici et ailleurs*. The first sequence is that of the "revolutionary additions," and the second that of a photo and the name of Henry Kissinger. During these

Jean-Luc Godard

NUMERO DEUX
1975

collage manipulations, the voice-over keeps repeating: "Any image from everyday life will thus become part of a vague and complicated system that the whole world is continually entering and leaving. . . . There are no more simple images. . . . The whole world is too much for an image. You need several of them, a chain of images. . . ." No longer a single image, but, rather, multiple images, images dissolved together and then disconnected. The electronic mixing that replaces montage *within* the image is indeed, for Godard, this "vague and complicated system that the whole world is continually entering and leaving."

In *Numéro deux*, the most powerful sequence, declined three times, allows us to see in a specifically videographic mode both the central couple of the parents in the sexual act (Pierrot taking Sandrine from behind), and their little girl, Vanessa, who, in close-up, "observes" the scene indirectly, by means of electronic keying within the image.[5] Here are sexual violence, the primal scene, and voyeurism; sexual transgression is

here transgression of images: a matter of looking, a family matter, a matter of body and of mediums, all rolled into one. The extraordinary visual and emotional charge of this scene (the intertitle introducing it features the word "MONTAGE") derives from the completely organic way in which the little girl's face, indirectly, by means of a variable keying, seems to burst out of the very interior of the embracing bodies of the parents, *as if emanating directly from the body of the parental image*. It's a little as if she were the hallucinatory conscience of this image she seems to spring from and by which she ends up being engulfed at the whim of the luminous, fluid variations of the figure. Only video that is processed like this, in its very image-matter, allows such an integration of image/body/text, out of the apparatus of "montage" (montage of bodies as well as montage of mediums), in a sort of metaphor of assumed trauma represented to a filmgoer's eyes by the electronic processing of a film image. We are all Vanessas, witnessing more or less silently the sodomizing of cinema

ICI ET AILLEURS

co-director: Anne-Marie Miéville

1974

Henry Kissinger

Adolf Hitler

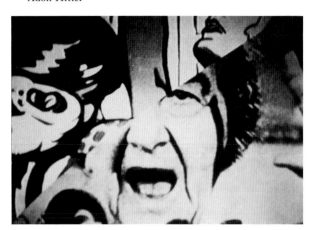

Golda Meir

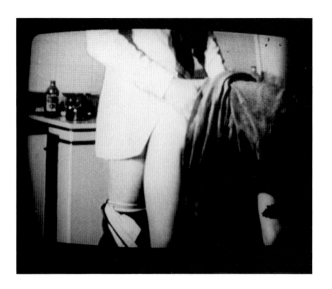

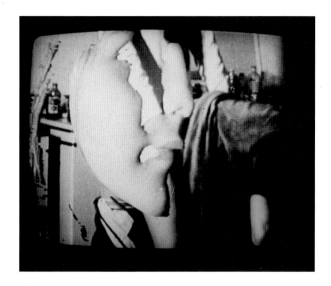

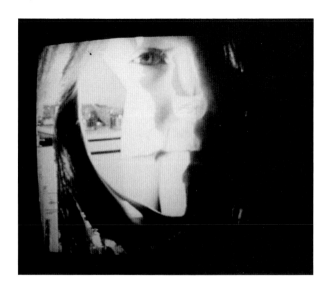

NUMERO DEUX

1975

by video: Vanessa herself says, "Sometimes I think it's nice, Mama and Papa, and sometimes I think it's caca."

In *Comment ça va*, the electronic mixing of images is played out largely in the great central sequence, in which the two photographs of the protesters are super-imposed. On the one hand, there's the photo from Portugal, taken during the Revolution of the Carnations: a protester in the crowd, fist raised, and soldiers in uniform. On the other, there's the photo taken four years earlier at the time of the Joint Français business, showing a protester face-to-face with police officers. The entire Socratic undertaking is set off by the *visual alliance* of fluctuating superimpositions and wandering camerawork. A voice-over asserts: "A gaze is never profound. What's profound is the extent, the extent of a certain relation between the unknown and the known. Thinking. Bringing together in order to think. Simply bringing two images together. Two images that are simple because they show people who are simple, but who set into motion something complex because they dare to rebel. Yes, to begin to think as you look." It couldn't be said better: to bring together, actively, in the mixing of images, in order to be able to see. Because **seeing (with video) is thinking (live, with the image).**

3 • Experimentation with speed

De-composition, analysis, breaking down the editing, slowing down the process ("Let's go more slowly, we gotta de-compose," says Odette/Miéville in *Comment ça va*). We must de-compose to find anew a power of seeing, to turn the act of seeing into an event once more, to see if meaning can still be constructed with images. Hence photography's essential role in these films as an arrested image, an atom of cinema, "the truth twenty-four times a second." In *Ici et ailleurs*, it's the famous "pedagogical" sequence, where, in a theatricalized setting, the "photographic bodies" (five extras, each carrying a photo with a name) embody before a *video* camera the very principle of the procession of images that constitutes the cinema-effect. It's an insistent figure that Godard will re-create much later in *Grandeur et décadence d'un petit commerce de cinéma.* The "lesson" is clear: cinema, when stopped, when one takes the time to look at it, is a matter of photographs. And in order to see that, one has to pass through video as a tool with which *to analyze* cinema, the thing that flushes out the photography on which it is based. As Odette/Miéville says in *Comment ça va*, "To proceed from an image, only one, like an atom, to see how it moves and how it all holds together. . . ."

COMMENT ÇA VA
1976

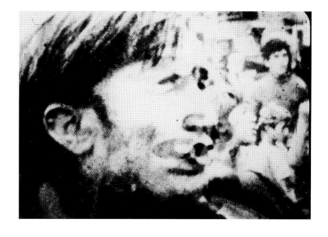

ICI ET AILLEURS

co-director: Anne-Marie Miéville

1974

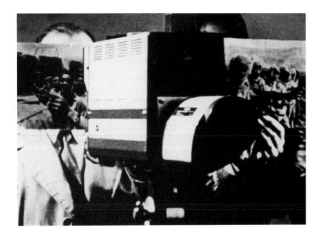

2 • To use video as you would cinema, and to use cinema as you would television, is to make a television that doesn't exist, and a cinema that no longer exists. Film people reject video absolutely. The advantage of video, however, is that you can see the image you're making before you make it; you can decide whether or not you want to lay claim to it.

—Jean-Luc Godard[6]

The second great moment of our journey would be the television series of 1976 to 1978. This time, Godard took the plunge. Continuing to develop his small, autonomous production structure, *Sonimage*, he appeared to be deserting cinema, going over to the enemy completely—which he then attacked from the inside. In coproduction with the INA, he made in 1976 *Six fois deux/Sur et sous la communication*, and in 1977 and 1978 *France/tour/détour/deux/enfants*. On the one hand, these are productions that one can call, from the outside, full-blown **television** ("I functioned as a network programmer, that is, by making a programming grid").[7] There are a structured series, standard formatting, and the classic televisual enunciation—interviews, commentaries, presentations, reports, and so on. At the same time, however, the series are also, from the inside, a type of **antitelevision**, a complete turning of televisual conventions against themselves. Thus, even as he uses in all its forms the postures of the omnipresent word, Godard knows precisely how to play off their opposite: silence, and stammering. **Silence** is what television dreads above all, and what Godard knows how to operate like full speech. The art of silent television can only call itself video ("Nous trois"—not a sound for nearly fifty minutes!—or "Jacqueline et Ludovic"). Along with the silence, there is language—floating, uncertain, hesitant, stumbling. Godard erases none of the gaps in speech, the trials and errors, the verbal digressions, neither his own nor those of others. It's a sort of fundamental **stammering**, which Deleuze identified so well, and which is exactly the language *of* video. With video, Godard speaks as he thinks and thinks as he speaks, *at his own speed*. He tries speaking live from his thoughts. Even today, I see no television programs that can *stand up* to those made by Godard between 1976 and 1978.

On the other hand, these two great series seem to me to form a less homogeneous group than they have been said to do ("the video years"). The first, *Six fois deux*, still bears traces of the earlier essay films and acts as a kind of last extension, an end point in the analytical/critical sense of both the sociopolitical field and the mediums of communication. The second, *France/tour/détour*, is more the announcement of what will come at the beginning of the eighties: a writing in which one

**SIX FOIS DEUX/SUR ET
SOUS LA COMMUNICATION**

co-director: Anne-Marie Miéville

1976

"Nous trois"

FRANCE/TOUR/DETOUR/DEUX/ENFANTS

co-director: Anne-Marie Miéville

1977–78

senses the dawning of a more philosophical and poetic perspective, turned rather toward artistic creation than toward a social problematics. In this sense, *Six fois deux* would be Godard's last political film: it's still the video-scalpel, like the essay films, only inside TV. And *France/tour/détour* would be the first lyrical, densely artistic film of the Godard of the eighties, already tending toward *Sauve qui peut (la vie)*, but at the heart of a televisual apparatus. Godard recounts: "When the series was commissioned by Marcel Julian, it had been understood that we would try to make it at the same time a novel and a painting, which I believe can be done today with sequences of images. . . . Cézanne with Malraux's mediums. . . . Or philosophy as chamber music. . . ."[8]

The clearest sign of the gap between the two series can be found in the difference between the figures subjected to his electronic processing of images. While *Six fois deux* still mixes images (superbly) with wipes and keying (for example, in the episode "Nous trois"), *France/tour/détour* is the result of a radically new processing that marks the passage to another form of writing, and thus to another way of conceiving things. What Godard discovers here, in a still very experimental way, is of course the famous "changes of speed" that appear in the form of **slow motion and jump cuts**. We notice this in particular at the beginning of each of twelve "movements," in the images of children's gestures in everyday activities—getting undressed and dressed, walking in the street, and so on. This work on slowness continues, in a way, what in the preceding essay films was an analytical will to go less quickly in order to see and understand better the processes of the world. But this time, the de-composition is not at all intellectual (critical analysis, the search for the elemental atom in order to undo the chain). It is, rather, organic, material, physical—in other words, *carnal*. It affects the body of the image. De-composition no longer refers back to photography; it is henceforth entirely and specifically of the videographic order.[9]

Two major effects seem to me to result from this work with changing speeds: an effect of painting, and one of being restored, of the gaze being renewed. Take the **painting effect**: the video slow motions of *France/tour/détour* are neither smooth nor continuous; on the contrary, they are irregular, unpredictable, and variable, giving the impression of experiments with the image's very time-matter, attempts to bring to the surface the raw base of representation, a sort of repository of forms and emotions, knowledge and technique, a residue of image-matter as such. On the other hand, it's also a matter of slowing down, much as a pilot would an airplane: *by sight*, hand on the speed-control lever,

eye riveted to the control panel. Video slow motion is controlled *by the finger and the eye*, and the operator *discovers the effect live*, at the very moment he executes the operation, which can, moreover, be altered any time he chooses, all the while watching the result shown instantaneously on the screen (this is its essential characteristic, compared with cinematic slow motion). It's as if he were really seeing this image, which he's *already* shot, only now for the first time; as if it were a virgin image, never before seen, whose potential he discovers as he watches it unmake and remake itself. And we're aware (the spectator is here strictly in synch with Godard) that with each maneuver, with each change in speed, we feel violently **the pleasure of a perceptual revolution**, the "aha" effect of "so that's what's *in* images, and what I'd never before seen *that way*." At the same time, we feel a fundamental loss, which is why images always end up eluding us, and why we're always in a way blind. Video slow-motion effects are an absolute experience of the look lived as an event. They taught Godard to look at the world, and images, with fresh, new eyes, cleansed of all irrelevancies. They allowed him to (re)turn to a cinematographic image that is still possible, that can still be looked at as new, and therefore to be made. *Sauve qui peut (la vie)*, the film that is punctuated from first to last by these moments of staccato slow motion, is the film that marks this return ("My second first film," says Godard).

3 • I'm at a point now where I want to go out and do some research, and show what I've found, like an explorer, then use it afterwards to make my ballets, my operas, my novels. Television would be ideal for doing such scenarios, but, *in vivo*, so to speak, living the scenario as it takes shape. And then, from that, I'd make a three-hundred-page work, either in an hour and a half, or in four hours, in a certain form.

—*Jean-Luc Godard*[10]

The third phase would be that of the **video-scenarios** that surround the great films of the early eighties: the rebirth/renaissance film, *Sauve qui peut (la vie)*, and the "trilogy of the sublime":[11] *Passion*, *Prénom Carmen* (1983), and *Je vous salue Marie*. We know that most of these landmark films were the subjects—before, after, or during—of one or more small video works presented as moments of personal reflection on questions the film was putting, had put, or would put into play *in its own way*. Most often referred to as "video-scenarios," these works, which are, of course, much less well known than the corresponding films, are by no means to be considered programs or foreshadowings of the films. Shot with low-budget, "homely" means (*Sonimage* at Rolle), meant for primarily internal or private use (the production, the crew, the actors), basically hardly finished, if at all, they are like rough drafts, sketches, or research notes, essays in the strict sense. The only one of these "scenarios" that is at all well known is *Scénario du film Passion*, which was made after the film (in 1982), commissioned by Télévision Suisse Romande, which produced it. It's the only one that is truly a finished work, made for itself, and distributed.

Here, then, is a new posture of the video essay: no longer *in* the film (mixed in with its organic matter, with its body), no longer *in* the TV (as its interior, repressed expression), but *next to* the films (and, even, later, we will see, next to cinema)—in other words, *parallel* to them, close by, always "within reach," but separate, independent, *conscious of the distance that separates them*, and aware of how to make this well-thought-out separation of forces creative. The beginning of the eighties sees cinema and video *in stereo*, proceeding side by side, observing each other, one-upping each other, reflecting each other, the one thinking here what the other creates there.

In this phase, the "video state" is thus not only an interiorized mode of looking, but it begins to materialize in objects, still only half-formed (rough drafts, journals, notes), but nevertheless semiautonomous, existing in and even *by* their stammerings. For these "video-scenarios" are in fact stammering itself. They're simultaneously interior and exterior musings. Godard, impassioned, tries his hand at writing, thinking, looking, manipulating images, juggling sounds, inscribing words, scrutinizing, combining, starting over, erasing, adding, clarifying, displacing. And it's all done spontaneously, immediately in images and sounds, giving the extraordinary impression of witnessing live the very movements of thought by and in images.

Godard's video-scenarios are machines for experimenting with "language games" in the sense of Wittgenstein's *Philosophical Investigations*. He uses video to try out figures, see what happens, adjust them as he goes along, working in his laboratory to refine the data, the image-thoughts. These image-thoughts are in turn invested elsewhere, in particular in the creation of the "master" works, the films, whose *genesis* would thus be constituted by them. It is in this sense that the video works are "scenarios." Because for Godard the filmmaker, video is the only instrument that permits him to practice writing directly **with** and **in** images. The great thing is to always try for the "live" effect: I see at the same time as I do. In video (and, according to him, nowhere else, especially not in the written word), seeing is thinking and thinking is seeing, both in one, and completely simultaneously. The most beautiful mise-en-scène of this basic posture is, of course, found in the entire scenographic apparatus of *Scénario du film Passion*: Godard at the controls, in his Master Control room, the only master on board, surrounded by his machines, and facing the screen, facing the site of images. The images then appear, little by little, very slowly, in waves, as if bubbling up from the bottom of his thought-in-process, superimposing themselves on the silhouette of his own body, which haunts the "laboratory." We see here the entire road traveled since the opening and closing sequences of *Numéro deux* (where Jeannot, too, posed among his machines, except that there the relation to the images, the live connection between the work on images and the work of thought, wasn't at all portrayed as such).

This also explains how the "scenario" can sometimes come after the film. It signifies that when the image and thought are live, you're always in the "scenario"; it happens before the film (the conception), during shooting, or at the editing stage—even after the film is finished. What counts for Godard is not *to have made* a film, nor preparing one, in the classical sense, with the usual separate and progressive stages; it's rather being always in the process of making one, whether or not he's shooting, whether or not he's editing. For him, making a film is an extensive and total thing: it's being and living, and at every moment being connected to images, seeing and thinking together. This is why video as a state corresponds so well to his very mode of existence. This is why he lives with it daily, as if it were breathing itself.

These "videographic language games" that Godard experiments with in his scenarios are of four types, all explicitly presented by Godard himself in the first of the video-scenarios, that of *Sauve qui peut (la vie)*:[12] the relation of the image to writing (through the emblematic figure of the typewriter); the work of the image-chain (by superimposition); the work on speeds (with slow motion/de-composition); and the relation of music to the image (through the presence of the orchestra in the image).

I will not detail here each of these figures. Suffice it to say that, overall, some of them passed almost unchanged into the films. This is the case, for example, with the slow-motion de-compositions: the film *Sauve qui peut (la vie)* includes some eighteen moments of "variations of speed," which are so many tactile experiments with the time-matter of images and the movement-matter of actors' bodies seized in newly significant gestures. According to Godard:

One must use the combined techniques of cinema and television to get slow motion, changes in rhythm, de-compositions. . . . As soon as you freeze an image in a movement that includes twenty-five others, you notice in a shot you have filmed, according to how you

stop it, that suddenly there are billions of possibilities; all the possible permutations among those twenty-five images represent thousands of possibilities. I had concluded from this that by changing the rhythm, when you analyze the movements of a woman, movements as simple as buying a loaf of bread, for example, you notice that there are entire worlds contained within the woman's movement—corpuscles, galaxies, different each time—and that you can travel from one to another in a series of explosions. Slow motion is much less interesting with a man, where there is always in the end the same directing line. . . . In *Tour/détour*, I had stumbled upon this as a simple intuition, without going further, since I had to discuss it with some colleagues, so that they could bring in their own, scientific experience. Then, from a laboratory experiment, I made a novel.[13]

In the same way, as we know, his experiments with putting music in the image also passed directly into the films. In the final scene of *Sauve qui peut (la vie)*, after the "slowed-motion" fall of the hero, his ex-wife and daughter walk away ("That doesn't have anything to do with us") and pass *in front of* the orchestra, which is there, lined up on the sidewalk, playing the music of the film. "You see the music, as if you were seeing inside what accompanies us."[14] We also know that this diegetic presence of the music will be the central formal *and* scenaristic figure of *Prénom Carmen*, where it's pushed to the extreme, as it founds the very structure of the film.

On the other hand, there are other figures of writing experimented with in the video-scenarios that are not transposed to the films, but that in fact work beneath the surface, indirectly, because their effectiveness has been displaced from the formal terrain to the narrative territory. The best example is that of the numerous superimpositions that visually dominate in all the video-scenarios. In the video-scenario of *Sauve qui peut (la vie)*, Godard speaks of superimpositions in terms of dissolves, **chains of images**:

Use dissolves. Begin not from an image, but from a chain of images as an image, from an image of concatenation, a moment in a chain, from somebody being drawn into something. The person and the thing that slides across the person, into which the person slides. . . . Dissolves allow you to see if there isn't something that will open up, or is closing. And so you get the idea of a door, of making someone go through a door. A chain as a moment of the film of the events that you're going to do. *A dissolve as the idea of a scenario.*

In other words, if superimpositions as such are absent from the image in the film *Sauve qui peut (la vie)*, it's because they've passed into the diegesis, the narrative logic, into the modes of connection of the moments (and "movements") of the story. Video superimposition is what allowed Godard to find relations between his characters, or between actions. But these relations, which ultimately defined the logic of the film's editing, do not come from abstract or preconceived ideas. They

do not come, for example, from the dialogue; they come from the images themselves, from a visual, not a verbal, logic. Godard elaborates, still on the same scenario: "Those are all the models of dissolves there are, for example, in television. You see that in fact it's about time passing. . . . And at certain moments, rather than doing shot–reverse shot, which came from a conception of dialogue, or from Ping-Pong, you might want to see if you wouldn't rather go from one image to another *through an image event*, plunging as you plunge into the story, or as the story plunges something into your body." In the same way, the work of superimposition that is at the center of *Scénario du film Passion* cannot be found as such in *Passion*, but is clearly the basis for the entire logic of the re-creation of the classical paintings as tableaux vivants. *Superimposition transformed into the idea of a scenario*: "by plunging [into the image] as you plunge into the story."

Whether he uses slow motion or superimposition, Godard is always experimenting in video with figures that permit him to think in images, and not in language, and to interact with them instantaneously, which allows him to see at the moment he conceives. And from these visual reflections, from this video-laboratory of images, where the work happens live, spontaneously, he will sometimes derive visual forms, or the elements of the story (with Godard, it amounts to the same thing), which will make and be the film: *video thinks what cinema creates.*

4 · In the bowels of the dead planet, tired old machinery stirred. Pale tubes flickered into uneven life, and slowly, reluctantly, a main switch was wheezed out of its negative into its positive position.

—*Jean-Luc Godard*[15]

The fourth and last posture in our journey is that of the video works on their own. With no connections to specific films, these videos stand alone, parallel to Godard's cinematographic production, which they scrutinize wryly from afar. They appeared at intervals from 1986 to 1990, beginning with *Grandeur et décadence d'un petit commerce de cinéma à l'époque de la toute-puissance de la télévision*, which is both a fiction work and an essay, a sort of anthology of all of Godard's production after 1974: here, gathered together by the casting, we find the "analytical" vision of cinema as it unfolds before a videocamera, the slow-motion de-compositions of the image, the relation to painting through dissolves, the mise-en-scène of literature, the discourse on production and money, the false detective plot, as in *Détective* (1985), and so on. This video work is followed by two conversational essays, *Soft and Hard (A Soft Conversation between Two Friends on a Hard Subject)*, a sort of two-

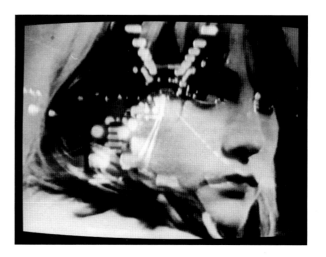

person autobiography (Miéville/Godard), and *Meetin' WA* (1986), an encounter with Woody Allen shot by Godard while he was in the United States for the preproduction of *King Lear* (1987). These are two "dialogues," where Godard lets speech between two people go at varied speeds. This engenders a certain increasingly rhythmic transport produced by the editing, a rapid alternation between text and image, and especially by the absolutely sumptuous work of a sound track that is both incredibly fragmented and incredibly complex, but that remains completely organic in its multiplicity and overlappings. These few independent tapes, all from 1986, are a sort of taking-stock of the results of Godard's research thus far, and correspond, moreover, to an exposure time that lasted about three years, between *Détective*, which closed his lyrical-aesthetic period, and *Soigne ta droite* (1987) and *King Lear*, which opened the latest, philosophical-literary phase of his cinema. Thus, they mark a transition to a new formula that Godard found after 1988 in the video works alone, where his mastery of speed became total, developing as much in the direction of slow motion as in a new direction, a conquest of acceleration.

Godard's work on speed becomes amplified majestically in a new figure of style: the repetitive, blinking effect of super-fast flash shots. *On s'est tous défilé* offers a first, dazzling, and "pictorialist" articulation of this, based on the undulating movements of a fashion show for Marithé and François Girbaud. But the best example is incontestably *Puissance de la parole*, which makes it the central figure of its functioning at every level: technically (the 35mm editing table, its ribbon of images unwinding like a river, at variable speeds; its deformed sounds that boom and rush: "tired old machinery stirred"); formally (electronic and computerized editing, with the pulsing of flash shots alternating super-rapidly and generating effects of accelerated beats: an exercise in perception closer to vibratory sensation than to visual recognition); thematically (the vibrant scene of the telephone liaison); and, above all, philosophically, the axis that gives to the rest of the work its meaning. The reference, from the short story by Edgar Allan Poe that lends its title to the tape, is to the "theory of vibrations" as the foundation of the universe: "As no thought can perish, so no act is without infinite result. We moved our hands, . . . we gave vibration to the atmosphere which engirdled [the earth]. This vibration was indefinitely extended, till it gave impulse to every particle of the earth's air, which, thenceforward, *and for ever*, was actuated by the one movement of the hand. . . . And while I thus spoke, did there not cross your mind some thought of the *physical power of words?* Is not every word an impulse on the air?"[16] After the analytical video-scalpel of the midseventies, after the visual experiments (to see better) of the staccato slow-motion exercises of *France/tour/détour*, after the musings on *écriture* and the stammering images issuing live from thought in the video-scenarios, we have here, in the complete and autonomous works, a **video-vibration**, like a cardiac pulsing that carries into and echoes throughout the whole universe the infinite marks of thought and speech.

This same figure of vibratory and infectious acceleration can also be found in the first programs of the series *Histoire(s) du cinéma*. There, the rhythm of the electronic *memory* typewriter determines the rhythm of the editing and all the wild visual and acoustic matter Godard manipulates with visual and acoustic explosions, infinite combinations of images and sounds coming from the whole history of cinema, and an extraordinary emotion that grows and draws on this galaxy of mixed possibilities embedded in one another. With *Histoire(s) du cinéma*, we reach a point of perfect seesawing between cinema and video: the autonomy of video is now not only total (this time we can truly speak of video *works*, without referring to a corresponding film), but will go much further than we have seen so far. It's no longer a matter of speaking of a film (by JLG), or of a conversation between two subjects, but of embracing cinema itself, of grappling with it in all its dimensions. I believe that the *Histoire(s) du cinéma* are the only truly great Godardian project today.

To continue making films, one more film, is good; it's vital work, necessary to a certain existential equilibrium. But over and above the films that no longer seem to be anything other than production "moments," there is a sort of immensity that only Godard can dream of being able to take on. There's the crazy, impossible project that has long held his imagination, since at least his Montreal lectures and his harbinger book, *Introduction to a True History of Cinema*.[17] It's an outsized project, in which there would be a wild immersion, where cinema as everything, as nature and culture, would be contained in a single, videographic hand. Faced with such a prospect, Godard plunged into a sort of absolute of image-being, where video as a state, a mode of being, thinking, and living, became a second skin, Godard's own second body. "I exist more as an image than as a real being, since my whole life is **making** images," he said in 1980 (the era of the video-scenarios).[18] "Since his whole life is **being** images," I would say today, ten years later. In the end, it's the films that Godard is *making* today that are the "little essays." The video he's immersed himself in totally with *Histoire(s) du cinéma* is not something he makes or does; it has become what he actually is: a body of images, a thought of images, a

**PUISSANCE DE LA
PAROLE**
1988

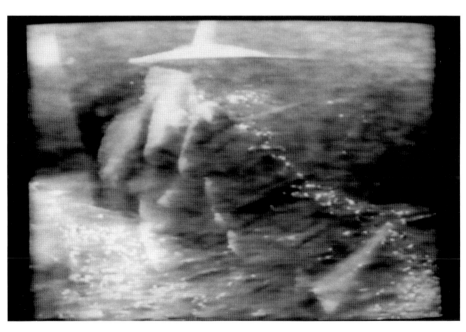

world of images—an image-being of everything. The Godard of today exists entirely in this tension between **still making**—films: circumscribed, identified objects that serve as reference points—and **completely being**—a state of gaze, of video-thinking, the all-being of images, which opens onto the infinite, and where the risk, obvious but avoided, is to be sucked in, absorbed, dissolved into an ocean.

Notes

1   In the text heard in voice-over in the "script" of *Sauve qui peut (la vie)*, *Quelques remarques sur la réalisation et la production du film*. The complete transcript of the tape was published in *Revue Belge du Cinéma*, no. 22/23 (1989), *Jean-Luc Godard: Le cinéma*, a special issue edited by Philippe Dubois, pp. 117–20.

2   Interview, *Le Monde*, September 25, 1975.

3   A phrase uttered by Odette/Anne-Marie Miéville in *Comment ça va*.

4   Serge Daney, "Le Thérrorisé (pédagogie godardienne)," in *Cahiers du Cinéma*, no. 262–263 (January 1976), a special issue on *Numéro deux*, pp. 32–39.

5   A sequence already analyzed by many, notably by Colin Mac-Cabe in his book *Godard: Images, Sounds, Politics* (Bloomington: Indiana University Press, 1980), pp. 96–98; and in detail by Raymond Bellour, "D'entre les corps" in *L'Entre-Images* (Paris: La Différence, 1990), pp. 174–86; and, finally, by myself, in the collective text "Cinéma et vidéo: Interpénétrations," by Philippe Dubois, Marc Melon, and Colette Dubois, in *Communications*, no. 48 (Paris: Editions du Seuil, 1988), pp. 299–305.

6   From an interview in *Le Monde*, March 30, 1980, reprinted in Alain Bergala, ed., *Jean-Luc Godard par Jean-Luc Godard* (Paris: Cahiers du Cinéma, 1985), p. 406.

7   Interview with Claude-Jean Philippe, *Les Nouvelles littéraires*, May 30, 1980, reprinted in *Godard par Godard*, p. 410.

8   *Les Nouvelles littéraires* interview, p. 411.

9   See on this subject the lovely text by Alain Bergala, "Enfants: Ralentir," in *Cahiers du Cinéma*, no. 301 (June 1979).

10 *Les Nouvelles littéraires* interview, p. 411.

11 According to Marc Cerisuelo's happy expression in his *Jean-Luc Godard* (Paris: Lherminier/Quatre-Vents, 1989).

12 See note 1.

13 Jean-Luc Godard, "Propos rompus," July 1980, in *Cahiers du Cinéma*, no. 316 (October 1980), reprinted in *Godard par Godard*, pp. 461–62.

14 See note 1.

15 *Puissance de la parole*. English text from A.E. Van Vogt, "Defense," *Destination: Universe* (New York: Berkley Medallion, 1964; originally published 1948 by Avon Book Company), p. 94.

16 *Puissance de la parole*. English text from *Poe: Poetry and Tales*, ed. Patrick F. Quinn (New York: The Library of America, Literary Classics of the United States, 1984), pp. 823, 825. Emphasis the author's.

17 Jean-Luc Godard, *Introduction à une véritable histoire du cinéma*, vol. 1 (Editions Albatros, 1977).

18 "Propos rompus," p. 468.

ARIA
(a compilation film)
1987
"Armide"

L'ETERNEL RETOUR

PETER WOLLEN

In 1923, Jean Cocteau gave a lecture at the Collège de France, entitled "On an Order Considered as an Anarchy," during the course of which he named Erik Satie and Pablo Picasso as his masters.[1] He went on: "How many times have I heard Satie and Picasso reproached for not knowing where they are going. One day Picasso is giving up cubism. The next, Satie is starting to regress. Yet, wonder of wonders, both of them are treated as if they were absolute beginners [translation mine]." Jean-Luc Godard's development has followed much the same pattern. His films have changed genre and style at an alarming rate, moving from Nouvelle Vague innocence to an embittered avant-gardism and thence to his idiosyncratic "late" style. Beginning, in the Nouvelle Vague days, with a turbulent mélange of Romanticism and existentialism, he underwent in turn the intellectual influence of the *Arguments* group, of Barthesian semiology, of Althusserian Marxism, of French feminism, and finally of postmodern thought, leading him inexorably back toward aesthetics and even religion. From the start, Godard was unusually open to the fashionable and the topical. In itself, this openness was a strength, but its end result was to send his artistic and intellectual compass pointer swinging wildly around the dial. When Luc Moullet commented that it was easy to identify central themes in the earlier work of Godard, but that, in the "late" period, the films proved much more difficult to categorize and describe in thematic terms, he was simply pinpointing the effects of this rapid and repeated change.[2] As with Picasso, Godard's underlying obsessions and compulsions have surfaced in a protean array of styles and subjects.

Almost ten years have passed since I last wrote about Godard, at the time of *Passion* (1982).[3] During the eighties and into this decade, Godard's films have further developed an "aesthetic" discourse, encompassing music, image, and text. Formal strategies have remained surprisingly constant, but quotation from the great works of the past has taken the form of providing classical reference texts to serve as an armature for a series of loosely linked episodes, fragments, and digressions. Beethoven quartets, the Gospel story, Shakespeare's

King Lear, all have played this role. At the same time, the films are pervaded by a second layer of quotation and allusion, a complex interplay between text and image, and a proliferation of wordplay and metaphor. It is possible to see in these "late" films many elements of earlier work, visible like archeological strata, together with quite new elements and preoccupations—images of the local Swiss landscape, theological speculations, the appearance of Godard himself as magus and fool. But the climate of these films is no longer that of either modernism or political engagement. The urban, metropolitan, consumerist world of the sixties has now been decisively rejected, along with the values of "modernity" and the politics of "Leftism."[4] Nonetheless, Godard still sets his films in the present and still alludes to topical events. He is still fascinated by image technology. But there is a new type of mesh between past and present, in which the contemporary, instead of being pervaded by images from the past, is seen almost as an allegorical reworking of the past: airplanes are angels, the message of the Annunciation is delivered by videocassette, and Rubik's Cube is an emblem of cosmogony.

One of the strangest of these allegorical texts is "Armide," an episode made for the British compilation film *Aria* (1987). Most of the directors are English (among them, Derek Jarman, Nicolas Roeg, and Ken Russell), but they also include Robert Altman and Jean-Luc Godard. Each was asked to make a short film, without dialogue, set to an operatic aria. Godard chose, as his classical reference text, Armide's recitative aria from act 2, scene 5, of Jean-Baptiste Lully's tragédie lyrique *Armide*, commissioned by Louis XIV and first performed at Versailles in 1686.[5] The libretto, by Lully's longtime collaborator, Philippe Quinault, is drawn from Torquato Tasso's *Jerusalem Delivered*. Armide is the daughter of the King of Damascus, whose realm is threatened by invading Crusaders from France. Through her beauty, she captivates and enslaves the Frankish knights, except for their leader, Renaud, who resists her charms and frees his comrades. Humiliated and burning with a desire for vengeance, she invokes spirits to enchant him and place him at her mercy. However, torn between love and hate, she is unable to deliver the fatal blow. This is the scene in which the aria takes place. Godard prefaces the film episode with lines from this aria:

I yield to this Victor, by Pity I'm won . . .
My greatest wish that thou liest dead . . .

For his film, Godard sets the story in contemporary times: in a gymnasium. The Crusader knights are represented by bodybuilders in shorts working out with elaborate machines. Armide and her companion are transmuted into cleaning women, attracted by the muscle-men. The two women wear loosely belted housecoats, with nothing underneath. They set out mopping and dusting the floor and the equipment, moving on to polish the bodybuilders themselves. However, the men carry on with their disciplined workout, impervious to the women's charms, even when the women strip naked and pose in front of them. As in the opera, Armide threatens to kill a bodybuilder who ignores her, to stab him with a butcher's knife, but is unable to carry out her purpose. In the end, after further attempts at seduction, thoughts of revenge, and repeated frustration, the women are left behind as the bodybuilders march out in a parade line. Armide cries out, "Yes!" and "No!" alternately and stands transfixed in a tableau with her companion. (In the opera, too, the enchantment is eventually broken and the knights leave, taking Renaud with them. But then Armide, in a rage, destroys her magic palace and is carried off by her demons.)

At first sight, we are confronted by a semipornographic discourse, in which servile women are shown as attracted by muscled men. They fondle themselves, touch the men, strip, and pose provocatively. The men are impervious and reject the desirous women. Thus, the normal conclusion of a pornographic video—the involvement of the women with the men: perhaps an act of masturbation or fellatio—is never reached. In this sense, the film deliberately frustrates the expectations of the pornographic spectator/voyeur (who, like the filmmaker, we may assume is male). In the opera, Armide is torn tragically between love and hate, between an overpowering fascination with the phallus and a conflicting desire to castrate and decapitate the invader. In the film, although Armide remains the protagonist, the emphasis is shifted away from her interior conflict and the magical tragedy is reduced to a disenchanted tale of sexual frustration. Renaud and his companions simply ignore Armide, despite her seductive provocations. The implication is that the men are impervious to female desire because of their narcissistic relationship to their own male bodies, and this is sealed by their final bonding into an exclusive male group. It all ends as if the women have wandered by mistake into what is, after all, potentially gay porn, dooming them to frustration. Yet, in this misogynist world, homosexual desire itself is perhaps only the innuendo that conceals a deeper renunciation of all sexuality, each body trapped in the glass of its own narcissism.

"Armide" is reminiscent, in many respects, of two earlier films by Godard, *British Sounds* (1969) and *Numéro deux* (1975). In the first of these, two sequences are juxtaposed: workers on the assembly line at the Ford car factory in Dagenham, with a sound track of machine noise, and a naked woman descending a staircase, with a feminist discourse on the sound track. In "Armide" it is as if these two sequences are combined into one. The sound track is broken up between fragments of machine noise and fragments of recitative (mainly, but not solely, the female voice). The image is of seminaked women juxtaposed with men locked into machines, themselves "machinized" as they pursue their discipline of rhythmically repetitive movement. The atmosphere is that of the factory assembly line, and their final departure, in a parade line, is like the stream of products leaving a factory, but the men we see are manufacturing not alienated commodities, but their own butch bodies. This self-production by the workers is like the production of a permanent and nonorgasmic erection, a "phallicization" with no fear of final expense or loss—no castration. The female voice, alternating between "Yes" and "No," is an ambivalent and divided voice, a split between accepting and rejecting this regime that excludes its enunciatrix.

In *Numéro deux*, the sexual overtures of the woman are rejected by her husband, exhausted by his mechanical work in the factory. As in a much earlier film, *Une Femme est une femme* (1961), the first in which Godard breaks the music up into intermittent fragments, she then turns in frustration to another man, but whereas in *Une Femme est une femme* (a loose remake of *Così fan tutte*) all ends happily with the reconstitution of the couple, in *Numéro deux* the husband is enraged and performs a violent, anal rape on his wife. Here, it is the humiliated man who acts out his revenge on the body of the woman. In "Armide," on the other hand, the men remain invulnerable, and the woman is doubly humiliated by her inability to carry out her revenge and kill the man she desires, but who refuses to acknowledge her. In psychoanalytic terms, perhaps we could say that while, in *Numéro deux*, the repressed fear of being the victim of anal rape by the male is acted out hysterically on the woman, in "Armide" the fear of being the victim of castration by the female can be belittled, in fantasy, and turned against the woman through the image of the phallus as a narcissistic and magical object of male self-identification.

Godard, as far as I know, has never directly confronted male homosexuality as a central issue in his films. In "Armide," we are as close to it as we get. It is hard to watch the film, as a cinéphile, without thinking of Anger's *Kustom Kar Kommandos* or Cukor's *Chapman Report* (on Godard's "Ten Best" list for 1963). Godard's treatment of homosexuality, however, reflects a heterosexual ambivalence toward women, in which an infantilizing voyeurism is combined with the acting out of an exaggerated misogyny, appropriating the imagery of homosexual desire as the signifier of the exclusion of the female from the male world. Ostensibly "Armide" has a female protagonist, but, as in Howard Hawks's *Gentlemen Prefer Blondes*, the child-woman is exhibited within a tableau of male hypermasculinity. The governing antinomy in the film is that of "soft and hard" (the title of a video that Godard made with Miéville earlier the same year, in which, once again, questions of gender are discussed). In Lully's tragédie lyrique, women are associated with love and desire, men with discipline and glory. In Godard's film, the women are associated with softness and wetness, with dripping mops; the men with hardness and tautness, with pumping iron. In one sense, of course, this scenario is a trivialization. But it is also a defensive schema, an exaggerated reduction of sexual difference to a cartoon of stereotypical extremes unable to meet or make contact, a strategy by which to evade the terrifying consequences of contact. Godard's films resonate with the drums of the "war of the sexes." In "Armide," the refusal to join battle is presented as the ultimate male victory.

It would be possible, perhaps, to read Godard's "Armide" as a critique of patriarchy, seen as a "homosocial" structure, a "bachelor machine," based on the displacement of repressed homosexual desire into the self-contained male world of work, power, and prestige. But, on the other hand, seen in the context of Godard's career, it seems more plausible to see "Armide" as an elaborate defense against adult or assertive femininity, against feminine "hardness." Godard's late films valorize "softness" ideologically, in contrast to the political "hardness" of his Maoist period, in their love of the countryside and the beauty of nature. In a different, more questionable way, he valorizes feminine "softness" in his repeated choice of youthful actresses with firm breasts and flawless skins, soft but insipid. Powerful heroines, like Carmen or Armide (or, in another way, the Madonna), are reduced to the same innocuous model. What is important here is that "softness," as signifier of femininity, is coupled with the tentativeness, confusion, and servility dis-

played by the young women. In "Armide" Godard gives the heroine a female companion, who is absent from the parallel scene in Lully's opera. Possibly this was suggested by Poussin's painting of Renaud and Armide, where Armide is restrained from murdering Renaud by an allegorical Amor. But more likely, it is a reminiscence of another, allied art-historical subject, the biblical story of Judith and Holofernes. Judith is a heroine who succeeded where Armide failed. In Godard's film, however, we are presented, not with a resolute heroine and her assistant, but with two ineffectual handmaidens, who can be distinguished only by the color of their hair and their housecoats.

A pornographic subtext runs through Godard's films from the beginning, restrained at first by stricter censorship laws. The theme of prostitution is central to his early work, in which consumerism is presented as a kind of pornography: "*la civilisation du cul.*" At the end of the sixties, in *One Plus One* (aka *Sympathy for the Devil* [1968]) and *Le Gai Savoir* (1968), pornographic discourse is transposed onto the sound track as well as appearing on the image track, and the fascination with the obscene and scatological is given a political twist. In fact, toward the end of the sixties the pornographic imaginary is a dominant dimension in Godard's increasingly apocalyptic vision of the world. Pornography, as in Pasolini's *Salò*, provides a vision of the world in which human relations are reduced to a cruel and abstract dialectic of pleasure and pain, of domination and subjugation. The emblematic artists of the sixties—Burroughs, Warhol, Godard—were all obsessed by pornography, and with the relationship between sexuality and an alienating commodity culture.

In "Armide," however, the mise-en-scène of pornography is set in motion, but enjoyment itself is blocked. Godard presents a world in which female desire, so threatening in so much of his early work, is doomed to disappointment by male indifference. Burroughs and Warhol, of course, had an explicitly homosexual world view, in which women were, by definition, unnecessary as sexual partners, and in Burroughs's view unnecessary *tout court*. In Godard's case, "Armide" takes him over the edge into superficial "camp," but the underlying framework of the episode is still heterosexual. Female desire is to be resisted and annulled through the displacement and renunciation of male desire. The male desires only to be the object of desire for woman and it is in this that his triumph lies, in the essentially heterosexual act of humiliating the woman who desires him and gratifying himself in her humiliation. The bodybuilders' indifference is felt as perverse, though necessary in its passive aggression. Yet, perhaps, this renunciation is the only solution Godard can now envisage to the problem of a destructive (and self-destructive) male sexuality.

However, Godard's fascination with pornography should also be seen as a formal feature of his work. Throughout his career, Godard has sought ways to distance himself from conventional narrative. In the sixties, he deliberately mixed Lumière with Méliès, fictional storytelling with documentary and cinéma vérité, juxtaposing different narrative regimes. In *Le Gai Savoir*, he took a further step, toward the experimental film and the film essay or lecture. In the seventies, when he drew back from this radical avant-gardism, he began to introduce tableaux into his films. Pornography, of course, is based around the tableau. As Roland Barthes points out, in his *Sade/Fourier/Loyola*, it has a permutational rather than a teleological structure.[6] In this perspective, we can see Godard's leaning to pornography, not simply as a question of taste or choice of problematic subject matter, but also as a new strategy for de-composing conventional narrative, having exhausted most of the other options in his previous work.

Significantly, there is a single reference to the story of Renaud and Armide in Godard's early critical writings. In 1958 he went to the Festival of Short Films at Tours, where he saw Jacques Demy's first film, *Le Bel Indifférent*. This is a film version of a short dramatic sketch by Cocteau, which he wrote for Edith Piaf in 1940.[7] It is the monologue of a woman, whose beloved takes no notice of her. He ignores her words and herself completely, and, for most of the play, spends his time lying on the bed in her room reading the newspaper, refusing to respond, impervious to her desire. Godard defended Demy's film in an article in *Cahiers* headed "Ignored by the Jury," and, invoking Cocteau, likens the film to another play of his, *Renaud et Armide* (written the next year).[8] Godard must have been aware not only of the similarity in the subject matter of the two works, but of the transposition between heterosexual and homosexual versions. It is perhaps not surprising that Godard's "Armide" should be so reminiscent of Demy's own later film work, in its visual style, its musicality, and its use of choreography and recitative. However, the association with Cocteau is also suggestive: are not Godard's bodybuilders also transposed versions of *Orpheus*'s motorcycle-riders? Is Godard not transposing Cocteau's homosexual text to suit his own heterosexual dilemma?

In fact, I would argue that it is the spirit of Cocteau who reigns over Godard's recent films, especially through the idea of "the eternal return," *L'Eternel Retour*, the reworking of classic and mythic texts in contemporary form. Cocteau, of course, is also the great French exemplar of the independent filmmaker, man of the arts, pursuing his uncompromising yet wayward journey through the wasteland of the cinema industry. Cocteau's own acquaintance with the story of Renaud and Armide came, I imagine, through the Michel Fokine ballet "Le Pavillon d'Armide" (first danced by Pavlova and Nijinsky), which was part of Diaghilev's repertoire. Godard's later works also echo the Cocteau of the Ballets Russes period, in their prolific borrowing from the other arts, their reworking of classical material in the garb of life-style modernism.[9] Cocteau and Godard both drape themselves in the mantle of the classics while extolling the charms of narcissistic youth.

It was precisely this strange mix of classicism and modernism à la Cocteau that first attracted me to Godard's films when he made his own debut as a filmmaker. I was living in Paris the year *A bout de souffle* came out and I went back to the cinema to see it many times. 1960! This was also the time of Samuel Fuller's *The Crimson Kimono*, and soon afterward came Budd Boetticher's *The Rise and Fall of Legs Diamond*. To me, Godard's *A bout de souffle* had the extraordinary merit of combining the Cocteau tradition with the American "B"-picture tradition. *A bout de souffle*, too, was a small film, a film set on the fringes of the underworld, a grittily urban film, but with a difference: Godard's self-conscious modernity. Boetticher was actually mentioned in *A bout de souffle* (one of his films is showing at the cinema that Michel Poiccard, played by Jean-Paul Belmondo, dives into on the Champs-Elysées), but he was there alongside Apollinaire (whose poetry was dubbed over what should have been the dialogue from *Westbound*). This was certainly film made by an intellectual. Yet it wasn't purely in the Cocteau tradition, nor in the allied tradition of auteur heroes such as Rossellini or Bergman, however much their films were the preconditions for its possibility. It was a movie, as well as an art film. It wasn't simply rejecting Hollywood, aiming for a "European" alternative, more cultured, more sophisticated, more sensitive. *A bout de souffle* was a "refunctioning" of Hollywood, and, by implication, of American mass culture. It was more like a work of *détournement*.

The connections between Godard and Cocteau that stand out in "Armide" have led me to reevaluate the impact of Cocteau on Godard's career as a whole. Cocteau, after all, was the cinematic godfather of the *Cahiers* group and the principal example, in France certainly, of a director who combined a successful career with outsider status. My first view of Godard concentrated on his "Americanism," linked to the auteurist rediscovery of Hollywood undertaken by *Cahiers du Cinéma*. Seen this way, Godard's early films, his Nou-

"Armide"
1987

velle Vague films, echoed important trends in my own English culture: the emergence of Pop art after the "This Is Tomorrow" exhibition, for example. Richard Hamilton's painting *Interior 1*, showing Pamela Knight in *Shockproof* (Douglas Sirk, from a Samuel Fuller script), followed soon after *A bout de souffle*, and seemed to echo its preoccupations. Lawrence Alloway, who was critical spokesperson for the This Is Tomorrow group, was the nearest thing there was in England to the *Cahiers* critics, and a patron of the parallel English magazine, *Movie*.[10] In the end, as the sixties progressed, this cannibalizing and reworking of American mass culture became more and more dominant in Britain. In the world of music, it produced the Beatles and the Rolling Stones. Indeed, English mass-cultural "modernism" began to be hegemonic, in certain sectors, even within the United States itself.

Godard's films appeared as the products of a similarly cosmopolitan intelligentsia when compared with the much more "domestic" and "French" work of Claude Chabrol, Eric Rohmer, or François Truffaut, whose "modernity" and "Americanism" soon began to seem skin-deep. Indeed, ironically, Godard filled a gap left within English cinema itself, where the cosmopolitan sixties never found a native interpreter. (Expatriate American directors like Joseph Losey and Richard Lester wanted to make European art films—look at *Eve* or *The Knack*—only to be eclipsed by the real thing: Michelangelo Antonioni.) In this situation, Godard's films were the best possible substitutes for their missing English counterparts. *Performance* (Donald Cammell and Nicolas Roeg) and *Leo the Last* (John Boorman) did not appear until after Godard's own English film, *One Plus One*. But by then Godard had moved a long way beyond *A bout de souffle*.

In retrospect, I now see my "Americanist" fascination with Godard's sixties films as one-sided. There were two further, often conflicting impulses at work in Godard's cinema, both of which were deeply French in origin. First, there was the strong strain of his own lifestyle modernism, which combined a journalistic sense of the topical with a more sociologically oriented mode of investigation and an attachment to the "critique of everyday life," to use Henri Lefebvre's phrase.[11] It is this dimension of Godard's work that made him seem both a cultural "barometer" and an emergent political critic. In cinematic terms, this strain owed a great deal to the films of Jean Rouch, which provided models of filmic urban anthropology, first in Africa, then, with *Chronique d'un été*, made with Edgar Morin, in Paris itself. In intellectual terms, it was from the *Arguments* group, to which Morin belonged, that Godard drew most, but also, I am convinced, from the neighboring, yet bitterly

antagonistic, group of Situationists. Godard's films exhibit any number of Situationist characteristics—not only his topography of the "society of the spectacle," but also, for example, the ideas of "*dérive*," of "*détournement*," and of plagiarism as a deliberate policy. Indeed, the films made by Guy Debord, the central figure in the Situationist movement, predate many of Godard's own later preoccupations and strategies.[12]

Secondly, there was Godard's profound and yet paradoxical attachment to the idea of art, both as a repertory of great works, an available cultural heritage, and also as an anarchic project in process, which simultaneously required the reinscription and destruction of that heritage. It is here that Cocteau's heritage also made itself felt. Like those of Cocteau, Godard's films showed a contradictory reverence for the art of the past and a delinquent refusal to obey any of its rules. This applied both to the cinema and to the other, older arts. Godard's films seem to be made in a consumerist version of Malraux's "imaginary museum," a society full of posters and postcards of great paintings, records of great music, shelves of paperback books, and people who can quote instant lines of poetry to each other. But rather than seeing the consumer society as antagonistic to art, as did many antimodernists, Godard saw the pervasive availability of art as an integral part of consumerism. Art had left its sanctum to become a prominent feature of "everyday life," alongside pinball machines and advertising posters. In this aspect of his work, Godard often seems to oscillate between a critique of consumerism and mass culture and a fascination with it. In this respect, too, Godard's work resembles Cocteau's. It was Cocteau, after all, who introduced the modern imagery of cabaret, café, and sports arena to the world of the aesthetic spectacle, while distancing himself from it through constant allusions to the classics and "high art," through a strategy of citations, rewritings, and parallelisms.

Eventually, of course, Godard's trajectory took him on toward a Leftist political commitment, crystallized by the events of May 1968, which threw his aestheticism into crisis. Everyday life itself became more and more politicized, until the streets were filled with militant demonstrations, and home, factory, and film set became sites of political ferment. Unlike Cocteau, Godard did not recoil from politicization. Indeed, his whole filmmaking career was bound up with a determination to be topical, to keep abreast of events (and particularly of the life-style of vanguard urban youth). Once this politicization passed a certain point, it triggered a transformation of the whole system. Godard's cinema entered its militant phase. At first, this seemed likely to stabilize around some idea of "Brechtian" or "guerrilla" cinema, but it soon became clear that Godard's radicalism was impelling him toward a kind of "Cinema year zero," although, even here, we feel echoes of earlier work: the Lettrists and Maurice Lemaître's *Le Film est déjà commencé*.[13] Cocteau broke with the Surrealists when they began to move to the far left, but Godard moved rapidly leftward with the Situationists and beyond, to join a Maoist groupuscule, as André Breton had joined the Communist party.

Instead of the Romanticism of Poe, Dostoyevsky, or García Lorca, it was the voice of Marxism-Leninism and Mao Tse-tung Thought that now overloaded the sound track of his films, providing an interminable and pitiless metalanguage, and a series of inquisitorial monologues, designed, like a Lettrist film, to provoke the audience. Yet, in many respects, elements of Godard's former strategies survived. Films were still structured in blocks and modules (often numbered), voices were divorced from characters, "real people" were mingled with fictional roles, genres were mixed in the same film, dialogue was replaced by direct address to the camera/audience, cinematic devices and techniques were foregrounded, image track and sound track were filled with quotations. There was also a new emphasis on the semiotic character of the cinema, its codes and "signifying practices," which were explicitly interrogated within the films themselves. Here we see the influence of Roland Barthes (another former member of the *Arguments* group), both in his inquiries into the rhetoric of the image and in his insistence on the necessity of verbal language to anchor the meaning of photographs.[14]

The films of this brief but intense period, which lasted from 1968 to 1972, were didactic and essayistic rather than narrative or dramatic. Even when there was a fictional "story" it was subordinated to a more or less explicit "master text." However, following the breakup of the Dziga Vertov Group, this dominance of the "master text" started to dissolve and, after Godard's removal from Paris to Grenoble and the beginning of his partnership with Anne-Marie Miéville, a new tentativeness began to be felt. At the same time, Godard began to be seriously interested in video as a form and to develop an ongoing semiotic inquiry, not only into the meaning of photographic images as such, but also into the specific differences of video and film, as opposed to television and cinema. This period saw a revival of Godard's interest in semiotic investigation and the contrast between the cinematic and the televisual sign. In *Ici et ailleurs* (1974) and *Comment ça va* (1976) Godard picked up threads that had been dropped since *Le Gai Savoir*. Although his films were still political, they lost much of the dogmatism of the previous period. In particular, his view of politics had changed and, in the wake of feminism, he now took into account the ways in which the "personal" was intertwined with the "political," a trend that eventually led him to the impasse of "Armide." His films and especially his videotapes now investigated the relationship between apparently "personal" categories like "love" and social categories like "labor." This was an extremely rich period in Godard's career.

Then, after 1976, when Godard moved again, this time from Grenoble to Rolle in Switzerland, his films took yet another new turn, toward a preoccupation with landscape, with metaphysics, and with cosmic speculation. It is often assumed that this was because he was now living and working in the country, rather than the city. However, it is also possible to see the shift of emphasis as part of a much more general shift within French culture itself. Leading Marxists and structuralists began to abandon the master narratives and semiotic systems of the sixties. As the Enlightenment and "modernity" were increasingly called into question, a process accelerated by post-1968 disenchantment, many French intellectuals turned away from "knowledge-based" approaches to the humanities and toward the more speculative domains of aesthetics, philosophy, and theology, or urged a decentralized vision of "dissemination," "rhizomes," and "molecular" microstructures. Godard's films, too, abandoned the center, not only geographically, but thematically as well, breaking down narrative into a mosaic of microelements. At the same time, there was also a clear and significant return to the tradition of Cocteau, in the development of personal mythologies and in a return to the classics, however heterodox the homage. Godard's revived classical aestheticism grew as his political commitment shrank.

As we look back on Godard's career, it is hard to find the red thread that unites his work, even though any one film or video is unmistakably Godardian. We tend to expect consistency in the work of an auteur, a single pattern of repetition and variation. But Godard has changed direction time and again, often seeming both to veer back and to advance simultaneously. In this respect, his career resembles that of his early model and mentor, Roberto Rossellini, who moved in turn from wartime propaganda to the founding classics of neorealism, then onward through the Ingrid Bergman cycle to the uncertainties of the late fifties and early sixties, and eventually, after *La Prise de pouvoir par Louis XIV*, to the pedagogic biographies of his final period. It has proved hard for critics to respond with equal enthusiasm to every period of Rossellini's work. The early wartime films were often conveniently forgotten. Critical opinion divided sharply over *Viaggio in Italia*, when erstwhile supporters condemned Rossellini for abandoning neorealism, and others hailed him for enriching it with personal themes. His *Louis XIV* and his *Pascal* found him an entirely new generation of admirers, as well as bringing back some of the old, who now placed him alongside Jean-Marie Straub or, indeed, Godard himself, rather than with Luchino Visconti or Vittorio De Sica. The same heterogeneity is found in Godard's cinematic career, too, and consequently the same critical uncertainty and mutability. In France, critics have tended to line up for or against Godard in fixed battle order, but elsewhere only a few could follow all his periods with equal enthusiasm. Some looked back in nostalgia to the Nouvelle Vague and the sixties. Others regretted that he abandoned and disowned his 1968 political and avant-garde period. New admirers appeared to hail his "late," Swiss films.

In 1964, just five years after he began work on *A bout de souffle*, Godard once more cited Cocteau in a review in *Cahiers*, this time as the author of *A Call to Order!*[15] After the ebb tide that followed May 1968, it seems Godard now felt the need for his own call to order. But his postmodern return to the classics, to religion, to opera, could not be so pure as Cocteau's. Troubled, as always, by confusing questions and fragmentary insights, Godard challenged the classical lucidity of his reference texts. Yet, as Cocteau observed, "a masterpiece can never look like a masterpiece. It must necessarily be incomplete and full of defects, since it is the triumph of its errors and the consecration of its faults that make it a masterpiece."[16]

Opinion is still divided as to whether Godard's "late" films, however grave their errors and their faults, should be considered as masterpieces, even accursed and defective masterpieces. Yet, after seeing his extraordinary *Nouvelle Vague* (1990), a reworking of his own origins as classic reference text, I suspect that, once again, beneath the surface, something problematic, new, and strange is already stirring that will compel another troubled critical reassessment at some time in the future. As if to unsettle both his admirers and his detractors, the perennial absolute beginner has given us yet another breathtaking and disconcerting debut.

Notes

1   Jean Cocteau, "D'un ordre considéré comme une anarchie," address given at the Collège de France, Paris, on May 3, 1923. Published in *Le Rappel à l'ordre* (Paris: Stock, 1926).

2   Luc Moullet, "Suivez le guide," *Cahiers du Cinéma*, "Spécial Godard," supplement to no. 437 (November 1990).

3   Peter Wollen, "Godard's *Passion*," *Framework*, no. 21 (Summer 1983).

4   Godard's distance from modernity is explicitly addressed in *Nouvelle Vague*, in which he speaks of a civilization doomed to extinction.

5   Jean-Baptiste Lully's tragédie lyrique *Armide* was first performed at the Académie Royale de Musique, Paris, on February 15, 1686. It was the last of a series he wrote for Louis XIV, with Philippe Quinault as the librettist. In *Aria* Godard uses the recording made for Erato in January 1983, conducted by Philippe Hereweghe and sung by Rachel Yakar as Armide and Zeger Vandersteene as Renaud, with the choir and orchestra of the Chapelle Royale, Paris. The album notes for this recording contain the libretto in the original French and in English translation. The two lines cited in the text are from this libretto.

6   Roland Barthes, *Sade/Fourier/Loyola* (Berkeley and Los Angeles: University of California Press, 1976; originally published in Paris: Seuil, 1971). See especially the passages on the tableau in the section "Sade I," and on the conveyor belt and the machine in "Sade II."

7   Jean Cocteau, *Le Bel Indifférent*, in *Oeuvres complètes*, vol. 8 (Paris: Marguerat, 1949). The monologue was written for Edith Piaf and first performed by her in 1940. *Renaud et Armide* was published in Paris by Gallimard in 1940.

8   Jean-Luc Godard, "Ignorés du jury," first published in *Arts*, no. 700 (December 1958), and "Chacun son Tours," *Cahiers du Cinéma*, no. 92 (February 1959), reprinted in Alain Bergala, ed., *Jean-Luc Godard par Jean-Luc Godard* (Paris: Cahiers du Cinéma, 1985), pp. 152–55 and 156–63. The English translation, *Godard on Godard* (New York: Da Capo, 1972), has detailed scholarly and critical notes compiled by Tom Milne.

9   For "life-style modernism" in Cocteau's work, see Lynn Garafola, *Diaghilev's Ballets Russes* (New York: Oxford University Press, 1989), especially chapter 4, "The Twenties"; and Dore Ashton and others, *Jean Cocteau and the French Scene* (New York: Abbeville, 1984).

10 See *This Is Tomorrow Today*, the catalogue of an exhibition in New York curated by Brian Wallis for the Institute for Art and Urban Resources, 1987.

11 Henri Lefebvre, *Critique de la vie quotidienne* (Paris: Editions Grasset, 1947, and new extended edition, Paris: L'Arche, 1958).

12 The Situationists mentioned Godard adversely in three successive issues of *Internationale Situationniste*: 10 (March 1966), a discussion of the difference between *détournement*, as a Situationist practice, and collage, as practiced by Godard; 11 (October 1967), a programmatic article by René Vienet, noting Godard's alleged recuperation of Debord; and 12 (September 1969), remarks on Godard's "false novelty" and "belated and useless plagiarism," in the context of a juxtaposition of Godard's *Le Gai Savoir* (1968) and Debord's *Hurlements en faveur de Sade* (1952). *Le Gai Savoir* shows Debord's title *La*

Société du spectacle in one of its close-ups of books. For Debord's films, see Thomas Y. Levin, "Dismantling the Spectacle: The Cinema of Guy Debord," in Elisabeth Sussman, ed., *On the Passage of a Few People through a Rather Brief Moment in Time: The Situationist International, 1957–1972* (Cambridge, MA: MIT Press, 1989).

13   See Maurice Lemaître, *Le Film est déjà commencé* (Paris: André Bonne, 1952). The film itself was first shown at the Ciné Club du Quartier Latin, Paris, December 7, 1951.

14   See Peter Wollen, "Godard and Counter-cinema," *Afterimage,* no. 4 (Autumn 1972), reprinted in *Readings and Writings* (London: Verso, 1982). Roland Barthes was asked by Godard to appear in a film as "himself," but refused.

15   Jean-Luc Godard, *"Orphée," Cahiers du Cinéma,* no. 152 (February 1964), an issue containing seven articles written in memory of Cocteau. Tom Milne's note in *Godard on Godard*, op. cit., is especially informative on details of Godard's debt to Cocteau.

16   See note 1.

LA CHINOISE
1967
Juliet Berto

EIGHT OBSTACLES TO THE APPRECIATION
OF GODARD IN THE UNITED STATES

JONATHAN ROSENBAUM

"Jean-Luc cultists," complains Judith Crist in the *World Journal Tribune*. God bless them! They constitute a line of defense against every manipulative insult the entertainment business throws out, there are more of them each year, and they may even be winning.

—Roger Greenspun[1]

Greenspun's rallying cry of a quarter of a century ago testifies to the passion and debate that used to be stirred up in the United States when Godard's name was mentioned. The gradual phasing out of that debate and the depletion of that passion cannot be explained simply, and to understand it at all requires some careful thought about how American culture as a whole has itself changed in the interim. For a director still closely identified with the sixties in American film criticism, Godard is regarded today with much of the same fear, skepticism, suspicion, and impatience that greet many other contemporary responses to that decade. And his status as an intellectual with a taste for abstraction may make him seem even more out of place in a mass culture that currently has little truck with movie experiences that can't be reduced to sound bites. (One might add that he has still fared somewhat better in this respect than Antonioni, whose American reputation has suffered an almost total eclipse.)

Roughly speaking, Godard's career as a critic spans sixteen years, from an auteurist appreciation of Joseph Mankiewicz, published in the 2d issue of *Gazette du Cinéma* in 1950, to "3000 heures de cinéma," published in the 184th issue of *Cahiers du Cinéma* (November 1966). His career as a director of features has lasted almost twice as long and reveals a comparable ambivalence toward the U.S., with both a love of William Faulkner and Robert Aldrich and a mockery of American power and influence extending all the way from *Breathless* to *Nouvelle Vague*. But in contrast to this sustained love–hatred that, through all its vicissitudes, has never ceased to be both pursuit and flight, embrace and recoil, the relationship of the U.S. to Godard has, broadly speaking, been one of increasing fascination (roughly 1961 to 1973), followed by decreasing interest (roughly 1974 to 1992).

It should be recalled, however, that, even at the height of his popularity as an art-house director, Godard was always something of a minority taste among critics and audiences alike. While the American critics and institutions that were originally most supportive of his work—Richard Roud, Susan Sontag, Andrew Sarris, Pauline Kael, and Vincent Canby, among the former; the New York Film Festival, The Museum of Modern Art, and New Yorker Films, among the latter—have been highly influential, mainstream resistance to Godard's work has remained constant over the past three decades, becoming increasingly decisive over the second half of this period.

The remarks that follow will attempt to pinpoint some of the sources of that resistance. Without pretending in any way to be exhaustive, I think that the principal obstacles to the American appreciation of Godard that have existed—and, in many cases, continue to exist—point toward a complex of cultural attitudes that ultimately have bearing on much more than Godard's work. Nevertheless, insofar as Godard's name has remained both a symbol and a rallying point for a certain kind of cinema since the beginning of his career, it seems useful to delve here, however incompletely, into the question of what that kind of cinema has meant, and continues to mean, in an American context.

While much of my emphasis will be on the American reception of Godard's work since 1974, it is important to bear in mind that Godard's American reputation prior to this period, beginning in 1961 with the release in the United States of his first feature, *Breathless*, affected his subsequent reputation in two largely antithetical ways. That is, part of the resistance to Godard in this country since 1974 can be construed as a backlash to the former centrality of Godard's name and work in certain circles, while another part of that resistance is due to a lack of awareness of his former centrality, especially among younger viewers. (Two significant instances of this latter situation, both dating from the early eighties, are worth citing here. By his own account, Jim McBride was able to finance his American remake of *Breathless* only because most producers he approached had heard of the film but had never seen it; and when Godard's *Passion* received an uncharacteristically wide American release a year or so later, it was most often billed—in ads, on marquees, and even in recorded phone messages at theaters—as "Francis Coppola's *Passion*.")

Although many of the topics addressed below represent ongoing problems of reception rather than obstacles posed in a particular period, and some of these are overlapping rather than sequential, I have given these topics in a very rough chronological order, from problems associated with Godard during the sixties, to the recent present.

1. *The Nouvelle Vague context.* Clearly, the fact that *Breathless* was originally perceived as part of a larger artistic movement helped immeasurably in providing Godard's first American audiences with a loose context in which to understand his work. *Breathless* opened in New York the same year as Claude Chabrol's *The Cousins*, after Alain Resnais's *Hiroshima, Mon Amour*, François Truffaut's *The 400 Blows*, and Louis Malle's *The Lovers* had already appeared, and while information about "the Nouvelle Vague" in the American press tended to be somewhat vague and confused—characteristically, both Resnais and Malle were often assumed to be *Cahiers du Cinéma* critics along with Truffaut, Godard, and Chabrol—the sense of Godard being part of a larger movement was already fairly pronounced.

While the Nouvelle Vague continued to be regarded as a viable journalistic hook by American critics throughout most of the sixties, subdivisions and discriminations became more apparent as more films and information became available. It was eventually understood that directors who had started out as critics on *Cahiers du Cinéma*—Godard, Truffaut, Chabrol, Jacques Rivette, and Eric Rohmer—represented a particular core group in the Nouvelle Vague, identifiable by their eccentric taste for American genre films, their low-budget methods of shooting, and their relatively freewheeling styles. (Regarding the latter, it was widely believed that most or all of these directors depended a great deal on improvisation. The appearance of John Cassavetes's *Shadows* around the same time as *Breathless* led some reviewers to make certain connections between the two, without discriminating between the actor's improvisations in *Shadows* and Godard's practice on *Breathless* of working without a complete shooting script; some time passed before it was understood that Jean-Paul Belmondo's asides and rambling monologues at the beginning of *Breathless* weren't the actor's own inventions.) Many other popular French films of this period, such as Marcel Camus's *Black Orpheus*, Resnais's *Last Year at Marienbad*, Malle's *Zazie*, and the early films of Jacques Demy and Philippe de Broca, were often labeled "Nouvelle Vague" as well, and it was

a while before the efforts of the better-informed critics made it apparent that some of these films, like those of Resnais and Demy, were more related to the tastes and methods of the core group than certain others, like those of Camus and de Broca.

The eventual dissolution of the original concept of "Nouvelle Vague"—with reference both to the core group and to its wider applications—was gradual, and largely came about when the ideological, temperamental, and stylistic differences between members of the core group became too glaring to overlook. Godard's increasing move toward Leftist politics articulated one of the most striking of these differences (see #5, below), and if one draws certain approximate parallels between the dissolution of the *Cahiers* core group and the breakup of the Beatles (which occurred during the following decade), it is clear that Godard was the John Lennon of the group. (Following the same rough parallel, Truffaut was the Paul McCartney and Rivette was the George Harrison, although one clearly couldn't postulate either Chabrol or Rohmer as an equivalent to Ringo Starr.) By the time that "Nouvelle Vague" became appropriated as "New Wave" to refer to a kind of rock music, the original meaning of the term had passed out of the working vocabulary of the American mainstream—so much so that contemporary American academics who teach Nouvelle Vague films generally feel obliged to speak of the "French New Wave" in order to avoid confusion.

One final comment regarding the original *Cahiers* core group is worth stressing. As many of the "eccentric" film tastes of these critic-directors gradually passed into the American mainstream—so that it eventually became less shocking to regard Alfred Hitchcock and Howard Hawks as serious and important directors—the polemical force of *Cahiers du Cinéma*'s position regarding American cinema was largely dissipated. Thanks in large measure to the early critical efforts of Andrew Sarris, terms like "*auteur*" and "*mise en scène*" (the latter with hyphens added) entered the language, and the notion of treating popular American mainstream and genre directors as serious artists became not only acceptable but firmly entrenched, eventually lent even more credence by the expanded role played by promotion (and the promotion of certain directors) in the reception of big-studio Hollywood features. Broadly speaking, the attention once accorded to figures like Godard and Truffaut (and other foreign directors like Bergman and Fellini) as "artists" is lavished today on directors such as Martin Scorsese and Woody Allen. Meanwhile, current American interest in *Cahiers du Cinéma* is so slight that a respected writer for the *New York Times* could recently state that the magazine "is no longer fascinated by Hollywood"[2]—a remark nearly fifteen years out of date.

2. Release patterns. According to the filmography in Richard Roud's *Godard*,[3] the first book about Godard in English, Godard's early features opened commercially in the United States in the following order and years: *Breathless* (1961), *Vivre sa vie* (1963), *Contempt* (1964), *A Woman Is a Woman* (1964), *The Married Woman* (1965), *Alphaville* (1965), *Band of Outsiders* (1966), *Masculine Feminine* (1966), *La Chinoise* (1968), *Les Carabiniers* (1968), *Weekend* (1968). During the same period, his other early features made their first U.S. appearances at the New York Film Festival: *Le Petit Soldat* (1965), *Pierrot le fou* (1966), *Made in U.S.A.* (1967), *2 or 3 Things I Know about Her* (1968), *Le Gai Savoir* (1969); the rarely shown May 1968 documentary, *Un Film comme les autres*, had its first screening in the United States on the premises shared by the New York Film Festival, Philharmonic Hall, early in 1969.

Putting these lists together and noting specific dates, one can say that Godard's first features appeared in the U.S. in the following sequence: 1, 4, 6, 3, 8, 2, 9, 7, 10, 11, 12, 5, 14, 13, 15, 17, 16. This almost continuous disruption of what might be regarded as the logical development of Godard's work from one feature to the next was bound to lead to certain confusions. (In France, by contrast, the sequence was broken only by the initial banning of *Le Petit Soldat*, Godard's second feature, which opened in Paris the year after *Vivre sa vie*, his fourth.) Haphazard programming patterns also tended to obscure certain linkages that enhanced and clarified many of the films in question; for example, *Made in U.S.A.* and *2 or 3 Things I Know about Her*, made concurrently in 1966, premiered at the New York Film Festival a year apart, in 1967 and 1968, respectively. The latter film was eventually released in 1970; the former, due to legal problems involving the Richard Stark novel that was the film's putative source, has never been released in the United States at all.

3. The price of innovation. As far back as the midsixties, it was already a commonplace that many of Godard's most "innovative" practices—such as his jump cuts, employment of direct sound and interview formats, fractured story lines, references to other films, freewheeling uses of pop culture, and essayistic digressions—were no longer as startling as they had initially been, because of their widespread influence on other filmmakers. But even though a considerable residue from his eclectic strategies was finding its way into other films, including those of the mainstream, Godard had the talent to remain ahead of his imitators by continuing to develop in unforeseeable ways—a talent significantly shared, and always to his commercial detriment, by Orson Welles.

Unlike such relatively "bankable" European filmmakers as Bergman and Fellini, Godard could never be trusted either by producers or by spectators to "deliver the goods," in the sense of repeating the formula (or at least the surface appearance) of a previous success—the means by which most well-known contemporary American directors make themselves known. As recognizable as Godard's style may be to aficionados, it has never adopted such obvious signatures as the white-on-black credits of Woody Allen films, "Spielberg lighting," or, after 1968, a near-exclusive use of the same actors. Today, when the dominance of advertising has had an increasing effect on criticism, any film or filmmaker that can't be marketed as an immediately identifiable quantity runs the risk of disappearing quickly from sight.

4. Aesthetic conservatism. Perhaps the most thoroughgoing American attack on Godard's work published to date is John Simon's essay "Godard and the Godardians: A Study in the New Sensibility."[4] In the second paragraph of this lengthy broadside, Godard is linked by Simon to currents in the other arts that Simon equally disapproves of, including "aleatory and electronic music," "action painting, Pop and Op art, junk sculpture," "rock 'n' roll and its sundry derivatives in popular music," and "happenings, events, environments, and other 'mixed media.'" Significantly, the only area of film that Simon chooses to relate Godard to in this paragraph is neither "the New Wave" nor any other European film currents, but "'underground movies' or 'New American Cinema,'" a movement whose most vocal figures during this period were not among Godard's strongest defenders. (While Jonas Mekas and a few writers in *Film Culture* praised some of the early features, it was generally felt in American avant-garde film circles that Godard's reliance on narrative and on professional actors disqualified him from serious consideration. Significantly, the only "Nouvelle Vague" figure recognized in the permanent collection of the Anthology Film Archives was—and still is—Marcel Hanoun. Mekas wrote in 1970, "With *Pravda* Godard finally abandons commercial cinema and joins the underground." Mekas declared *Pravda* Godard's best film to date, but this review proved to be an isolated case.)

The bulk of Simon's essay is devoted to point-by-point refutations of Godard's leading American supporters at the time—Sontag, Kael, Sarris, and Roud—along with John Russell Taylor and A. Alvarez in England. His principal charge throughout is that Godard is an undisciplined, unstructured filmmaker for whom "anything goes," and it is worth adding that in spite of Simon's many objections to the claims of Godard's defenders, there are some points of agreement about where to situate Godard in relation to currents in the other arts. Indeed, Sontag's evocations of a "new sensibility" in *Against Interpretation*⁵—which also contains a philosophical analysis of *Vivre sa vie* attacked by Simon—and her passionate and extended appreciation of Godard in *Styles of Radical Will*⁶ allude to most of the same artistic currents as Simon does, although for her these connections are positive rather than negative factors. On the other hand, faced with Sarris's positioning of Godard alongside "Stravinsky, Picasso, Joyce, and Eliot," Simon argues, "About the only place where Godard's position might be comparable to that of the other four is on the toilet seat. But Godard, alas, also expels his work from that position."

Rereading Simon's hysterical diatribe today, one is struck by how much of his anger is directed at Godard's respectful (if eclectic) attitude toward popular culture, Hollywood movies in particular. His opening and pivotal example from Godard's work that elicits his deepest scorn is the offscreen recitation of Apollinaire's poem "Cors de chasse" during the screening of a Western. "What business," asks Simon, "have the characters in a vulgar American western reciting one of France's finest 20th-century lyrics at each other—and antiphonally at that, as though it were dialogue that they were improvising?" (Later in the same essay, Simon is equally dismayed by Kael's respectful attitude toward American gangster movies, in her review of *Band of Outsiders*.) In short, the major issue at stake for Simon was literary high culture versus the encroachments of popular culture, and he regarded Godard (rightly, I think) as a major force in making such encroachments acceptable. (A specialist in theater and European literature, Simon exemplified a certain literary bias in relation to film that was considerably more prevalent among intellectual circles prior to the beginnings of film studies as an academic discipline during the seventies.)

5. *Political conservatism.* A love–hatred relationship with America has been apparent in Godard's work ever since *Breathless*, but the increasing political thrust of his work throughout the sixties—given especial focus by his determination to attack the U.S. role in Vietnam in every one of his films in the midsixties—made this relationship particularly acute. The vehemence of Godard's anti-Americanism by the late sixties may have drawn some politically oriented viewers to his work, but it also clearly alienated many others, and in many respects it continues to do so.

It might be said that, in the sixties, Godard's love for American cinema and his hatred for American imperialism echoed a kind of ambivalence that was felt in certain sectors of the United States as well. One of his last texts written for *Cahiers du Cinéma* in the six-

ties, "3000 heures de cinéma," expresses this ambivalence succinctly: "Mystery and fascination of this American cinema. How can I hate Robert McNamara and adore *Take the High Ground*, hate the John Wayne who supports Goldwater and tenderly love him when he abruptly takes Natalie Wood into his arms in the next to last reel of *The Searchers*? [translation mine]"

As long as this sort of romanticism was reflected in Godard's films, he still had a substantial and vocal constituency in the United States, particularly among students. In early 1968, many of these students at Columbia University went to see *La Chinoise* again and again only weeks before some of them participated in the takeover of campus buildings, and their campus uprising occurred only a short time before the May Events in France. One could argue today, of course, that *La Chinoise* may have been more of an effect of that period than a cause; nonetheless, the sort of centrality that Godard's work in the midsixties had for *some* viewers in the U.S. makes the notion of such a chain reaction plausible. And it is even more important to recall that the feeling of spontaneous combustion that ran from Berkeley to Paris and from Rome to Kent State in that period created a cultural climate highly receptive to Godard's impudence, as well as his feeling for the contemporary. One went to see Godard movies in that period with an expectation not unlike that of opening a newspaper.

But after 1968, Godard's violent rejections of cinephilia and other forms of pleasure in his Dziga Vertov Group films—coupled with his willingness to make films in "underground" conditions—led to a gradual disaffection among many of his American fans, including many of the most political. The theoretical concerns of these films seemed remote to most of the student activists (whose resistance to theory has often been remarked upon), and the relative absence of the romanticism and pleasure that had fueled the popularity of films like *La Chinoise* and *Weekend* was equally offputting. The same qualities that led Mekas to praise *Pravda* were alienating to most art-house audiences and mainstream critics (with a few notable exceptions, such as Penelope Gilliatt), and it wasn't until Godard made a conscious return to 35 millimeter, narrative, and stars in *Tout va bien* (1972) that he was to regain part of their interest.

6. *The move from Paris.* Godard had been viewed in the United States as a French, and specifically Parisian, director. When he moved, first to Grenoble, in the midseventies, and then more permanently to Rolle, Switzerland, a few years later, the gradual effacement of his perceived identity led to confusions about how to "place" him that have persisted ever since. Two compa-

rable cases of confusion about national identity in the public mind are those of Michael Snow, a Canadian who has worked on occasion in the United States, and Chantal Akerman, a Belgian who has worked on many occasions in France. The same unconscious form of imperialism that has tended to ignore both the Belgian aspects of Akerman's work and the Canadian aspects of Snow's has resisted regarding the bulk of Godard's work since *Every Man for Himself* (1979) as Swiss. This has unfortunately obscured the degree to which Godard's Swiss identity might be construed as a significant factor in the meaning of his recent work, carrying specific inflections to the uses of Swiss landscapes, the meaning of borders, the prominence of banks and bankers, and so on—elements that seem especially prominent in *Nouvelle Vague*, but are also surely relevant to many of the others.

7. *Historical amnesia and cultural gaps.* The subject of cultural amnesia has been a central preoccupation of Godard's since the mideighties—most evident in *King Lear* (1987) and *Histoire(s) du cinéma* (1989–), two works that have so far failed conspicuously to receive a comprehensive critical response in the United States. And not so coincidentally, it would appear that cultural amnesia is itself at the root of this failure. Jonathan Baumbach's defense of *King Lear*, unpublished in 1987 but printed three years later in the collection *Produced and Abandoned*, epitomizes as well as describes the memory hole that Godard's work since the midseventies has fallen into, particularly for American viewers:

Between 1959 and 1968, Godard produced virtually all his major work. . . . After that there was a period of agitprop films, in collaboration with Pierre Gorin [*sic*], where Godard attempted to efface himself as an artist. And though he returned to making commercial films in 1981 with the admirable *Every Man for Himself* (his second first film, as he called it), he was no longer at the center of our consciousness. He was speaking to us, or such was the perception, from a vanished time.[7]

Missing from this chronology (along with the "Jean" in Jean-Pierre Gorin) is any recognition of five major Godard works that followed his collaboration with Gorin and preceded *Every Man for Himself*, all made in collaboration with Anne-Marie Miéville: *Ici et ailleurs* (1974), *Numéro deux* (1975), *Six fois deux/Sur et sous la communication* (1976), *Comment ça va* (1976), and *France/tour/détour/deux/enfants* (1977–78). None of these works received anything more than minimal exposure in the United States, frequently without subtitles, although I believe the political and formal importance of this massive block of work—comprising collectively over eighteen hours—far exceeds that of the "period of agitprop films" (1969 to 1972, about nine hours)

that were fetishized by certain English and American academics (see #8, below). Many of these academics clearly found it easier to quote the theoretical discourses and slogans in *Le Gai Savoir*, *Vent d'est*, and *Tout va bien*—all of which were eminently teachable precisely because they were more easily reducible to their verbal texts—than to analyze the complex audiovisual and verbal interplay in *Numéro deux* and *Ici et ailleurs*, which were far more resistant to verbal paraphrase, or to situate the two TV series as particular political interventions conceived in relation to France and its state-run television in that period, a specialized context that was equally hard to grasp. This latter period in Godard's work seems marked by two tendencies that are closely connected: the first is a grappling with TV as both subject and metaphor (in *Ici et ailleurs*, *Numéro deux*, and *Comment ça va*), on the one hand, and as a medium to work in and through (in the two TV series), on the other. The second tendency is to grapple more directly with political and social engagement, an approach that is quite distinct from the grappling with theoretical positions found in the previous films. Thanks to this loss of continuity, every subsequent Godard feature appears to come, as Baumbach puts it, "from a vanished time."

8. *Hermeticism and declining interest in intellectual cinema.* In *Under the Sign of Saturn*, Susan Sontag expressed a growing disaffection with the "diffident logorrhea of Godard's late films," compared with Syberberg's "supreme confidence in language, in discourse, in eloquence itself."[8] Significantly, in the same volume (though in an essay written seven years earlier than "Syberberg's Hitler"), she also alluded in passing to "the irresistible ascension of Woody Allen."[9] In fact, it would not be unduly fanciful to argue that the principal American model for "intellectual art cinema," once Godard's films, became, about ten years ago, those of Allen—films whose complete trust in narrative, disinterest in formal abstraction, and more modest intellectual aims place them in a different universe of discourse. This is certainly plausible if one compares Vincent Canby's remarks about both directors in the *New York Times* over the same period—beginning, say, with his rapturous review of *Manhattan* in 1979, continuing with his stern advice to Antonioni in 1982 to study the films of Allen, and concluding in 1990 with his dismissal of *Nouvelle Vague* as "featherweight," in a review that ends: "Only people who despise the great Godard films, everything from *Breathless* (1959) to *Every Man for Himself* (1979), could be anything but saddened by this one. The party's over." Setting aside the question of whether the self-pity, defeatism, and nearly suicidal impulses of *Every Man for Himself* ever constituted much of a party to begin with, Canby's

pronouncement resembles Baumbach's in that it describes a break in Godard's work rather than either a continuity or a development. And surely an implicit element in Canby's dismissal is Godard's abandonment of a relatively lucid narrative: from this point of view, it might be argued that the more legible, "realistic" narratives of films like *Breathless* and *Every Man for Himself* constitute, for some of his viewers, promises that Godard has not always kept.

Canby, one should note, is a relatively late defector from the Godard camp; Andrew Sarris and Pauline Kael, by contrast, who were two of Godard's biggest defenders in the midsixties, ceased to show much sustained interest in his work from the late sixties on, and most other mainstream critics have tended to follow suit. (Sarris expressed a grudging support for *Nouvelle Vague* "as an essayistic meditation on a dying world," but added that Godard is "caught in a losing wager" because "the cinema did not end with *Breathless*" and "the world did not end with *Weekend*.")[10]

On the other hand, American academics became increasingly interested in Godard around the same time (the early seventies) that mainstream reviewers were backing away—a period that corresponded roughly to the beginnings of academic film study, when Godard himself was, ironically, converted by certain academics into a kind of Aristotelian model of a theoretically informed counter-cinema. I'm thinking in particular of Peter Wollen's essays "The Two Avant-Gardes" and "Godard and Counter Cinema: *Vent d'est*,"[11] although a similar tendency can be found in the writing of Robin Wood about *Tout va bien* over roughly the same period. Thanks to the efforts of these and other critics, films like *Le Gai Savoir*, *Vent d'est*, and *Tout va bien* became valued classroom texts that were presented as virtually offering recipes for the establishment of a politically progressive "alternate" cinema. But by the time that Godard moved to Switzerland, even this interest seemed to diminish; Fassbinder began to supplant Godard as the exemplary contemporary European director among academics, much as Allen replaced Godard in the mainstream, and, apart from *Camera Obscura*'s special Godard issue in 1982,[12] the rest has mainly been silence.

Nevertheless, one can't deny that a certain loss of evangelical urgency has made Godard's recent work somewhat less accessible, to Americans and non-Americans alike. "I think I'm not a very good screenwriter who *can* be a good director," Godard once said to me in an interview.[13] Certainly, a discrepancy between his mastery of and confidence in *mise en scène* and his uncertainty in furnishing a story and dialogue accounts for many aspects of his films, particularly his more recent

ones: the inability of the director-hero in *Passion* to come up with a story; the appropriation of "classic" stories in *First Name: Carmen*, *Hail Mary*, and *King Lear*; the use of a story line furnished by others (Alain Sarde and Philippe Setbon) in *Detective*; the scattered serial narrative of *Soigne ta droite* interrupted by rehearsals of pop music (recalling the form of *One Plus One/Sympathy for the Devil*; dialogue consisting exclusively of literary quotations in *Nouvelle Vague*. This problematic search for story and dialogue ultimately points to a search for a unifying belief or system that could impose continuity. Over the years, Godard has sharpened his ability to film nature, to light shots, and simply to fill certain moments with sound, color, shape, and movement; what he seems to have less of—in the absence of his former cinephilia and Marxism—is a pretext for getting from one of these moments to the next.

Sometimes, as in *Passion* and *King Lear*, this pretext becomes simply spite and anger—emotions undervalued in more cowardly periods such as the present, just as they were perhaps overvalued twenty years ago. Godard has been honest enough to reveal the envy that underlies, in part, his spite and anger, and obviously these emotions may seem less than heroic. But as a source of energy and invention all three can still have heroic consequences, epitomized in a line spoken by a character in William Gass' story "In the Heart of the Heart of the Country": "I want to rise so high that when I shit I won't miss anybody."

Rising as high as Godard may entail some measure of self-protection in this respect, as well as elitist alienation, but this has never been the inclination of American intellectuals, who are likelier to reject the very terms of such an aspiration. Significantly, my editor at *Soho News* changed the title of my 1980 Godard interview from "Catching Up with Godard" to "Bringing Godard Back Home"—home in this context apparently being located somewhere in the vicinity of Vincent Canby's party. But until we address ourselves to catching up with Godard, the point of The Museum of Modern Art's retrospective, we haven't any home to bring him back to.

Notes

1 Roger Greenspun, "Film Notes," *Cahiers du Cinéma in English*, no. 6 (December 1966), p. 5.

2 Molly Haskell, "Auteur! Auteur! Cahiers du Cinéma Takes a Bow," *New York Times*, Arts and Leisure section, Sunday, March 1, 1992.

3 Richard Roud, *Godard* (Bloomington/London: Indiana University Press, 1970).

4 John Simon, "Godard and the Godardians: A Study in the New Sensibility," reprinted in his collection *Private Screenings* (New York: Macmillan, 1967). The quotes cited here are from pages 306–32.

5 Susan Sontag, *Against Interpretation* (New York: Farrar, Straus & Giroux, 1965).

6 ———. *Styles of Radical Will* (New York: Farrar, Straus & Giroux, 1969).

7 *Produced and Abandoned: The Best Films You've Never Seen.* National Society of Film Critics Members Staff, ed. Michael Sragow (San Francisco: Mercury House, 1990), p. 166.

8 The quotes cited here are from "Syberberg's Hitler," in Susan Sontag, *Under the Sign of Saturn* (New York: Farrar, Straus & Giroux, 1980), pp. 137–65.

9 Ibid., p. 4.

10 *New York Observer*, December 3, 1990.

11 Peter Wollen, "The Two Avant-Gardes," and, idem, "Godard and Counter Cinema: *Vent d'est*," both reprinted in his collection *Readings and Writings* (London: Verso, 1982).

12 Three essays from this issue, *Camera Obscura*, no. 8-9-10 (Fall 1982), are reprinted together in this volume, under the title "Sexual Difference and *Sauve qui peut (la vie)*," pp. 42–55.

13 *Soho News*, September 24–30, 1980.

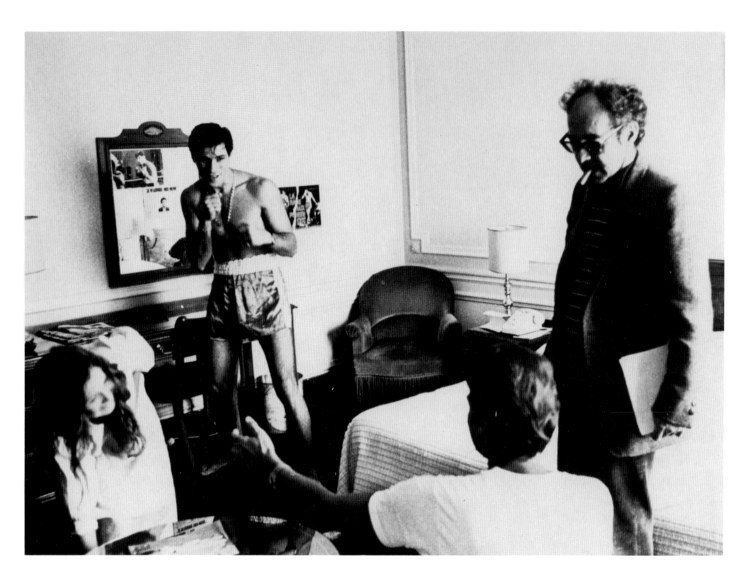

Jean-Luc Godard on the set of

DETECTIVE

1985

with Stéphane Ferrara and Johnny Hallyday

THE MEDIUM

JACQUES AUMONT

It was 1962 or 1963. It was a time for settling accounts: France was still struggling to emerge from the postwar period, decolonization was shaking up people's minds, unmaking habits. French cinema still believed it was making some waves, when the new wave of 1959 was no more than a bit of foam. Film was about to explode, but we didn't know it yet: from a classicism only lately achieved,[1] it was to pass with almost no transition to the innumerable baroque effects of the "new" types of films, to neo-Hollywood rococo. It was 1962 or 1963, and already Godard was a bit more, a bit less, a bit *other* than a filmmaker, already he was both exasperating and astonishing. The year that Godard was filming *Le Mépris* (1963), a critic for the review *Positif*, the review of the Left's perpetual "good conscience," denounced what he saw as the imposture the Nouvelle Vague was putting over, comparing it to the "new" Gaullist republic: smoke, the both of them— superficial publicity stunts. Godard was the worst of the lot, because he didn't even pretend to be serious.[2]

At a distance of thirty years, it is easy to say that a critic was wrong; it is more useful to recall what was symptomatic in his attitude. The Nouvelle Vague, especially the *Cahiers du Cinéma* school, which was both its spearhead and its kernel, so to speak, was causing annoyance with its cutting statements, with a naked ambition that was often taken for pushiness, and by its sense of self-promotion. But, already, Godard looked different. The banning of *Le Petit Soldat* (1960), which everyone considered provocative and scandalous, and the raging battle over *Les Carabiniers* (1963)[3] had already singled him out; *Le Mépris* and *Pierrot le fou* (1965) completed the process, by proving that he could also make big-budget films that appealed to more than cult audiences.

There was immediately a Godard "case"; today it is even more evident, and more complex. There is a Godard case because Godard is an important person, and today this important person is very visible, often occupies the downstage, becomes literally inevitable.

It's also true that times have changed; the Gaullist republic and the Nouvelle Vague are distant historical references, washed over by other waves and replaced by other references. Godard, who was already singular thirty years ago, is more so than ever. The proof? There is plenty—take your pick. If, for instance, you decide to interview some writers, philosophers, or artists, to find out which one filmmaker has influenced them, that filmmaker is not one of the trendy figures—a Lynch or a Wenders—not someone great and dead, but inevitably Godard![4] If a French film school inaugurates an editing workshop in which the students will observe, *in vivo* (or maybe *in vitro*), a Master in the process of creation, the person offered the contract, even provisionally, is neither Rivette nor Straub—brilliant editors—but Godard. If a chic TV channel— Canal + or SEPT—wants to add a cultural feather to its cap, again, it's Godard who they'll get to be their guaranteed, solid-gold draw (for a substantial contract).

There really is a Godard-effect, everywhere: in the press, in thought, teaching, and TV. In prey to the effect, everyone has a portable Godard: artist, theoretician, producer, boss, artisan, businessman, actor, historian, critic, prophet; the litany is inexhaustible—except perhaps by a trivial "Godard as one-man band." Godard surprises by the variety of roles, social and subjective, public and private, that he maintains with such skill: but the roles really only add up to one, unchanging and obsessional.

Godard is an effect, a case, a role, a public person. As an individual he astonishes, to the point that we often forget that he is a director, that he also makes films. The most remarkable thing about him as a public person is probably his capacity to surprise in roles that are always unexpected. As a Leftist, he got his glasses broken by a police truncheon in April of 1968 (during the demonstration for Langlois), but, fifteen or twenty years later, for a season, he became a sort of salon curiosity for TV, we saw him all over the place, on the TV news, on the literary shows—the mass audience ones as well as the somewhat snobbish ones, opposite Duras or Sollers; just recently, *Soigne ta droite* (1987) disoriented a lot of critics, who found the film obscure but had at least learned to be a bit humble in the face of Godardian obscurities, and could point out only the talent Godard showed as a slapstick actor, as if this were a revelation.

Certainly, the astonishment is often excessive. The very people who were surprised by *Soigne ta droite* had probably forgotten the comparable roles that Godard had played brilliantly in *Vladimir et Rosa* (1971), *Prénom Carmen* (1983), *Soft and Hard* (1986), *King Lear* (1987), and in that old TV clip that was shown again recently, in which Godard walked on his hands in front of an amazed Jacques Doniol-Valcroze—in short, they had forgotten Godard's old and intimate relationship with burlesque, a genre that the dictionary defines as the contrast between a coarse, commonplace style and a noble, heroic subject. But Godard also knows how to distill his effects, to play with them skillfully and with obvious amusement.

An effect, a public person—a celebrity. No doubt the period we live in has a particularly strong need for celebrities, because it is the age of generalized biography, of permanent, mediatized autobiography—that is, when all is said and done, the age of advertising. The principle underlying the celebrity of public personalities resembles that of manufacturers' brand names: when the name becomes famous, what it represents, the reality it covers, is of infinitesimal importance; it is enough to supply an image of it that is regularly renewed, nourished at reasonable intervals. So it's hardly important that Godard surprises, if his celebrity is that of a *provocateur*, classified as such once and for all, sorted into the lot for recognized *provocateurs*, from the more brilliant to the less so, from Picasso to Sollers.

Godard's celebrity cannot be compared to that achieved by any other filmmaker, apart from two or three prodigies like Eisenstein or Welles. Today, at least in France, he is the absolute celebrity, a sort of unquestionable monument that is sometimes confused with a (deliberately funereal) monument to film. Year in, year out, Godard directs (and—we'll come back to this—produces) films, at a sustained rhythm, but what the public retains of Godard nowadays is not the films. The Parisian public, the cultivated or petit-cultivated (as we say "petit-bourgeois"), goes to see the latest Godard the same way that you fulfill a cultural duty, between the latest Fellini and the latest Kurosawa. Of course, you also go to see *Détective* (1985) because of Johnny Hallyday, and *Nouvelle Vague* (1990) because of Alain Delon, but it would be more correct to say: to see what Godard did with Hallyday or with Delon. These films are not so much seen for themselves (as Rohmer's and Straub's still are, after all) as for the way they evoke in the Godardian public, the general public, their own reactions toward Godard: surprise, fascination, and slightly mocking and always vaguely suspicious wonder.

However—another Godardian paradox—Godard differs from his contemporaries in his extraordinary lack of pretensions to the autobiographical, in fact, in a lack of any noticeable interest in himself. He is not his own biographer, either in the here and now or in the long term. Even when he puts himself personally into a film, and often in sites of intimacy (the intimacy of work, in *Scénario du film Passion* [1982], in the analysis of a scene from *Soigne ta droite* for the television program "Cinémas cinémas," in the intimacy of his affective life, in *Soft and Hard*), he avoids indiscreet confidences, of course, but even the most harmless allusions to himself. Even when he takes up the whole scene (*Lettre à Freddy Buache* [1981], *Scénario du film Passion*), he doesn't put himself forward. He's not trying to conceal anything, nor to conceal himself, as Eric Rohmer does, for instance, but his intimacy, when shown, is shown in a mise-en-scène that is never erased, that never seeks to appear *lived*.

Quite obviously, Godard is hardly interested in himself at all; that is sufficiently rare to be remarkable, and rather attractive. But there is more (and it is more surprising): the lack of attention paid to himself extends to his works. He is practically the only one, of all the filmmakers, even the least vain of them, who doesn't talk about his relationship with film by detailing the theory of his past works. He barely mentions these works—you might think at times he had forgotten everything about them. The current work is never explained or justified in the name of past work, even when everything shows that the current projects correspond to past ones, at least in the form of his infinite reprises. And also: this same filmmaker, who will do anything to exercise the greatest possible control over his work, is not interested in either showing his films or in preserving them. Far from anticipating a Godard exhibition in some imaginary museum, he gives up the rights on his completed films as he goes along, as if getting rid of them.

What is the meaning of this figure, of this strange status achieved by a filmmaker in his own lifetime? It is difficult to explain it absolutely, but a few reasons can be suggested.

The Godard character consists, first of all, of a few images. Correct images, just images? That depends—there is, no doubt, a bit of both. Just images: from the most superficial—let's say the cream pie smashed into his face at Cannes by a young Belgian who specializes in this stunt—to images that are more precise but that we still feel belong in the category of representation. Godard accepting a special César award, apparently only half-awake ("I sleep ten hours a night"), wrapped in a muffler, acting the eccentric, the "artiste."

The image that is infinitely more accurate, despite—or because of—its multiple resonance, is that of Godard in his Rolle cave, as he presented himself on "Cinémas cinémas" to comment on film clips (from *Full Metal Jacket*, *La Primera Carga del machete*, *Soigne ta droite*), or better, the way he staged himself up until *Histoire(s) du cinéma* (1989–).

A cave must be inhabited by a sorcerer, and in these images of Jean-Luc Godard, who, with an air of mystery and concentration, manipulates mysterious machines, or (in *Histoire(s) du cinéma*) pronounces enigmatic, incantatory formulas, there is much of the image of the sorcerer, a Faust who hasn't yet received Mephistopheles' visit. The image of the sorcerer is ambiguous, reversible: the sorcerer is the one who works the bad magic, who casts the spells, but he is also the one who allows a bit of the supernatural to be glimpsed as a possibility. "The filmmaker . . . has the vocation, like a sorcerer, to make his body the medium for words, the way that others are the mediums for the words of God or nature."[5]

The cave is also that of the (mad) scientist, the more or less bizarre laboratory of the experimenter. Godard is readily fascinated by stories of inventors who are prisoners of their inventions, or even just by stories of prisoners (like the anecdote, used in a recent press handout from JLG Films, about Poncelet reinventing Desargues's theorem of the projection of cone shapes when he was in prison). From this point of view, his comparative analysis of sequences in "Cinémas cinémas" served to illustrate Godard's often iterated belief in science (his library, we are told, consists primarily of scientific works). He works amid machines, with a library, a print room, and a record library close by: the most exact possible replication of laboratory conditions.

Finally, the third aspect of this image of the experimenting sorcerer is also perhaps the most accurate: the one that emphasizes his corporal investment. The tightrope-walker's perfection and the acrobatic precision of the burlesque body, which were so striking in *Soigne ta droite*, are not essentially different from what was going on—but in a different register—in *Scénario du film Passion*: the bold mise-en-scène of a body embracing the fantasy-screen, clasping it, declaring its love. Though Godard communicates with what must, despite himself, be called his oeuvre, with his films as with his cinema, he also does so with his body.

As we see in his acrobatic performance at the beginning of *Soigne ta droite*, or his walking on his hands in front of Doniol-Valcroze, Godard's is an athlete's body. He keeps in shape playing tennis every day; there is a sly allusion to this in *Soft and Hard*. But the image systematically omits his muscles (they come back, for example, in the short film "Armide," in a way that is all the more obscene for grotesquely setting these protruding muscles against a sound track connoting delicacy [Lully, baroque opera]). Godard's body always looks a little *displaced*, as though apologizing for being there, even as it wholeheartedly offers its absolute presence. The images of this body, inside and outside the films; the presence of the voice, with its touching huskiness; the way he takes up the whole frame while appearing to have entered it on tiptoe; these evoke life in the cave, the life of the scientist and the sorcerer, shut up day and night, physically and spiritually, with the object of his study: the cinema. They evoke a complete gift of the self. This has been the gift of all the great filmmakers, to be sure, but the gift of the body is rarer, very few have given it completely, and those who have—Keaton, Vertov, Straub-Huillet . . . —have done it differently from Jean-Luc Godard.

The visionary scientist, with sometimes a touch of the absentminded professor: *Tintin*'s Tournesol or Christophe's Cosinus, the ardent experimenter, no longer living any other life than that of the prison he has chosen for himself, bending his body to it to the point of torture; these are only images, of course, and potential legends, but perhaps they are more true than the truth, together forming the image of Godard the artist. Moreover, the artist probably does not dislike this image of himself, and the myth of the sorcerer-scientist is corroborated in reality at least by the fact that Godard is more and more interested in projects that, like *Histoire(s) du cinéma*, keep him in his laboratory, and claims to be less and less interested in anything else, fictional films included.

The putting into play of the body, much cultivated and emphasized by Godard, certainly does not explain everything. Yet, it is as crucial as his personal involvement. Godard, as he has constantly repeated at least since *Numéro deux* (1975), thinks of himself as an experimenter. As an avid and inveterate reader of scientific writing, he knows that modern science does not exclude the experimenter; on the contrary, he or she is included in the experiment and is part of the measurement's result, and, at the very least, of the method. The experimenter is present in what he or she examines, present in the examination and the result; nor does this make the latter any less scientific.

This is a fortiori true of artistic research, and the artist, even more than the scientist, only remains one by becoming consubstantial with the art, the science. (What's more, even if art and science were not one and the same thing for Godard, they are at least on the same side of a boundary beyond which lie commerce, television, and that logobabble we call culture—toward which he feels less than tender.) He perceives the elders, Rossellini and Hitchcock, to have "died in their art."[6] This was even true of Fassbinder, who was in fact younger than Godard, and, in Godard's view, that death has become a poisoning, a death by "overdose of creative obligations." Consubstantial with their art, prisoners of their art, dead in their art.

So the filmmaker's presence in his work is something quite other than a manifestation of narcissism, since what interests Godard passionately about himself is neither his person nor his oeuvre, but his method.

A number of descriptions of this method have already been given, but most important, from the point of view of what we are investigating (the constitution of a general equivalent of the art of cinema), is less the nature of this method than its point of application. Or, more precisely, it is less this or that particular application of his method (in a film, in an essay, in life) than the general methodology. This method is thus first of all a *position* of work, a posture (Godard is certainly not given to *im*posture). Defining its object will be less easy, because there are several, or, rather, because this object can be illuminated under such diverse kinds of light that it seems to shimmer indefinitely.

With his formulation of a "between method,"[7] Gilles Deleuze accurately identified by implication one of these objects, namely montage. This is obviously one of Godard's major concepts, which he believes to be essential to cinema itself, because it is basically what the century needed, and what only cinema was able to invent. "One image does not necessarily show. A true image is a group of images."[8] But if we insist unilaterally on editing, we would forget that it edits something, and that, on the contrary, Godard has always insisted on the importance of the recorded image, of the image seen, of seeing, and of knowing how to see: "You have to be able to see, and if you are, to exercise this ability at the right moment."

Now, the striking thing is that for Godard, seeing is less an analytical activity than an immediate, synthetic *relation* (and relation also means "between"). What is seen is all seen at once, by virtue of a more or less innate aptitude that always partakes of the miraculous. In the same way, a barely allegorical emblem would be its *vision*, in the mystics' or visionaries' sense of the word, and, in the *Libération* interview cited above, Godard approvingly tells the story of Bernadette Soubirous, who immediately "recognized" the person in her apparitions, not from the garish prayer-card Virgins that she was shown, but from a Byzantine icon, and thus "saw" instantly, beyond appearances.

Seeing is peculiarly different from *hearing*, as the syn-thetic is from the analytical, the horizontal from the vertical. The Western tradition of polyphonic music, which Godard loves and knows well, involves the kind of listening that, in a metaphor that is hardly even odd, we designate as horizontal: listening with an ear that is able to follow the overall form, as well as the musical lines drawn by each voice, and is not led astray by the fleeting, vertical synchronies between notes. Merging listening and vision, Godard is totally on the side of the horizontal,[9] the general, the general image. He sees or wants to see the way that musicians hear: lines ("vanishing traces," as Jean-Louis Leutrat puts it),[10] visual "overall forms," and motifs. "Motif" is particularly apt, with its semantic ambiguity that covers both the form—a musical motif—and the referent—a pictorial "motif."

Like Vertov earlier, Godard applies himself to "extracting thought from the visual" (the famous equation "seeing = re-see-ving" [*voir = rece-voir*] means precisely this), but he adds a dialectical beat, in which thinking returns to the visual in the form of the image. But Jean-Luc Godard has said everything on this subject himself, on the link between cinema and abstract image, on the privilege granted to seeing (with intensity but without intention) over looking, even on the almost Cratylean belief that makes him want to try "to call things by *their* name."[11]

It has been said that Godard manifestly takes less interest in his fictional films; recently, the project about which he had the most to say was *Histoire(s) du cinéma*; similarly, it was perhaps in *Puissance de la parole* (1988) that he gave the most stunning demonstration of his art of musicality and of the horizontality of editing. Yet *Soigne ta droite* and *Nouvelle Vague* both give the impression of an ever-increasing mastery in this art of vision. The accident scene at the beginning of *Nouvelle Vague* is particularly impressive in this regard. A slow traveling shot, depth of field, and an extraordinarily well-selected point of view show—without designating anything in any authoritarian way—the countess' car on the road in the distance (she is driving fast, dangerously), then the huge, gloomy tree trunk in the foreground; the shot comes out onto the road, this time very near to us, at the very moment when Delon is hit by the car, and hurled against the tree. Here is economical use of the cinematographic gesture: this single frame inscribes the entire event, including its extravagant rhythm (the encounter between the speeding vehicle driven by the young woman and the tramp's body struck slow, struck almost motionless). There follows a surprising low-angle shot of the tree branches from underneath, while crows screech offscreen, in stereo: a vision if there ever was one, a black, malign vision, a vision of light and sound from hell, the exact opposite of the "divine" visions of *Je vous salue Marie* (1985). (Indeed, a number of critics noted, maybe a bit too simplistically, that the tree is none other than the Tree of Knowledge.)

What is more, the Godardian "vision" is anything but a hallucination, a fantasy, a dream, or delirium. Godard has said several times, in a way that apparently half-contradicts his exaltation of vision, that if he had to choose, it would be easier for him to do his job as a filmmaker blind than without hands. (Like a reprise of the fable of the halt and the blind, this parable of the eye and the hand already underlay a key scene in *Comment ça va* [1976].) As always with Godard, the paradox is obvious, barely provocative: hands are indispensable to the filmmaker, who is, in posse, blind because the images of things have more to do with the things themselves than with a vision of them, and also because the film is what has to become another body. The vision of the malign tree of *Nouvelle Vague* is the rough, gloomy vision of the bark of a tree, the knotty vision of a trunk, the buzzing vision of branches—and what is visible through the foliage is not so much a supernatural apparition as an excess of air and light. Or, again, from the same film, the art of terror exercised in certain shots of the cars that belong to the denizens of the business world. Monstrous, menacing boats, as fatal as the sharks who own them—and it's a matter of framing, as much as of the tactile sensation of smoothness, of shininess, of the aggressive lacquered metal that they are made of. Not the "visual touch," in Hildebrand's sense of the word, of sculptors and painters, but a relation of the whole body to vision: contact, but at a distance.

Another, more euphoric example: Rita Mitsouko, in their first appearance in *Soigne ta droite*; like hairs in the soup. With the very first shot of them, we understand that they are artisans, working (very seriously) at home; in the second shot we see Fred Chichin look at Catherine Ringer, and we say to ourselves: "This man loves this woman." The love-work equation, so dear to Godard, is perhaps an image in the rhetorical sense. This was somewhat the feeling the equation gave in *Sauve qui peut (la vie)* (1979) and *Passion* (1982). Here it becomes a vision, not so much because there are two shots united by a common mode of looking, but because the distance at which this love and this work are shown seems appropriate.

We ought to dig even deeper, and speak, for example, of the acoustic visions that Godard's films now seek to arouse. In *Soigne ta droite* and *Nouvelle Vague*, everything is said as though at a distance, chiseled, cutting; the impression is that of an excessive tidiness and precision. If the Brechtian actor must always seem to be quoting, then Godard's actors are all Brechtian in these

two films. But elsewhere, in the essays, the voices will be grainier and more modulated, the sound recording will be softer, and the sound mixing will no longer produce voices like knife wounds. It is no longer a question of showing the same thing; the pathetic miscommunication of the two young heroes of *Puissance de la parole*, for example, required these echoes, fade-outs, and interference. Godard the filmmaker wants to look at sounds and voices the same way he looks at the things of this world—with his whole body.

We understand that he no longer has the time, or the desire, to write stories and dialogues; that the texts of *Puissance de la parole* are taken entirely from Van Vogt, Poe, and Cain; that *Nouvelle Vague*, by Godard's own admission, contains not a single word of dialogue by him;[12] that the *Histoire(s) du cinéma* mix up all kinds of quotations, films, photos, and music. It is not so much that Godard wants to deny himself the possibility of fully creating, or that he refuses to add a text to the culture's texts (he is not Straub, even if there are an increasing number of points in common between the two filmmakers), but rather that his ambition is to engage more directly with things (the subtitles of *Nouvelle Vague* are: *De natura rerum* [*On the Nature of Things*]; *res non nomina* [Things, not names]), even as the text, any text, appears to be a kind of thing.[13]

Godard the creator is, as he has often claimed, a meticulous artisan. We should add: a solitary artisan, preferring to work in his laboratory, or, if he is in a team, against the team; his solitude is such that despite his obvious courtesy, despite, in fact, the impression of goodness he sometimes gives, he cannot speak to you, nor can you speak to him.[14] Furthermore, and semi-inconsistently, he does not present himself as an author, taking himself neither for an origin (a creator) nor for a singularity (a signature), but at the most for someone who deals with poetics, as a poietician. The people he admires and his explicit homages are very revealing on this point: are almost always minor, forgotten, or even unknown creators. One film is dedicated to Clint Eastwood, another to "small movies"; in a reply to the audience at his Pantin retrospective in 1989, Jean-Luc Godard admitted to feeling a kinship to Dylan in the stubbornness, the "in-spite-of-it-all-ness" of the work pursued, and to having cited him *for that*. In *Scénario de Sauve qui peut (la vie)* (1979), it's a few frames, given by way of example, that had been shot by a Swiss film-school student who is still unknown today. Godard's declarations of admiration for the great are comparatively more rare. Yet it's not (only) that Godard refuses to recognize any master, but that this is the way he signifies that creation is not a matter of genius, that poetry is artisanal, a matter of work and workers, that everybody should do it, not just one (Godard-Rimbaud: one more equation—or, better still, Godard-Ponge, they who are on the side of things).

The image is starting to get complicated: the magus thinks of himself as a worker (Pasolini, 1968: "A manual laborer who goes to work every day");[15] the artist thinks of himself as an artisan.

There is an insistent idea informing Godard criticism nowadays, that Godard no longer makes films, he makes cinema. Now, what does this formula mean, beyond its somewhat facile elegance? If we look coolly at what follows from it, we see clearly that it places Godard, not on the side of the invention of forms, of style, of the *Kunstwollen*, but on the side of the ("scientific") exploration of cinema's powers as a machine for signifying. If we look laterally, however, rather than sequentially, to what should we attach this idea?

To this, first, from the interior of cinema, from the interior of the history and criticism of cinema: in the view of Alain Bergala and Serge Daney, there is a more or less explicitly accepted heritage of cinematographic "modernism," its invention attributed to Rossellini, a modernism defined by the renewed risk of an unprecedented encounter with reality with each new film. Nothing to counter to this plausible explanation.

But we can also try a few others, equally plausible, and related to Godard's idea of cinema's present position within current practices (signifying practices, social practices in general). First of all, there is his stubborn insistence on placing cinema on the same footing as the most recognized of the arts, the ones earliest established, or at least as some of these arts. Godard is a poet, certainly a painter, and a musician, but neither a writer nor a photographer. The script of *Nouvelle Vague* reveals an unquestionable talent for writing,[16] a style close to Duras's "lyrical-objective" short sentences, but this does not mean that Godard's films are prose. They are perhaps a poetic prose, woven of unexpected images, incongruous conjunctions, and thus closer to certain American novelists, such as Brautigan. In the same way, the shots on the shore of Lake Leman that punctuate the film, each of them more sensual than the next, are by no means "beautiful photographs." Their effect owes less to the slightly obvious sumptuousness of the fall colors than to the exactness of the distances chosen, and the precision of the editing. To take one example, toward the middle of the film the narrator's voice says: "The lake was no longer where it usually was, and when they caught sight of it through the trees it was no longer the same." Image: the lake, in the distance through a gap in the trees, while in the center of the frame stretches an undulating beige surface, a prairie that has been crossed, and that for a moment we mistake for the lake. We admire this shot, at the same time as we understand its place in the sequence of shots of the lake: it establishes a sort of visual metaphor between the beige of the field and the gray of the lake.

Painting, on the other hand, is deeply present in the Godardian gesture,[17] but so is music. "Making cinema, no longer making films" thus means ceasing to make his activity conform to the laws of the film market, no longer manufacturing "presentable" products one after the other, but thinking about his work in general terms, and, especially, thinking of it from a "creatorial" point of view. Godard is striking (and sometimes shocking) in his apparent indifference to the fate of his films, at least to their commercial fate, since he is a bit concerned about the critical response to them. This follows from his decision that the filmmaker's activity consists not of breaking records, but of pursuing an oeuvre.

So cinema is art, a major practice, something distinct from the general cultural mass. As we have mentioned, Godard cannot speak harshly enough about culture. We could take this, too, as provocation, paradox for the sake of paradox, snobbishness: How can this be? this son of the bourgeoisie is himself so cultivated, and so on. Yet his systematic rejection of the cultural is perfectly coherent, it is only the logical response to what Godard, working in France, can observe there particularly clearly: the ravages of a confusionist ideology of culture, which reduces everything to a common denominator, and especially evaluates everything at the same level. This leads to a general neutralization of values, a true indifference, all the more overwhelming in that it often decks itself out in moralizing justifications. The notion of culture, emptied of substance when the epithet "classical" that had long qualified it fell into disuse, becomes what has to be resisted, not by unculture, but by singular acts that cannot be bought or sold, in short, acts that cannot be appropriated by the culture industry (there is no more culture nowadays outside its industry).

This illustrates how, and how intimately, Godard's personal involvement, his discourse on method, and his ethical preoccupation are merged. Godard often compares cinema and the filmmaker to the *résistant*—the one who embodies the Resistance to the culture's oppressive Occupation. Resistance is a duty, but this duty is only a contingent aspect of a fundamental obligation, of a necessary responsibility toward oneself, others, the world, the truth. "I understand responsibility as responsibility for others, thus as responsibility for what isn't my doing, or even my lookout; or, precisely for what does look out at me, is approached by me as a face."[18] Whether or not he understands it the same way as Lévinas, Godard aligns himself with the notion that our closeness to others lies in our responsibility *for them*, rather than in even the most perfect knowledge of them. This is Godard the phenomenologist—united with Lévinas in his admiration for Heidegger and Sartre.

"No more films, just cinema"—if cinema really has become primarily a site of (necessarily solitary) resistance, of responsibility (opposing it to the irresponsibility of the media). This position is, in fact, neither really political nor simply moral. It is not a question of having one's hands clean at any price, still less of changing the world. It is a question, pragmatically, of preserving a possible space for one's own activity, of marking it as one's own (in a more ecological than legal or economic sense), in the hope that the existence of this singularity as such will authorize other singularities.

Resistance and responsibility: one must resist for oneself but also for others (even if the others do not know, do not want to know). It is not a question of setting up an example, nor of proving anything at all, simply a question of making something exist outside.

Images, a body, visions, a posture, films, the cinema—these form a somewhat idyllic patchwork to make up the Godard persona. The final touch was missing, the one revealed by the anticulturalism, and completed by Godard's institutional image. This recluse, this *résistant*, is set up, as we said at the beginning, as solid gold, the gold standard, a more or less universal model of cinema-value. Even if this value has become weak (cinema is a soft institution, which from many points of view does no more than perpetuate itself), everyone, friends and enemies alike, will recognize in Godard a sort of personification of cinema, and this recognition is not the least paradoxical feature of his persona.

For Godard is also—it is time to say it again—a producer. De jure, since he directs a small production company, formerly JLG Films, which has just recently become Peripheria. De facto, because, in addition, and above all, he is unanimously perceived as being skilled and clever, someone who knows how to put a project together and find the financing for it with no trouble, who knows how to talk from one position of power to another, as one boss to another, with Gaumont, Canal +, or Monsieur Télécom. Undeniably, it was the expert producer of cinema, cinema understood also as a small or medium-sized business, who was awarded a special César (just as, conversely, it was given to Tati for managing to ruin himself financially for *Playtime*).

The producer's trade has its mysteries; financially setting up films like *Détective*, *Soigne ta droite*, probably *Nouvelle Vague*, whose profitability is uncertain and precarious, is a matter of talent, luck, and a strength of conviction that sometimes has to border on charisma.

Charisma, that is, charm—personal and professional. The seductive/repulsive portrait of the producer played by Jean-Pierre Mocky in *Grandeur et décadence d'un petit commerce de cinéma* (1986), a film largely shot on the premises of JLG Films, obviously has a certain value as a self-portrait: a little candor mixed with a lot of swindling, or perhaps it's the other way around . . . As a matter of fact, Godard, who detests or despises culture and the culture vultures, has nothing but respect, even esteem, for his partners and sleeping partners in production. They have never, apparently, been the butts of the good-natured sarcasm of his famous formula "the professionals of the profession."

Godard's is a strange relationship to production. Or perhaps not strange, after all. The desire to participate in the sphere of production, to gain recognition there, is obviously understandable in the first place as a desire for freedom. This is one of the lessons Godard derived from his long acquaintance with Hollywood, from his reflection on cases of producer-directors and on the vicissitudes of those who were not (see, very early on, the quasi-theoretical fallout of these reflections in the characters of *Le Mépris*), a banal lesson learned equally well—and even, in commercial terms, a lot better—by Truffaut, not to mention Lelouch and Berri.

But this relationship is deeper, too: it is one of the privileged signs of Godard's vocation as the one who takes us across the forbidden zone. As such, as the mediator, he sees himself first of all as a medium, the one who calls up the spirits, makes the spirit of things descend into images, the one we encountered just now—the visionary. He is also the one who tries to let the discourses through. *Six fois deux/Sur et sous la communication* (1976), *France/tour/détour/deux/enfants* (1977–78), and the *Histoire(s) du cinéma* are not so much attempts to lay siege to television or to propose new and better models for it, as heterogeneous films that mix up several discourses (including an obsessional scientific discourse). And though as television broadcasts they may not always have been successful, the integration of discourses on art, science, and journalism is fundamental to all these films. We could go on, see Godard as taking us across the forbidden zone between film and video, as he has often been described as doing for the past twenty years at least, or, at a deeper level, we could relate this idea of passage to the between-two, the "between method" that Deleuze attributes to Godard. (That, however, may be going too far, giving Godard a more coherent, compact image than is appropriate.)

Godard started working in cinema, or "on" it, in the fifties, which is to say, as we have noted, just before the collapse of "classicism" (or its miscarriage). Cinema was instantly an art for him—and it has remained so.

The cinema-as-art debate was experienced as crucial by successive generations (that of 1920 and that of 1950), who set themselves the task of defining this art practically and theoretically; this debate was at least considerably displaced thirty years ago. Not that we should overestimate the interest of that eighties litany, the "death of cinema," but it is the general panorama of the arts, or, more precisely, the concept of art itself, that has vastly changed, as much in extent as in understanding.

A massive, major phenomenon marks this change: the definition of the work of art, its acceptability, and the recognition of it involve the inclusion in the work or its surroundings (its before and after) of the very means of art. Several theoretical accounts of this phenomenon have been proposed, of which the most important are the theory of institutions and the theory of creators. A recent, extreme representative of the former is Thierry de Duve, for whom the work of art only becomes one when it is elevated by the explicit discourse of an institution called art, and that has a large share of arbitrariness about it.[19] A representative of the latter, the theory of creators, is Arthur Danto, for whom the work is defined by its relation to an explicit artistic intentionality, both internal and external to the work.[20]

Intentionality is a dangerous criterion (and concept). Manipulated incautiously, whether naïvely or complacently, it formerly allowed a tradition of cinephilic criticism to be engendered, according to which the filmmaker, knowing what he is up to, possesses, and is alone in possessing, the meaning of the work, the film. The artistic intentionality envisaged by Danto demands more, a passage to the conceptual, theoretical plane. The majority of the (few) filmmakers who have made this passage in their discourses do so with an ideal aesthetic norm on the horizon, transcending any film: Rohmerian naturalism, Rivettian dramatic realism, Straubian spatiocorporeal coherence, and so on. Godard, however, has no ideal aesthetic norm, even though among the filmmakers of his generation, and among filmmakers in general, he is the one who makes most manifest his intentionality.

In his case—where cinematographic "modernity" and artistic "postmodernity" are joined—intention is an exploration of the nature of cinema as an instrument, so to speak, for encountering reality, and not a respect for some a priori conception of this instrument, however seductive or noble it might be. In this extra step, which, moreover, Godard takes with full awareness of what he is doing—with full awareness of the conventional aesthetic ideals—we can see the first trace of the remarkable *contemporaneity* of the Godard method.

This also explains why Godard's discourse is so important. At one time, the Benayouns of all varieties had at first retained from this discourse the most superficial effects, a casualness, a taste for wordplay, everything that had been hastily classified as "vaguely hilarious provocation." As the years went by, it became evident that this insistent, sometimes frankly obsessively repetitive discourse was not just babble amusingly stuffed with paradoxes and riddles, but that its very movement, as unlinear as it could be, proceeding more by meanderings, boustrophedons, and spirals, was and was meant to be an image of the movement of thought. For the past twenty years at least, Godard has been periodically delivering some formulas that bear his inimitable stamp, and that immediately become aphorisms. Over this same period, and without his ever giving the impression of wanting to mutate into a theoretician or historian as such, he has continuously published written versions of his monologues, or allowed them to be published, the first being the *Introduction à une véritable histoire du cinéma*, and the last, to date, an extract from his interview with Noël Simsolo for the radio.[21]

This discourse has a quantitative importance: Godard monologizes a great deal. And a pragmatic importance: his discourse explicates and often furthers the conceptions of cinema, art, and representation that are at work in the films. Finally, last but not least, there is its *aesthetic* importance. Whatever the intrinsic interest of what Godard says (often great, as great as his originality, and as a sort of purity conferred on him by the hermit's life he leads in the cave), this discourse is also important for its formal quality. I have already expressed my admiration for the screenwriter of *Nouvelle Vague*, but in the "aesthetic" monologues there is something else, beyond the style, or, more precisely, there is a perfect transposition, in the register of the oral-made-written, of the qualities of Godard's cinematic discourse. Godard's aphorisms become emblems the way that his trenchant shots sometimes do; his complicated, unfinished sentences have the same relation to meaning as some of his inconclusive edited sequences. Godard is the only filmmaker whose speech is like his filmmaking, no doubt because his filmmaking is also like his speech. (Whence, no doubt, the quite special importance of "metadiscursive" works like the *Lettre à Freddy Buache*, the *Scénario du film Passion*, the *Petites Notes à propos du film Je vous salue Marie* [1983], in which the encounter between two discourses materializes; yet, this encounter seems even more perfect when it is less explicit, less controlled, for instance, in the composition obtained by juxtaposing the *Histoire(s) du cinéma* and, let's say, the interviews Godard gave parallel to the project.)

If Godard is so essential (and, indirectly, if he is the celebrity that he is), it is precisely because he is the only one to have succeeded in splitting himself between all these positions: an old-fashioned love for movies, adaptation to the media, *aggiornamento* of the representational credo and its marriage with the desire for the imaginary, and finally an *up-to-date* theoretical position on the very nature of what art is—not only the art of cinema, but simply art, all of art.

Perhaps—certainly—there are touches missing from this portrait—which of course does not aspire to being "to the life." It must suffice as it is to give an outline of Godard's originality, of the Godard persona (of the "real" Godard, we obviously know nothing here), and to go some way toward explaining his celebrity and his special status.

Godard coincides absolutely with himself: his person with his work, his oeuvre with his method, his posture with his position. Because he asserts it in several areas at once, his discourse appears more coherent, above all, more convinced. The relationship with Godard is thus, necessarily, an intense, strong relationship: if we are interested in him, we are interested in everything about him; if we love his work, we love it unconditionally—not in the naïve way of the old auteur politics, which maintained that we could identify the man in the oeuvre, but still by being aware of what there is of his persona in his work. If we see Godard in his films, it is also because we see all his work and all his discourse there.

At the same time, this presence of Godard in his work, and this interpenetration of the person, the discourse, and the films are anything but narcissistic self-satisfaction, since they signify, in fact, that Godard nowadays embodies cinema, in the full sense of the term.

How, then, should we define Godard? I see no other way but this: he is the man who was cinema. Not that he was so ten or fifteen years ago (and no longer is), but the man who, *now*, was cinema. Without nostalgia.

Notes

1　This is Eric Rohmer's insistent thesis, in his ground-breaking articles from the fifties: cinema has not yet had its classic period. See "L'Age classique du cinéma," in *Goût de la beauté* (Paris: Editions de l'Etoile, 1984), pp. 25–99.

2　Robert Benayoun, "Le Roi est nu," *Positif*, no. 46 (June 1962), pp. 1–14. Samples of Benayoun's judgements on Godard: "a Weltanschauung of incompetence"; "At the present stage of his career, M. Godard no longer makes films, at most he is trying not to look too much as if he is making them"; "Of course, we have to allow for the desire to provoke in this series of vaguely hilarious affirmations," and so on.

3　See Jean-Luc Godard, "Feu sur *Les Carabiniers*," *Cahiers du Cinéma*, no. 146 (August 1963).

4　Carole Desbarats and Jean-Paul Gorce, eds., *L'Effet-Godard* (Toulouse: Milan, 1989).

5　Jean-Luc Godard, interview, *Le Monde*, June 27, 1986.

6　Interview with Serge Daney, *Libération*, December 26, 1988, and reprinted in this volume, pp. 158–67.

7　Gilles Deleuze, *L'Image-Temps* (Paris: Editions de Minuit, 1985), pp. 234ff.

8　See note 5.

9　This is also, in spite of an apparent paradox, owing to an unfortunate choice of vocabulary, the type of listening and looking implied and aroused by Eisenstein's "verbal editing."

10　Jean-Louis Leutrat, "Le Portrait ovale," *La Part de l'oeil*, no. 6 (1990), pp. 156–65 and his essay in this volume, pp. 22–33.

11　For previous examples of this same Cratylean temptation, see Mireille Latil-Le Dantec, "Jean-Luc Godard, ou l'innocence perdue," *Etudes cinématographiques*, nos. 57–61 (1967), p. 55.

12　Press conference at the Cannes Film Festival, 1990, *Cahiers du Cinéma*, no. 433 (June 1990), p. 11.

13　Again, this is not a new temptation: see the insistence on "les Mots et les Choses" in *Pierrot le fou*.

14　"I had never seen him. I recognized him by his solitude. It betrayed itself right from the start by a sort of constraint, a certain ungraciousness in being or appearing to be in a world that the solitary ones always look as though they were forced to enter." Michel Vianey, *En attendant Godard* (Paris: Grasset, 1966), p. 9.

15　Pier Paolo Pasolini, "Piccoli dialoghi sul cinema e sul teatro," *Tempo illustrato*, November 23, 1968. French translation from *Ecrits sur le cinéma* (Lyon: Presses Universitaires de Lyon, 1987), p. 224.

16　*Cahiers du Cinéma*, no. 432 (May 1990).

17　As I have attempted to show elsewhere; see the last chapter, "Godard peintre, ou l'avant-dernier artiste," in *L'Oeil interminable* (Paris: Librairie Séguier, 1989).

18　Emmanuel Levinas, *Ethique et infini* (Paris: Fayard, 1982), p. 102.

19　Thierry de Duve, *Au nom de l'art* (Paris: Editions de Minuit, 1989).

20　Arthur C. Danto, *The Transfiguration of the Commonplace: A Philosophy of Art* (Cambridge, Mass.: Harvard University Press, 1981).

21　This appeared in Sergio Toffatti, ed., *Jean-Luc Godard* (Turin: Centre Culturel Français de Turin, 1990), pp. 39–49.

LE MEPRIS

1963

(NOT) JUST AN OTHER FILMMAKER

RAYMOND BELLOUR

To use video as you would cinema, and to use cinema as you would television, is to make a television that doesn't exist, and a cinema that no longer exists.[1]

For me, cinema is Eurydice. Eurydice says to Orpheus, "Don't look back." And Orpheus looks back. Orpheus is literature causing Eurydice to die. . . . For me, images are life, and texts are death. You need both—I'm not against death. But I'm not for the death of life to that extent, especially during the time when it needs to be lived.[2]

There's no such thing as a mad filmmaker. There are few mad filmmakers. Images protect them, at least the images that keep their distance, and everything in an image that confirms, establishes, and forms this distance. Such an image comes from very far away: from an image of the world, of the God who focuses it, of the angels who bear it. It comes from churches, where it floats in space, stops on walls, freezes into immense tableaux that are so many screens for reflecting and capturing the mental light that the interior image of the divine inscribes in each of us. Cinema, a secular, mechanical art, recalls those holy spaces. Its images continue the spirit of the great paintings of landscapes and bodies, for, in relativizing that spirit—Benjamin's "lost aura"—cinematic images redirect it as well, bypassing collections and museums, to rejoin cinema's obscure place of origin, where so vital a religion of the image was born (the direction Bazin took). The movie theater is, accordingly, closer to a church than to a theater, in the sense that its power derives above all from the image, which early on played so dominant a role in the spread of Christianity. Cinema turns the image into a story to be contemplated, simultaneously individual and shared, the secret but effective object of a social community. Cinema's image is spectacular, like, and universal, within the limits of the world through which it spreads. Its image captures and restores life, even becomes life, bringing to light the sort of invisible power that revealed religions presented as their mystery, and which the image guaranteed was true. This is why cinema comforts us: its image was a revelation, wagering the image of the world against revelation. This is why the very idea of its disappearance, or even

just its transformation, is so disturbing, and could be maddening, if we can still imagine a place for a madness in which the reality of art would be at stake.

On March 1, 1894, Mallarmé brought some rather unique and important "news," as he called it, to his audiences at Oxford and Cambridge. He essentially announced to them: "Verse poetry has been attacked." He noted how it used to be that even when governments changed, verse always remained intact; that revolutions come and go, without dreaming that "this ultimate dogma might vary." This is how Mallarmé christened the appearance of free verse, which was supposed to allow everybody, henceforth, "to express themselves as they pleased."[3] In this liberation of the voice, he recognized an opportunity, and a risk, both manifesting a partial, but increasingly distinct, autonomy of literature as such with regard to historical development. The opportunity comes from a desire for expression and knowledge whose limits would be pushed back further than could have been foreseen. The risk comes right along with it: a rupture with all forms of reality, even those of language. The result is an extreme solitude of both work and self, which Mallarmé evokes emphatically. Such a solitude approaches madness, whose threat was certainly no stranger to Mallarmé. This comes out in his letters to Cazalis, about the time he began to form the idea of The Book. It's also evoked in a remark to Valéry, in response to the proofs of Un Coup de dés: "Don't you find this an act of insanity?"[4] It recurs to the point that Mallarmé often gives the impression of knowing how to master this madness, which makes even more understandable the reasons for its vibrancy in the modern odyssey of literature and art, both before and after him. It's linked to a collapse of the world: an accelerated political, social, and scientific transformation, whose expressive forms crystallize the attendant anxiety. "Verse poetry has been attacked." Just as, one day, the image would have to be attacked.

Godard will have been the one who attacked the image; Godard kept on loving the image that dissolved in his

LES CARABINIERS

1963

hands, as he always had. This was the virtue of *Le Mépris* (1963), which allowed film to maintain its privilege. Associating Fritz Lang and Homer, and sliding Hölderlin back and forth between them, Godard defined the frame, articulating the Greek world, and classical cinema's gesture to it, like a new order of mythology. And between them, in them, based on them, henceforth, the fissure caused by the absence of the gods. Hölderlin's madness marks the quintessential moment of the ebb that forces poetic language to retreat further into itself, at the risk of losing itself. It is the index of that rupture out of which art appears as "the end of art," and continues to position itself as such, more charged than ever, between utopia and nostalgia. This is the destiny of literature, painting, and music from the nineteenth century through the twentieth, from Romanticism to the avant-gardes. For a long time, it was, essentially, cinema's deferred destiny as well. For half a century, it was, in its American form especially, the only "innocent" art, identified as if by nature with the societies whose image it constructed, so to speak, at a distance: the agreed-upon distance of a projection that enabled a social relation to perpetuate itself, in full view of each and every one. It is from the day this distance was broken that we can symbolically date the moment when cinema became one among the other arts. In a new proximity, it lost its aura, the conditions for which would henceforth have to be ceaselessly reinvented. The very year of *Le Mépris*, one of Godard's two "*carabiniers*," Michel-Ange, buddy of Ulysses (the other *carabinier*), goes to the movies for the first time in his life. He tries to peek into the image on the screen, to see what he can't see from his seat: a nude woman just getting into the bath. He approaches the image, which is projected onto his body, in another attempt to see what he cannot see. He caresses the woman's face for a moment, then decides to jump into the bath. Grabbing the edge, he pulls the screen down, and the image with it, though the image goes on projecting onto the wall behind the screen—like a 35mm film on a bad TV set. And so, Godard destroyed the image. He did so, of course, out of the excessive love he bears it—as if anyone could, still or ever, go to the movies for the first time—but it's also in proportion to the aura he lends the image. Think of the movement that hurls Ulysses, facing the real sea at Capri and the fictitious sea of Ithaca, in the last shot of *Le Mépris*: Ulysses, pushed toward the sea(s), toward this "unique phenomenon of a distance, however close it may be."[5]

This is the paradox of Godard, which Serge Daney recognizes: he is neither prophet nor revolutionary, but a radical reformist and an inventor.[6] As a filmmaker whose action may be described as that of unveiling, Godard is attached above all to the veil, to the thing that both hides and reveals what his movement unveils. He relies on the fixed point that orients him, toward which, like Orpheus, he looks back, because that is where his vision comes from. Godard is, in this, very close to Mallarmé, in the sense that Mallarmé, when he lingered over the "crisis of verse," never failed to underline to what extent free verse brought out the unique character of the "great verse of yore," the alexandrine, once so central to the idea of literary creation. And even when Mallarmé, with *Un Coup de dés*, dealt the blow against everything that preceded him, he still maintained his "worship" of the "old verse," and continued his explorations of the rhythmic requirements narrowly determined by what he dubbed so well "the combination, among them, of twelve tones."[7] Mallarmé thus succeeded in revitalizing literature by taking off from the tradition he overturned, but continued to desire. In a similar fashion, Godard, the strictly contemporary filmmaker "dedicated to the present," as Daney says, continually positions himself in relation to cinema's past. Take, for example, both the alternating and parallel montages in *Puissance de la parole* (1988): the accelerations that digital montage permits serve to multiply the narrative and conceptual possibilities that have been linked, since Griffith, to these two great forms of montage. Or, in *Passion* (1982), the various modes of shot–reverse shot that Godard subordinates to the combined pressure of the tableaux vivants, the video relays, and the ruptures of synchrony between image and sound. Godard tackles these old cinematic forms in a way that preserves what they express: both the old (cinema as it's always been done), and the new (the future of their own transformation). In Daney's view, "Utopia doesn't consist of doing something else, but of doing something differently." To do cinema in an *other* way, in order to be able to keep on doing it, mindful of all it can do, in order to keep lending it the power to do everything, indeed, to lend it even more power: this is the condition of the other filmmaker.

Let's begin by referring to this place of the other as television. Godard is the filmmaker who knew, even before Rossellini, although in part because of him, that it was impossible to think of cinema (to think cinema) without television. Think of Belmondo as the quasi–TV host, addressing the spectator at the beginning of *A bout de souffle* (1960); in *Charlotte et son jules* (1959), there's the effect of a live broadcast and the concentration on Belmondo's voice. Using the first film as an example, Jean-Paul Fargier has pointed out how one could generalize its significance and state only slightly paradoxically that Godard had never done cinema, and, on the other hand, never done other than television.[8] It's the primacy of the present, nonstop filming, a "theater of the moment": the work conceived as the result of directing several cameras at once. The hypothesis is persuasive, but should be inverted. Not: "Cinema has never existed. . . . Cinema has long been the putative name of what we didn't yet know to call television," but, rather: cinema must become the name of what we call television. Because that was the name given to a new passion of the image, to the mystery of its presence and its distancing.

Television is central in this mystery. From the beginning, it threatens it by producing other sites of the image. These are the sites you have to steal from it if you don't want cinema to fall outside the image, even if it means "changing the image." Television first creates another site: a celestial screen transformed into a domestic servant. TV is above all an object that you touch, like its image, to which you can "do anything." It offers a direct and indiscreet relation, a passing image, which you pass without having to stop, since it never stops. It is this sequential movement, and this speed founded on a multiplicity—of programs, channels, and so on—that we must learn to fight while simultaneously incorporating them. TV then creates, under its alias of "video" (or "electronic image"), still other sites within the image, that is, everything that comes from treating the image electronically, according to modes and frequencies still unknown to cinema: speeds, forms, tonalities, and so on. At the two extremes of social institution and individual puttering, television thus imposes a permanent modification of the conditions of production and reception of images and sounds.

This is what Godard sees and hears, and responds to, when he begins shooting a film. This was implicitly so during his first period. It became explicit beginning with *Ici et ailleurs* (1974) and *Numéro deux* (1975) ("a film conceived by television, but clothed by cinema").[9] These films mark the end of the utopias of the militant period, and open onto a direct confrontation with TV: Godard's two great series of the seventies—nearly twenty hours of authentic television. Godard's serialism, his sorting by categories (so well observed by Gilles Deleuze), all the forms of interruption and overlapping—self-quotation, freeze-frames, diverse fragmentation—and the various modalities of composition and de-composition of images, strategies of positioning and mise-en-scène: all this was meant to provoke open competition with television, a need to beat it on its own turf and with its own means, under pain of disappearing into TV, crushed by the weight of its incessant

drone. This attitude is, again, similar to what openly pushed Mallarmé toward a conception of The Book influenced by the growing presence of The Newspaper. And not only by the event itself, and its vanishing traces, and its dispersive value, but even the conception of the typography, the varieties of characters and their spacing: *Un Coup de dés*, this "forthcoming book," owes much to the present tense of The Newspaper. Mallarmé "rewards" its contingency of being multiple and imperfect, just as literature exploits the shortcomings of language. He embraces its injunctions against chance, in order to dissolve them in "an exact, spiritual mise-en-scène." Mallarmé even founded a newspaper, as we know: the aptly titled *La Dernière Mode* (*The Latest Fashion*), in which he edited everything ("down to the theaters and dinner menus"). This was the forerunner, the model for the "everything" of The Book, which he conceived as "the orphic explanation of the earth."[10]

Similarly, Godard polishes up his television programs, dreaming of becoming program director or station manager of a Third-World-country television station, and reserving, in view of this "everything"— both actual and virtual, in the work, his work—the harshest words any filmmaker has ever had for television: television crews are collaborators; the State is an occupying power; the cinema, his cinema, is the Resistance. This is how Godard speaks to television itself in *Changer d'image* (1982). His is truly the voice of a writer opposing his silence to the drone, the intolerable, incessant drone of this foreign voice that imposes its *dictare*, so like "dictatorship" (in the last chapters of Maurice Blanchot's *Livre à venir*). But the most writerly writer is the one who, in order to silence it, knows how to mimic the noise, almost to the point of confusion with it, so as better to take it in and transform it.[11] Hence the need, so clearly affirmed by Godard in the seventies, to keep his eye on the eye of the cyclone, and stay both "on and under communication"—in other words, at the heart of television, but simultaneously above and beneath it, so as to maintain his desire for cinema.

It is important to mention, even briefly, what characteristically sets Godard apart from Rossellini, since Godard is in so many ways his continuator and his double. When Rossellini chose to do television and conceived his "pedagogical project," he did it against the fiction-effect of cinema. In the name of communication and education, he divided facts from illusion in the body of the image. He subjected the innocence of the image, in which he had complete and excessive faith, to a theater of the voice, a kind of speech, to which, in the end, he almost reduced the image. He invented a utopian pedagogy of drama, supported by an obstinate will-to-knowledge. And at the last he declared, in the name of the superior objective he gave himself: "I am not a filmmaker." Whereas, in the name of an identical belief in the universal virtue of images, Godard is the filmmaker who, with a nonutopian but mad will, anchors in the cinema the carnival voice that transforms the image's value of illusion by doubling its seductive force, which has remained whole, with a knowledge-function: A Gay Science.

For in the beginning was the voice, the voices, their irrepressible multiplicity, their reverberation at the heart of a dispersed center. There is his voice, which is not only his master's voice, the better to avoid the slaves and "the monsters" (as Godard calls the normalized adults of *France/tour/détour/deux/enfants* [1977–78]). His voice was present, as we know, from the beginning, as if transmitted live through the body of "her old man" [in *Charlotte et son jules*], who delivers a monologue while circling around Charlotte. It is Godard speaking through Belmondo, as he does, in a sense, through *all* the characters in his films. Indeed, they are all so many possible fragments of a discourse that is at once inchoate, modulated, and open-ended. Godard increasingly used this discourse, starting with *Ici et ailleurs* and *Numéro deux*, addressing apparatuses of mise-en-scènes and writing that take us to the heart of the problem: the need to construct (with a little determination) an image of Godard as writer, more so than Godard as painter or musician, which has already been done, and done well.[12] This brings us back and nearest to our image. When Jacques Aumont emphasizes that Godard is interested above all in "the musical idea," that "if he's a musician, he is so everywhere other than in his use of music, or rather, everywhere *as in* his use of music," Mallarmé comes to mind again: Mallarmé justifying the key role of music in the endeavor of *Un Coup de dés*, in search of a superior synthesis ("Several means having seemed to me to belong to Letters, I duly reclaim them").[13] If Godard is above all a "writer," or like a writer, if this image of him seems more complete, not canceling the others, but, on the contrary, bringing them together, it's because it's a question above all of enunciation, of a posture attached to language, which only he allows, linked as he is to the image. This is certainly something new, this position with respect to Everything, peculiar to writers since the end of the eighteenth century, and today more visibly occupied by this filmmaker of an other kind than by any writer. That's what makes him an other filmmaker. He has put himself partly in place of the writer, from whom he borrows the value of quotation, precisely because he's a filmmaker. Thus, far from ending with Godard, this art

of our century returns in and through him, and signals a new form of accomplishment.

By "Everything," we mean the relation among knowledge, expression, and responsibility, which burdens the writer with a world forever more vast and ungraspable, within the limits of a Self the writer doesn't know. In the German tradition from Schlegel to Novalis and Nietzsche, "the subjective encyclopedia" culminates in disintegration, in *The Will to Power*, *Ecce Homo*, and *The Antichrist*. In French history, it's between Flaubert and Mallarmé, and later resonates so strongly, in desperation, here and there, in Joyce, Kafka, Musil, Artaud, Gombrowicz, Beckett, Michaux, and some others. The other filmmaker figures in this lineage as much as in that of the great filmmakers among whose number he continues to count himself—more than in that of the equivalent painters and musicians. Godard says so clearly, in a dialogue with a writer (of course, it's also his function to be able and obliged constantly to "say everything"): "As for us, we're the ones condemned to analyze the world, reality, ourselves, while neither painters nor musicians are so condemned."[14] The key word is clearly *analyze*. Neither painting nor music, as essential as they are to Godard's filmmaking—for their formal material, and affective effects, as well as for their referential value—can contribute fully to this analysis. It takes place on two levels, whose interplay expresses what is most new and different—most other—in Godard's films: on one level, everything that derives from literature and language; on the other, everything he weaves between the images.

In Godard's films there are four modalities that link text and speech to image, but also divide them. They turn speech into something that sticks to the image, while holding in check the text, from which the image can no more free itself than speech can truly circumvent it.

The first modality is the very visible and established book circuit, a continuous circuit with peaks and troughs. The book is the object in hunt-the-slipper: you can hold certain moments of it, which you hold out to the other, your partner, as the spectator. You expect a sort of grace from it, which is always deferred, since the real belief is in the image—before which the text is always lacking. An exemplary reference film (after *Une Femme est une femme* [1961], *Pierrot le fou* [1965], and others) might be *Détective* (1985), which is full of books: the enormous piles of whodunits tossed on a table (pointing up the film's origin), and those books we reach for at every turn to calm our anxiety. An ironic twist is Johnny Hallyday's mother giving him Conrad's *Lord Jim*: "She told me that at every serious moment of my life I had only to open it at random, and I'd always stumble upon something of value to me. It's been thirty years, and every time I open it, somebody comes in. I've yet to read a word."

Then there is quotation, issuing from books on this side and beyond: on this side to mark how references spontaneously exercise memory and the body, like available traces; beyond, to create impalpable dissociations—to contain, to veil the image as such, which is at once too simple, excessive, immediate, and out of reach. *Nouvelle Vague* (1990) is in this regard a paragon: in it, the image manifests a sort of fullness, making it Godard's most seamless film in a long time, almost a dream of the "classical" film. But the fragmented continuity of the quotations, as unavowed and fleeting as they are constant and ripe with meaning, strikes bodies with the force of their detachment, encompassing them with a negative aura that gives a nostalgic aspect to the wonderful chaos of the sound track. Think, too, of the body-quotations formed by the extras in *Grandeur et décadence d'un petit commerce de cinéma* (1986): each one is affected by a suspended fragment of a Faulkner phrase that he or she enunciates while moving toward the camera.

The third modality is also textual. It is common knowledge that Godard has privileged text over image, ready-made texts—ads, signs, graffiti—all foregrounded by the framing of the image. Or those pages of books or of texts that fill the screen—Pierrot's newspaper, the letters and postcards of the *"carabiniers,"* and so on. Words and phrases emblazoned across the image, composing and de-composing in place of the image, or penetrating the image, as in the credit sequences of films of Godard's first period, and so many films and videos of his second, from *Ici et ailleurs* to *Histoire(s) du cinéma* (1989–). The screen becomes treated as a writing tablet, the word, as a kind of matter that develops, between sense and nonsense, in a multiplicity of directions.

Finally, there are the voices. All the voices: those of the book and of quotation, and those of all the characters from whom Godard's voice stands out more and more frequently and insistently. But all share with his voice the singularity of always addressing the spectator, at least somewhat—even when talking to a partner, whether on- or offscreen. Thus, they constantly double the film with a critical layer that isn't commentary, since the voices remain engaged in the fiction. But this fiction is based, as much as or more than on plot, on an analysis of the conditions of fiction, the conditions of a possible (hi)story, in the context of a (hi)story of images and sounds. (The signature ending of *France/tour/détour* is "That's another story," while the leitmotiv of *Passion* is "So, what's the story?") So strong is this sense of a critical, questioning voice, that all the characters seem to be on a quest that, mediated by privileged intercessors (Paul Godard in *Sauve qui peut (la vie)* [1979], Jerzy in *Passion*, Gaspard in *Grandeur et décadence*), comes together in the voice of Godard quizzing himself directly on his creation (for example, in *Scénario du film Passion* [1982] or in *Changer d'image*). This doesn't mean his cinema can't offer the sharpest and most complete documentary take there is on contemporary reality; on the contrary. But it does contribute to continually bringing the capture of the world back to the conditions that make it possible, and, in the last analysis, to the person who has become the echo and repository of these conditions.

There are at least three ways of looking at this increasingly overt way of making a "cinema of cinema" by confronting the image with the powers of the book and the voice.

The first is descriptive. Forced to define it, we might say: in exploding the antinomies of fiction and documentary, in treating all stories as histories, that is, already anterior fictions (already filmed, written, painted, sung), and all situations as possible (hi)stories, by saturating all the modes in which history can be told (tragic, dramatic, parodistic, burlesque, and so on), Godard's work oscillates between critical mythology and epic catalogue. It's also expressed in the resonance of two words: the *essay*, with all it implies about a continual opening-up and the quest for knowledge; and the *self-portrait*, with what it implies about concern with the self. All this is borne out by the existence of so many "intimate" works, those based on "fictions," shot in video and not unlike those journalistic vignettes that novelists contribute to magazines from time to time (even if most of Godard's have been conceived for television). There is also Godard's increasingly substantive presence in the intimate works, the "essays," and the fictions. A film and a tape, nearly contemporaneous, give a good indication of the tension between two overlapping and merging extremes in these works: *Nouvelle Vague*, in which the novelistic is riddled with the echoing voices of all the literary ghosts that haunt it; and *Histoire(s) du cinéma*, in which, for the first time, a filmmaker dares to evaluate the history of his art, that of this century becoming his own, because he tells it with his body and his voice.

The second way of looking is historical and stylistic. We might base it, for example, on the distinctions made by Deleuze, in his three-phase study of the "components of the image," from silent film to contemporary cinema.[15] The silent film image is double: on the one hand, it's simply seen, in the image itself, the site of a "natural" truth; on the other hand, it's read, in the intertitles, the supports of a cultural—indirect—discourse. In the first phase of sound cinema (the cinema of "image-as-movement") the act of speech is direct; heard and no longer read, it becomes a component of the visual image. In Deleuze's novel scheme, the image is "denaturalized" by the complexity that comes with dialogue and the whole sound track, and "begins to become readable, for its part, *insofar* as it's visible or visual." The third phase is modern cinema (the cinema of "image-as-time"): here the voice wins its autonomy, according to a "free indirect style," and the act of speech separates from the visual image, itself, in turn, detached from its sensory-motor underpinnings. This is Deleuze's fundamental thesis, that, in modern cinema, images are no longer connected, but rather *reconnected* over and above the interval that separates them. So much so that each of the two images, acoustic and visual, becomes autonomous in relation to the other; cinema becomes truly audiovisual, and the two images have to be read, both together and independently, according to "a new Analytics of the image." Straub-Huillet, Duras, and Syberberg are here exemplary, each working through an ever more extreme tension between text, voice, and image. But with Godard, as Deleuze notes, there isn't a pure disjunction, but rather a "system of disconnections and microruptures in every sense: the ruptures crowd together, and no longer pass between the acoustic and the visual, but into the visual, into the acoustic, and into their multiplied connections." Godard may well be the only one who, given the complexity of the present media landscape, can manage all three registers at the same time: silent, classical, and modern cinema. He constantly revisits film history, settling on its most tangible forms and modes; he does this directly in his *Histoire(s) du cinéma*. Passing, for example, through a same character (let's say, Sandrine in *Numéro deux*) from the second phase of cinema (direct visible voice) to the third (indirect visible voice), in order to integrate and reformulate the first (pure image and written text), Godard proceeds to a critical evaluation: he works into the "*mise-en-histoire*," as into the mise-en-scène, whatever he is saying—or having someone say—on the central question he lives and breathes: the question of words and images.

The third way of looking is thus metaphysical: a vision of vision, of what draws closer and what pushes away.

Here, we must introduce one last voice: that of Godard speaking outside the context of his films to continue saying what he's already said in the films, and directed so many others to say. We know that Godard has always waged a troubled war against what he has variously called words, text, writing, language, litera-

ture—in other words, everything he borrows and feeds off at will, especially to zero in on what he wants to oppose it with: the image. The image, that is, in its most natural, truthful state: the silent film image, or any image that still partakes of that aesthetic. One has only to reread Godard's interview with Serge July after the death of Hitchcock to understand his passion and nostalgia for the possible end of cinema, the ebbing of the visual, the triumph of death, and cinema as "the childhood of art." Or to hear the following words, in another context, also in May of 1980: "The image doesn't name. Silent cinema was a great cultural and popular revolution. It didn't name, but we recognized everything and knew everything. With the sound film industry, we started naming again."[16]

Naming. Or seeing, an act prior to all verbs. This tension has long and most often been polemical and deliberately anti-intellectualist, a position Godard has sometimes taken in relation to theory and thought (which has earned him Deleuze's reminder: theory, too, is something that is done, neither more nor less than the films it concerns itself with, and a filmmaker who speaks becomes a theoretician or philosopher, even when he prefers to ignore it).[17] Godard gave the conflict between word and image its densest expression at the beginning of *Scénario du film Passion*, doubtless because the film *Passion*, in turning to traditional, grand painting, both secular and religious, was unconsciously making its way toward Christianity's central mystery: the conception of Christ as both God and man, man-God in the image of the Father, inscribed in the body of the Mother by the breath and Verb of the Father. "I didn't want to write the script, I wanted to see it. When all is said and done, it's a pretty terrible story, which goes back to . . . , it's terrible, perhaps, because it goes back to the Bible. Can we see the Law? Was the Law written first, or was it seen and then, later, Moses wrote it on his tablet? I think that we see the world first and write it later, and that the world *Passion* describes had to be seen first, to see if it existed, for it to be filmed."

The first question is thus that of the Law, including everything that's been outlined clearly since *Numéro deux* and *Sauve qui peut (la vie)*: excessive sex, forbidden sex, incest, and the image that could show these things—the aborted project with Myriem Roussel, *Père et fille*, itself doubled by a "Freud and Dora," which led up to *Je vous salue Marie* (1985), the distant echo, twenty years later, of another, impossible film on the desire of bodies.[18]

What does it mean, to see the Law? Does it assume an anteriority of the world, of things, before all language? But where would the Law be, how could there even be a Law, if it's not that which is written after, and whose nature would then always be second? Or does this presuppose that the Law, the words of the Law, could be visible before they were even written? Are we then to take "visible" in the sense of "heard," and imagine language as still immersed in the real, immediate presence of speech? This is what Deleuze is proposing, with his conception of a "seeable/readable" that characterizes sound cinema, in which language is part of the image. Several years later, *Puissance de la parole* upheld this sort of mediation, which is the entire significance of this work. In it, the phone conversation between the lovers translates an energy that is instantly expressed in terms of image, since the words are transported into space, where they resonate, and their very resonance seems to create the image. The conversation is about desire, what it lacks and its fulfillment, and—by the very fact that they're discussing it, and detaching it from its pure image-surface—its Law. What desire lacks, its fulfillment, is also what gives it its power and guarantees its transport, in both senses of the word. The conversation between the two angels, implicated in and by that of the lovers, confirms this. An emblematic phrase, borrowed, like their entire dialogue, from Poe's "extraordinary (hi)story," is revealing in this regard, insofar as it refers the images we see to an idea of divinity, and of creation founded on an identity among thought, matter, and speech: "And while I thus spoke, did there not cross your mind some thought of the *physical power of words?* Is not every word an impulse on the air?"[19] In other words, we have here an image-equivalent, a part of the image, a layer, a stage of what composes the image. To speak would then be to see, the opposite of Blanchot's affirmation "Speaking is not seeing," a phrase meant to tease out the writing within a speech unbound from seeing ("A word like speaking would no longer be unveiling by the light").[20] To the neat formula of *L'Entretien infini*, "written speech," one is tempted to oppose Godard's "spoken writing," which brings writing to the image by way of speaking, and maintains them in a painful, vital, furious dependency.

This implies for Godard the power to retransform all books, even The Book itself (the Bible and Mallarmé), by means of a speech that quotes them, plays with them, makes them enter the circuit of the film where they are torn from the page, their written space, as are, in *Puissance de la parole*, an A. E. Van Vogt story, "Defense"; the James Cain novel *The Postman Always Rings Twice*; and Poe's tale. This is a mode pushed to the extreme in *Détective* and *Nouvelle Vague*. It also implies the ability to treat written texts as images, an image, and the screen as a page. It implies removing writing itself from its own readability in order to turn it into the object of a "seeable/readable," which its plasticity *in vivo* guarantees in the time of inscription and unfolding (this is what, among other things, *Histoire(s) du cinéma* fully achieves). This also means surpassing the law of the book, and all that clings to it, in the act of creation itself, in order to (re)make cinema into something approximating life itself. This is the background for Godard's deployment of two origin myths into a mirror relation when, again in *Scénario du film Passion*, he accuses the merchants of having substituted writing for speech, and the accountants of having substituted written scripts for the spontaneous inspiration of shooting.

Godard's consistent reiteration of "Cinema is life" is well known, but in *Scénario* he repeats "Cinema that copies life, cinema that comes from life, that represents life." The second question, after that of the Law, is thus premised on seeing a scenario, rather than writing a script. How could cinema be taken for life? By "life," we mean both the reality that appears on the screen (image and sound, voice and text, indissolubly connected, even if the image is also always foregrounded for itself), and the way of life that permits this reality to appear. This is what makes Godard paradoxically the most writerly of filmmakers, even when everything in him rejects what this implies. The conflict emerges clearly in the following rather lengthy excerpt of an early conversation between Godard and a writer:

Le Clézio—Would you really take a sheet of paper and just write without really knowing, up to the last minute, what will come out?

Godard—But that's exactly why I can't write! That's why I'm always so touched by Flaubert, by the extraordinary pains he took to write. He'd think, "The sky is blue," he'd write it, and then he'd be sick for three days. He'd say to himself: Maybe I should have written, "The sky is gray," maybe instead of "sky" I should have written, "The sea is gray," maybe instead of "is" I should have written "was. . . ." And then finally he'd write . . .

Le Clézio—"The sky is blue."

Godard—Yes, but what suffering.

Le Clézio—Doesn't the filmmaker have the same problem?

Godard—No. In cinema, the sky is there, and I'd never say, "The sky is blue," if it were gray . . . I don't feel that I make a distinction between life and art. For me, directing an actress and speaking with your wife are the same thing . . . If a look makes me think of purity, I dissolve to another image of purity . . . If the sky is blue, I shoot it blue; if it turns gray, I shoot it gray . . . Because it changes . . . I get the impression that you, on the other hand, make a distinction between life and art.

Le Clézio—Yes. I have to. It's technique. It comes from writing in my room with pen and paper at night. If I wanted to write something equivalent to what I feel, I would do nothing but write constantly that I am in the process of writing."[21]

Le Clézio calls "technique" what really isn't, or isn't only technique. He thus gives a name to what made Voltaire "the last of the happy writers," and Rousseau the first of a different species, which is not yet extinct: a man alone and (a little) mad.[22] Le Clézio hints at the detachment that, from Hölderlin to Beckett, has made the writer into a being separated by the very power that guarantees him access to the entirety of the world: his writing, his language. Mallarmé also observes this, when he points to the consequence of the divorce between general action (life, History) and the restrained action of literature: "Solitude necessarily accompanies this kind of attitude." "Whoever achieves it, withdraws completely."[23] Blanchot has crystallized this experience by introducing an equivalence, at first blush an enigmatic one, between "literature and the right to die."[24] And this is what Godard fiercely rejects, in the name of cinema.

What he opposes to Le Clézio is as simple to grasp as it is difficult to formulate. On the one hand, we recognize the pragmatic ethic of a cinema inspired by Rossellini, which adapts to the given reality of things more than it constrains it. On the other hand, there's the indivisible character of the shots: that block of space-time called the image is not to be divided (unless it's by a trick: a trick shot). Thus, cinema represents life, whatever it may show, and in spite of the manipulations to which images and sounds are subjected in the editing as in the mixing. But this is already less true the moment the image becomes electronic and permits intervention within the components of the image, dividing the field into individual elements and making them the object of a sort of writing-painting. This is where you can determine the color of the sky, à la Flaubert, and as Antonioni did in *The Oberwald Mystery*, or, using more classical means but means already induced by this new mutation of images (for which Straub reproached him), in *Red Desert*.[25] It's clear that Godard, who was quite early on so strongly drawn to video, has up to this point traced a sort of demarcation: except for the four "sexual" sequences in *Numéro deux*, his exploration of the image stops short of denaturing it. Though it plays with the rhythm, the speeds, the thickness, and the coalescence of the images (by superimposition, simultaneous alternation, or both), this exploration effects no internal transformation of the

forms and colors, which would divert the image too much from the function Godard still assigns it: to be an emanation of life. Significantly, it's also more or less at the moment Godard takes on video equipment (in Grenoble, then in Rolle) that he chooses—to oversimplify a bit—the country over the city. This is also when his cinema becomes directly touched by nature, by the human, cosmic, documentary dimension of natural phenomena (even if it's already there in *Pierrot le fou* . . .). As if there were an equilibrium to preserve between a possible, necessary artifice and an ever more primal desire to touch things as they are. But he's still on this side of the particular destiny that drives him to make this capture of life *his* very life, to the point where in forming an image of life, cinema becomes the unique and absolute condition of that life. Again, Rossellini's example comes to mind, but from another angle—that of the films he made with Bergman. "Directing an actress and speaking with your wife are the same thing." Except that Rossellini, as Truffaut said, "prefers life." He preferred life to cinema, and that's why he, too, ended up choosing television over cinema. And of course his Nouvelle Vague admirers were the first to enjoy the ambiguous privilege of, as Godard says, "making cinema before having lived"[26]—that is, of having had or believing they had had cinema as their only life. If you think about it, this assumes that a ridiculous demand is being made of cinema, asking it to respond, on the spot, as if live, to a desire that no other art could satisfy, since no other art, none more than most cinema, is so manifestly attached to life.[27]

What is Godard thinking when he stresses that what he expects from a shoot is the possibility of dialogue, exchange, communication, always reformulated and forever inadequate? When he asks each person, each actor and crew member, to be at every moment absolutely present, dedicated to the work in progress? When he reiterates his famous phrase: the identity between love and work (we always have to try to think about what that means. Godard has Hanna Schygulla say in *Passion*, "What you want from me is too close to love")? When in relation to *Je vous salue Marie* he dreams that the gestation of the film is like a pregnancy, that the recording time prefigures and prescribes the projection time, in the image of a never-ending live broadcast—that film, television, might never stop?[28] When he implies that this experience, which is a collective one, and must remain so, nonetheless be identical with the will that compels him to retreat, alone or nearly alone, to his editing table and all his machines, in his studio/house at Rolle? He demands the impossible, and this is his strength and his greatness. In the name of cinema-as-life, of life-as-artifact, he demands what Christ did of his disciples, in order to touch in them the community of men. He demands that others, all others, be like him, be him, become in themselves identical to him, which draws them to the image insofar as to recognize himself as an image, to know his image(s)-being, he attracts to himself all images, which become so many images of him, as he insists.[29]

In the end, Godard's paradox is that he demands of cinema what the writer has demanded of language as long as "literature has existed, and, if you will, alone, outside of everything."[30] But this assumes a retreat, which the indirect character of language favors, once it is no longer the natural echo of an order of the world, and must suffice unto itself, as the writer ought to find sufficient his or her own uncertain image, which rises from it and dissolves back into it. It's within an extreme solitude that each writer makes the personal wager that he or she can be at the same time God and no one, and has the chance to see one day, or, as sometimes happened to Kafka, one night, "the world rolling at his feet." The extraordinary thing with Godard, with any filmmaker animated by a will such as his, is that this exigence takes place at the heart of an always more or less collective situation, as well as with respect to a more or less preexisting reality. It's in fact the population that's already there (sets, actors, and so on), that must be there, with all that they imply of material preparations and provisions, that Godard tries to persuade to improvisational, spontaneous shooting, with a mad, documentary passion, in the name of a never-ending desire for the present, for absolute presence, and for the coincidence of times. It is truly the eternal present, the always disjointed present of writing that Godard aims for and intends, ideally, to equal; he means to re-create it in another present, using means that, up to that point, implied other disjunctions, which he seeks to diminish. It's as if, in order both to conjure and attain the image of nocturnal solitude Le Clézio offered him, Godard would have to film and write just as well amid his crew on the shoot of *Passion* as in his house at Rolle, in his video studio, confronting his own image, finally finding it, seeing its *Scénario*, "before the invisible, enormous white surface, the white page, Mallarmé's famous white page."

Deleuze has said of Godard: "He's a man who works a lot, so he is, necessarily, absolutely alone. But his is not just any solitude, it's an extraordinarily populated solitude."[31] This populating, when it grows, often drives the writer mad, since he can only hear and understand it against a double silence: the silence it takes to hear his own voice, and the silence of language itself, when the voice disappears in the written word. In the same interview cited earlier, Le Clézio remarked that though there is no such thing as a mad filmmaker, Godard is one of those who could become one.[32] But Godard has on another occasion been quick to remark that very few filmmakers have been alcoholics, drug addicts, or suicides, compared to all the painters, musicians, and writers—and that Eustache must have been "an exceptional case."[33] (Did he perhaps have in mind Gottfried Benn's extraordinary list of all the creators afflicted in body and mind by the split between their "genius" and the world?)[34] If there are very few mad filmmakers, it's because the image protects them, so long as there are several (at least two) to make it and talk about it, and so long as the image doesn't stop, but continues to be seen and felt as a living thing through other moving bodies. Godard could have become mad, because he has surrendered more than anyone else to all the clashes that have driven the image to the edge of disappearance in our world, and because he has appropriated for himself all the obstacles that in our world threaten to immobilize all images. He has even chosen, the better to experience them, to live in part like a writer, to put himself at a distance, as a means of protecting himself. But it's principally to see the image better, as much as the nature on which it depends. His solitude is thus populated, not only with the whole social and professional field that makes him effective, "a force," as Deleuze says, but also with all the movements he employs to continually reanimate the image, in the excessive intimacy he has established with it. Thus, faced with his "white page [*page blanche*]," his "white beach [*plage blanche*]," as he calls it, his video screen, Godard knows he has "a writer's work to do." He might write, like Proust, "I have long gone to bed early," or like Rimbaud, "A white, E black, I red," and sketch the gesture, immediately filling the frame with an immense alphabet, as on a computer screen. "But you don't want to write, you want to see, to re-*see*-ve [*rece-voir*]." And gently he brings up the frozen, silent image in *Passion* of Hanna Schygulla running toward a car, a bouquet of flowers in her hand; he makes this image appear and disappear, causing the frozen image to beat. "But it's movement"—this movement he gives back to the image, body and voice, because it's the movement it's always had, as long as there's been cinema. Godard must preserve movement to the last, even in the situation that resembles most closely the process of writing, in which he creates, at his house, his back to his bookshelf, at his typewriter, his *Histoire(s) du cinéma*. A film take; a take on life. This is how strong the relation is between capturing a scene and capturing life, not only in the images surging onscreen, or the texts that take shape there, and the voice that guides them,

SCENARIO DU FILM PASSION

1982

Jean-Luc Godard

Hanna Schygulla

but in the deepest heart of writing itself: the electronic memory of the typewriter spits out live what it has first recorded, written words that become sound, a piece of living image.

In each of the apparatuses Godard prepares, he has to be able to "touch the image," approaching, as closely as possible, its invisible and forbidden part: the body, the true body, but also the bottom of the bottomless image itself. Godard-the-body-image puts his hands flat against the white screen in *Scénario du film Passion*, when he says "see." But he pulls them back toward himself when he says "re-*see*-ve," and the image of Hanna Schygulla comes up. He's like Joseph in *Je vous*

salue Marie, unable to actually touch Mary's belly, or only touch it by already withdrawing his hand, so that his desire, his "I love you," may conform to the Law. He must maintain with respect to the image, and to the life from which it emanates, the distance necessary for it to exist as an image, in its dimension of belief and revelation. You don't touch the Virgin's belly if you expect from her the aura destined to illuminate all images. The parable can be understood as a tension between Rossellini's famous and always too simple adage "Things are there; why manipulate them?" and the proposition derived from it of the intense need to retain images at the threshold of their disappearance, because of the increasingly vivid absence of things.

"Things—images—might still be there. How could you not manipulate them?" This is how one becomes, by digital means if necessary, a privileged artisan in the fight "between the digital and suffering." Between the analog image and what threatens it, we must seek a new foundation for the image.[35]

The thing is that there's always a residue of suffering in "the image itself," in its pure visuality, which one is continually isolating, identifying, and trying to reconstitute. This suffering distinguishes cinema; it is its site, its most intimate truth, the thing that protects filmmakers dedicated to making cinema "the repository of suffering." Godard elucidates this in a remarkable way, rearticulating with his final deduction a conviction of pure passion: "The image itself must remain our only chance of holding onto suffering. And our possibility of manufacturing what are called images—mentally or by means of visual aids—must be something where the visual aid is itself only a possibility of making images, *in other words, without a verb.*"[36]

Let's return for a moment to the silent film era, to the very beginning, before there were scripts, when nothing was named. Back then, cinema that was made up during shooting was in the process of constructing an imaginary unity, founded on distance, even if it was only half-aware of doing so. Its spectacle could be taken for life, because it fixed the life-moments it animated within an intangible frame, a frame no one was supposed to penetrate, neither the spectator nor the voice or avowed subjectivity of an author (this is what allowed the filmmaker-actor's body to be so present in burlesque: it's just an other body, instantly given over to the desire for spectacle). At the very moment it was being done, cinema could in this way participate in life's immediacy. But this cinema–life continuum became limited by the material and psychic divisions characteristic of an institution that stakes its claim in the social space, and would eventually quite naturally produce its own rationalizations as it became simultaneously an art and an industry: the script, shooting script, and so on. This is, in short, what happened to an art that would soon become classical, and in its own, new mode adopt a position similar to that of other arts in earlier historical epochs.

Godard's paradox, then, his "madness," would be that he aspired to a situation of impalpable origin, a sort of "primal scene" of cinema. Wholly dedicated to the image and to it alone, and set on maintaining a pressure on all earlier films, as well as on all films to come, Godard can thus intentionally ignore the prescriptive value of silent film's intertitles (as Deleuze aptly recalls), as well as the force of the script and the intangible minutiae of the shooting script in the work

of Hitchcock.[37] Godard is aiming beyond them, toward an ideal state destined to make an image exist, a unique image-body, as it were, disengaged from the (hi)story it's born in, because that would be its basis. This mythic view informs simultaneously the beginning and limit of (hi)story—this history of cinema that also becomes the history of the origin and creation of the world, of cinema as re-creation and restarting of the world. Godard has become heir, Messiah, interpreter, and witness to this history; from *Passion* to *Scénario du film Passion*, from *Puissance de la parole* to *Histoire(s) du cinéma*, it's one and the same question: the creation of a film, the creation of the world, the history of the creation of cinema. It's *Fiat lux* without the verb—always more or less obscurely guaranteed by the luminance of words, but also transcending them—which must be preserved and loved.

In the final text of *L'Entretien infini*, where he comes closest to "the absence of book," Blanchot describes two types of writing. First, there would be what he calls a "black writing," that of the witnessed and visible book, whose image is the Bible, the sacred book that sets down in script the speech from which it is born. But there would also be before it, always and forever, a "white writing," in which the Law would be in some way absent to itself, for this "first writing" evades discourse, communication, and commentary: it is "*outside speech*, and turned solely toward the *outside*."[38] The first writing is the one Godard restores to speech, both living instance and reference of a law whose presence and debate cannot be denied. The second writing is, on the other hand, the one Godard would like to commit to the image and to it alone, like the secret of a law that would surrender before the affirmation of a pure love and transparency, along with the nostalgia and suffering that flow from it.

Godard is, in a sense, quite close to old Nicephorus, who believed in the image, and thought that the evangelical message of the icon was not only equal but superior to that of the Gospel itself.[39] The image is all the more universal and absolute in that, unlike words, it is without contradiction—there is no counter-image—and its presence is whole and immediate, without delay. It is as much the object of public worship, in the holy places it illuminates, as it is the object of an intimate relationship, in the private dwellings it transforms by its grace, and by the mystery it holds and envelops. The image thus protects those who give themselves up to it. This is what Godard dreams of, when he conceives his films all at once, and seeks to reconstruct the image (*Nouvelle Vague*, "*Vague nouvelle*"), and when he peppers a video home movie (of a family or a couple) intended for television with black-and-white images

SOFT AND HARD

co-director: Anne-Marie Miéville

1986

Anne-Marie Miéville

Jean-Luc Godard

from great films of the past (*Soft and Hard* [1986], for example). Even if only as a Christian who becomes Christ without God, Godard is destined, like the Romantic writers and so many writers after them, to be the one and the other, or to pretend to be. This is why the image, which comforts him so, frightens him also, to the point where he can't live without the "other," without an other, the person one talks to, and to whom he also addresses the image, his image, since it is also with him or her that he has made it.[40]

It remains to write on Godard's behalf this "letter to the beloved," which he so eloquently claims lives in every work (see *Changer d'image*), and indeed is every work. We've known this since Rousseau, since the Romantics, since Schlegel and his "Letter" *On Philosophy (to Dorothea)*—Dorothea-Lucinda, the woman-light, she who gives form and life to light, when she stands behind both the man and the work.[41] Godard is a writer also because he was the first to give cinema such a clear and tormented expression of the question of the other, in its creative and self-reflexive dimension. The other would be the one on whom one depends, in reality and symbolically, to make the work arrive, to make it possible. "All texts are texts to the beloved, somewhere; whether it be the Revolution, a woman, or a man, all texts can be considered texts to the beloved."

The other could thus be the Revolution or the revolutionary, or each of the two Lumière brothers to the other, as Godard likes to recall, to reemphasize that cinema is, from the outset, a battle waged against solitude, since it's only made in a group. The other would then be the producer, the assistant, the technician, the collaborator, any other whom Godard uses for the work, and who becomes, ideally, an element of this expanding image, which assures at the same time the image of its creator. The other is thus any other, but also and above all a woman, and before any other, the beloved.

We ought to be able to say who this woman is, and how the work crafts an image of her, an image through which Godard seeks to recognize himself. She is both many and one. There is, of course, the actress, who was also the wife or the lover, Anna Karina, Anne Wiazemsky ("Directing an actress and speaking with your wife are the same thing"). They represent the riddle of what is simultaneously taken and given, through the body offered to the image, as through life merging with cinema. Then there is the actress again, the girl-woman/woman-child, too intensely coveted in the name of an impossible incest not to end in the image that puts her at the desired distance, once and for all: Myriem Roussel—the Virgin Mary, whom we find again at the end of *Je vous salue Marie*, very like Nana in *Vivre sa vie* (1962):

SOFT AND HARD

co-director: Anne-Marie Miéville

1986

You can look... look... look...

When it comes to the image...

woman between holy maternity–creation and prostitution, between love and work.

In a much more amorphous and undoubtedly deeper partition, there is his collaborator-companion, Anne-Marie Miéville. Godard's entire adventure between cinema and television, cinema and video, public and intimate images is bound up with her, across so many shared works, in part or entirely, from *Ici et ailleurs* to *L'Enfance de l'art* (1990), with the privileged moment of *Soft and Hard* along the way—that "Conversation Between Two Friends" about their life and things of this world. "Cruel mothering," said Daney of Miéville's voice, which covers and corrects Godard's in *Ici et ailleurs*, and extends itself via Sandrine's voice telling the man a thing or two in *Numéro deux*.[42] True enough, but her voice offers to whoever submits to it much more than simple masochism: it offers a renewed possibility of making an image, of placing his voice in the image, of reclaiming himself more as an image, as Godard has continually done.

Going toward this image, then, in the films themselves, there would be two times two women, in *Sauve qui peut (la vie)* and *Passion*. In the first film, we find again the whore and the woman who liberates herself, confronting Godard's double, Paul Godard, who destroys himself on contact with them. Isabelle and Denise are linked by a complicity that makes of one the mistress of her body and free of her pimps, even if they beat her, and of the other this strange and unique woman-writer, this almost too literal feminine double who exchanges television for solitude, and leaves Paris for Switzerland in order to finish her writing project. In *Passion* there are the two women, one on either side of Jerzy, the director, Godard's double in this film that is, more than any other, devoted to the present moment of the work. Hanna and Isabelle, "the one open and the other closed," are equally necessary to Jerzy in his endless quest for the light, which passes through their bodies, the bodies of women and actresses.

One could do as Godard has suggested (a moment of Godard's voice), and have literature be Orpheus and cinema Eurydice, in a never-ending conflict between word and image that would actually bridge the gap between the sexes. But in a less clear-cut view, closer in a sense to what Blanchot meant by "the look of Orpheus,"[43] we could also have Orpheus be cinema in search of its Eurydice, and doubly so: in addressing itself to Eurydice as to the other, the beloved, its double among doubles, cinema conceives itself in a new and painful intimacy, as literature has so often done. But even from the depths of this retreat that threatens its existence, cinema remains, first and foremost, the art that is more directly engaged than others, by

nature, in a struggle against solitude and loss. This is why, says Godard, commenting recently on his *Histoire(s)*, "cinema authorizes Orpheus to look back without causing Eurydice's death."[44]

Given this skein, this connection, there is surely no image more correct than the decision taken to assemble within a single reel, in the negative itself, in the deepest body of the film, both Miéville's short film *Le Livre de Marie* and Godard's film *Je vous salue Marie*. The exact weight of the words inspires dreaming: between the child Mary and the Virgin giving birth to the celebrated child, writing and speech, the action of grace, meet, and together tend toward, and into, the image.

Notes

1   Alain Bergala, ed., *Jean-Luc Godard par Jean-Luc Godard* (Paris: Cahiers du Cinéma, 1985), p. 406. Henceforth abbreviated *JLG*.

2   *JLG*, 415–16.

3   Stéphane Mallarmé, *Oeuvres complètes* (Paris: Editions "La Pléiade," Gallimard, 1965), pp. 643, 644, 363.

4   Paul Valéry, "Un Coup de dés," *Variété II* (Paris, 1930), p. 180.

5   One of the definitions of "aura" in "The Work of Art in the Age of Mechanical Reproduction," by Walter Benjamin, in *Illuminations*, edited and with an introduction by Hannah Arendt (New York: Schocken, 1969), pp. 217–51.

6   Serge Daney, "Le paradoxe de Godard," *Jean-Luc Godard—le cinéma*, special issue of *Revue Belge du cinéma*, no. 22/23 (second edition,1988), p. 7.

7   Mallarmé, 360–68, 455–56. On this work on number in *Un Coup de dés*, ed., Mitsou Ronat, "Cette architecture spontanée et magique," in her edition of Mallarmé's poem (Paris: Change Errant/d'atelier, 1980).

8   Jean-Paul Fargier, "Le Théâtre de l'instant," *Cahiers du Cinéma*, "Spécial Godard," supplement to no. 437 (November 1990).

9   *JLG*, 382.

10   Mallarmé, 363–64, 456, 663–64.

11   Maurice Blanchot, *Le Livre à venir* (Paris: Gallimard, 1959). See in particular "La Mort du dernier écrivain."

12   See Jacques Aumont, "Godard peintre," *Jean-Luc Godard—le cinéma*, special issue of *Revue Belge du cinéma*, no. 22/23 (1989), second edition; and Jacques Aumont, "Lumière de la musique," *Cahiers du Cinéma*, "Spécial Godard," supplement to no. 437 (November 1990).

13   Mallarmé, 456.

14   *JLG*, 287.

15   Gilles Deleuze, *L'Image-Temps* (Paris: Editions du Minuit, 1985), chapter 9. The quotations that follow can be found on pages 298, 319, 325.

16   *JLG*, 412–16, 408.

17   *L'Image-Temps*, 364–65.

18 "The only film I really want to make I will never make, because it is impossible. It is a film on love, or about love, or with love. To speak in the mouth, to touch the breast, for women, to imagine and see the man's body, his sex, to caress a shoulder, things as difficult to show and hear as horror, and war, and illness." (1966)—*JLG*, 294–95.

19 *Puissance de la parole.* English text from *Poe: Poetry and Tales,* ed. Patrick F. Quinn (New York: The Library of America, Literary Classics of the United States, 1984), p. 825.

20 Maurice Blanchot, *L'Entretien infini* (Paris: Gallimard, 1969), pp. 35–45, 41.

21 *JLG*, 286–87.

22 Roland Barthes, "Le Dernier des écrivains heureux," in *Essais critiques* (Paris: Le Seuil, 1964), pp. 94–100.

23 Mallarmé, 664, 481.

24 Maurice Blanchot, *La Part de feu* (Paris: Gallimard, 1949).

25 Jacques Aumont and Anne-Marie Faux, interview with Jean-Marie Straub and Danièle Huillet, *La Mort d'Empédocle* (Dunkerque: A bruit secret, 1987), p. 39.

26 "Jean-Luc Godard: la curiosité du sujet," interview with Dominique Païni and Guy Scarpetta, *Art Press*, special issue on Godard (1985), p. 14.

27 Among his innumerable axioms, there are the following:
"The cinema is a laboratory of life. Everything can be found there: relations of production, hatreds, loves, parent–child relations, worker–boss relations. And beyond all that, it's creating an artistic commodity. It's the paradise of being able to study life as you're living it." *JLG*, 449.
"The cinema is life, and I would really love to live life as I do cinema." *JLG*, 409.
The title of Alain Bergala's interview with Godard, which introduces the book, is "Art Taken from Life."

28 "What needs to be done is to show everything in unbroken continuity, which would make a film at least nine and a half months long. . . ." *Art Press*, special issue on Godard (1985), p.12.
"I would love it if there were a single television program that stretched on and on and continued uninterrupted, and never stopped." *JLG*, 458.

29 *JLG*, 467–68, 471, 450.

30 Mallarmé, 646.

31 Gilles Deleuze, "Trois questions sur *Six fois deux*," *Cahiers du Cinéma*, no. 271 (November 1976). Reissued in Gilles Deleuze, *Pourparlers* (Paris: Editions du Minuit), p. 55, and reprinted in this volume, pp. 34–41.

32 *JLG*, 288.

33 *JLG*, 503.

34 Gottfried Benn, "Le Problème du génie," in *Un Poète et le monde* (Paris: Gallimard, 1965), pp. 108–10.

35 "Invention, or creation, is always an analogical thing. Maybe that will change. Digital interests me as a thing in itself, or as a technique, but not as a ground for creation. Otherwise, the digital becomes the foundation and the analogical disappears." *JLG*, 604.

36 *JLG*, 608. Emphasis added.

37 The "silent" cinema that has never really existed as such is the one Henri Langlois used to show at the Cinémathèque Française: without music and often minus intertitles (he never cut them out of his prints, as legend has it, but he disliked them and was reluctant to include them among newly struck prints).

38 *La Part du feu*, 620–36, and especially 631.

39 Nicephorus, *Discours contre les iconoclastes*, translated and introduced by Marie-José Mondzain-Baudinet (Paris: Klincksieck, 1989), particularly pages 19, 26.

40 "I need an other so as not to be afraid of the image of myself," *JLG*, 511.

41 "Sur *La Philosophie (à Dorothea)*," in Philippe Lacoue-Labarthe and Jean-Luc Nancy, eds., *L'Absolu littéraire—théorie de la littérature du romantisme allemand* (Paris: Seuil, 1978), particularly pages 224–47; and Friedrich Schlegel, *Lucinde*, ed. Jean-Jacques Abstett (Paris: Aubier-Flammarion, 1971).

42 Serge Daney, "Le Thérrorisé (pédagogie godardienne)," *Cahiers du Cinéma*, no. 262–63 (January 1976), p. 40.

43 Maurice Blanchot, *L'Espace littéraire* (Paris: Gallimard, 1955), pp. 179–84.

44 This is the caption chosen by Godard for one of the photos illustrating his interview with Serge Daney on the subject of *Histoire(s) du cinéma*: "Godard fait des histoires," *Libération* (December 26, 1988), and reprinted in this volume, pp. 158–67.

LIST OF WORKS

Titles are listed in their original version first, followed by alternate titles, if any, in parentheses. English-language release titles appear in brackets. Dates given are, to the best of our knowledge, and following international archival practice, those of the first theatrical release, which might have been a festival premiere or a television broadcast. Two examples: *A bout de souffle*, which was filmed in August–September 1959, premiered in Paris in March 1960, and is accordingly dated; chapters 1A and 1B of *Histoire(s) du cinéma* were produced in 1988, and aired on French television in 1989, the date listed in this volume.

Opération Béton 1954. Pr co: Actua-Films. Pr, Dir & Sc: Jean-Luc Godard. Dir of ph: Adrien Porchet. Ed: Jean-Luc Godard. Mus: Handel and Bach. 35mm. 17 min.

Une Femme coquette 1955. Pr co: Jean-Luc Godard. Pr & Dir: Jean-Luc Godard. Sc: Hans Lucas (pseudonym for Jean-Luc Godard); based on the story "Le Signe" by Guy de Maupassant. Dir of ph & Ed: Hans Lucas. Mus: Bach. With: Marie Lysandre, Roland Tolma, Jean-Luc Godard. 16mm. 10 min.

Tous les garçons s'appellent Patrick (*Charlotte et Véronique*) [*All Boys Are Called Patrick*] 1957. Pr co: Les Films de la Pléiade. Pr: Pierre Braunberger. Dir: Jean-Luc Godard. Sc: Eric Rohmer. Dir of ph: Michel Latouche. Ed: Cécile Decugis. Sd: Jacques Maumont. Mus: Beethoven, Pierre Monsigny. With: Jean-Claude Brialy, Anne Colette, Nicole Berger. 35mm. 21 min.

Une Histoire d'eau 1958. Pr co: Les Films de la Pléiade. Pr: Pierre Braunberger. Dir: Jean-Luc Godard and François Truffaut. Sc: François Truffaut. Dir of ph: Michel Latouche. Ed: Jean-Luc Godard. Sd: Jacques Maumont. With: Jean-Claude Brialy, Caroline Dim, Jean-Luc Godard (narrator). 35mm. 18 min.

Charlotte et son jules 1959. Pr co: Les Films de la Pléiade. Pr: Pierre Braunberger. Dir: Jean-Luc Godard. Sc: Jean-Luc Godard. Dir of ph: Michel Latouche. Ed: Cécile Decugis. Sd: Jacques Maumont. Mus: Pierre Monsigny. With: Jean-Paul Belmondo (dubbed by Jean-Luc Godard), Anne Colette, Gérard Blain. 35mm. 20 min.

A bout de souffle [*Breathless*] 1960. Pr co: Société Nouvelle de Cinéma. Pr: Georges de Beauregard. Dir: Jean-Luc Godard. Asst dir: Pierre Rissient. Sc: Jean-Luc Godard; based on an idea by François Truffaut. Dir of ph: Raoul Coutard. Ed: Cécile Decugis, Lila Herman. Sd: Jacques Maumont. Mus: Martial Solal, Mozart. With: Jean Seberg, Jean-Paul Belmondo, Henri-Jacques Huet, Daniel Boulanger. 35mm. 90 min.

Le Petit Soldat 1960. Pr co: Société Nouvelle de Cinéma. Pr: Georges de Beauregard. Dir: Jean-Luc Godard. Asst dir: Francis Cognany. Sc: Jean-Luc Godard. Dir of ph: Raoul Coutard. Ed: Agnès Guillemot, Nadine Marquand, Lila Herman. Sd: Jacques Maumont. Mus: Maurice Leroux. With: Michel Subor, Anna Karina, Henri-Jacques Huet, Paul Beauvais. 35mm. 88 min.

Une Femme est une femme [*A Woman Is a Woman*] 1961. Pr co: Rome-Paris Films/Unidex, Euro International. Pr: Georges de Beauregard, Carlo Ponti. Dir: Jean-Luc Godard. Asst dir: Francis Cognany. Sc: Jean-Luc Godard; based on an idea by Geneviève Cluny. Dir of ph: Raoul Coutard. Ed: Agnès Guillemot, Lila Herman. Sd: Guy Villette. Art dir: Bernard Evein. Mus: Michel Legrand. With: Anna Karina, Jean-Paul Belmondo, Jean-Claude Brialy, Marie Dubois. 35mm. 84 min.

"La Paresse" (sketch in *Les Sept Péchés capitaux*) ["Sloth," sketch in *The Seven Capital Sins*] 1961. Pr co: Les Films Gibe/Franco-London Films/Titanus. Dir: Jean-Luc Godard. Asst dir: Marin Karmitz. Sc: Jean-Luc Godard. Dir of ph: Henri Decae. Ed: Jacques Gaillard. Sd: Jean-Claude Marchetti, Jean Labussière. Mus: Michel Legrand. With: Eddie Constantine, Nicole Mirel. 35mm. 15 min.

Vivre sa vie [*My Life to Live*] 1962. Pr co: Les Films de la Pléiade. Pr: Pierre Braunberger. Dir: Jean-Luc Godard. Asst dir: Bernard Toublanc-Michel, Jean-Paul Savignac. Sc: Jean-Luc Godard; based on documentation from *Où en est la prostitution* by Marcel Sacotte. Dir of ph: Raoul Coutard. Ed: Agnès Guillemot, Lila Lakshmanan. Sd: Guy Villette, Jacques Maumont. Mus: Michel Legrand. With Anna Karina, Sady Rebbot, André S. Labarthe, Peter Kassovitz. 35mm. 85 min.

"Le Nouveau Monde" (sketch in *Rogopag*) 1962. Pr co: Société Lyre/Arco Film. Dir: Jean-Luc Godard. Sc: Jean-Luc Godard. Dir of ph: Jean Rabier. Ed: Agnès Guillemot, Lila Lakshmanan. Sd: Hervé. Mus: Beethoven. With: Alexandra Stewart, Jean-Marc Bory, Jean-André Fieschi, Michel Delahaye. 35mm. 20 min.

Les Carabiniers 1963. Pr co: Rome-Paris Films/Les Films Marceau/Laetitia Films. Pr: Georges de Beauregard, Carlo Ponti. Dir: Jean-Luc Godard. Asst dir: Jean-Paul Savignac, Charles Bitsch. Sc: Jean-Luc Godard, Roberto Rossellini, Jean Gruault; based on the play *I Carabinieri* by Benjamino Joppolo. Dir of ph: Raoul Coutard. Ed: Agnès Guillemot, Lila Lakshmanan. Sd: Jacques Maumont. Art dir: Jean-Jacques Fabre. Mus: Philippe Arthuys. With: Marino Masé, Albert Juross, Geneviève Galéa, Catherine Ribeiro. 35mm. 80 min.

"Le Grand Escroc" (sketch in *Les Plus Belles Escroqueries du monde*) 1963. Pr co: Ulysse Productions/Primex Films/Lux/C.C.F./Vides Cinematografica/Toho/Caesar Film Productie. Pr: Pierre Roustang. Dir: Jean-Luc Godard. Asst dir: Charles Bitsch. Sc: Jean-Luc Godard. Dir of ph: Raoul Coutard. Ed: Agnès Guillemot, Lila Lakshmanan. Sd: Hervé. Mus: Michel Legrand. With: Jean Seberg, Charles Denner, Laszlo Szabo. 35mm. 25 min.

Le Mépris [*Contempt*] 1963. Pr co: Rome-Paris Films/Les Films Concordia/Compagnia Cinematografica Champion. Pr: Georges de

Beauregard, Carlo Ponti, Joseph E. Levine. Dir: Jean-Luc Godard. Asst dir: Charles Bitsch. Sc: Jean-Luc Godard; based on the novel *Il Disprezzo* by Alberto Moravia. Dir of ph: Raoul Coutard. Ed: Agnès Guillemot, Lila Lakshmanan. Sd: William Sivel. Mus: Georges Delerue. With: Brigitte Bardot, Jack Palance, Fritz Lang, Michel Piccoli. 35mm. 105 min.

Bande à part [*Band of Outsiders*] 1964. Pr co: Anouchka Films/Orsay Films. Dir: Jean-Luc Godard. Asst dir: Jean-Paul Savignac. Sc: Jean-Luc Godard; based on the novel *Fool's Gold* by Dolores and Bert Hitchens. Dir of ph: Raoul Coutard. Ed: Agnès Guillemot, Françoise Collin. Sd: René Levert, Antoine Bonfanti. Mus: Michel Legrand. With: Anna Karina, Claude Brasseur, Sami Frey, Louisa Colpeyn. 35mm. 95 min.

Une Femme mariée [*The Married Woman*] 1964. Pr co: Anouchka Films/Orsay Films. Dir: Jean-Luc Godard. Sc: Jean-Luc Godard. Dir of ph: Raoul Coutard. Ed: Agnès Guillemot, Françoise Collin. Sd: Antoine Bonfanti, René Levert. Art dir: Henri Nogaret. Mus: Beethoven, Claude Nougaro. With: Macha Méril, Bernard Noël, Philippe Leroy, Roger Leenhardt. 35mm. 98 min.

Alphaville, une étrange aventure de Lemmy Caution 1965. Pr co: Chaumiane Production/Filmstudio. Pr: André Michelin. Dir: Jean-Luc Godard. Asst dir: Charles Bitsch, Jean-Paul Savignac, Hélène Kalouguine. Sc: Jean-Luc Godard. Dir of ph: Raoul Coutard. Ed: Agnès Guillemot. Sd: René Levert. Mus: Paul Mizraki. With: Eddie Constantine, Anna Karina, Akim Tamiroff, Howard Vernon. 35mm. 98 min.

"Montparnasse-Levallois" (sketch in *Paris vu par . . .*) [*Six in Paris*] 1965. Pr co: Les Films du Losange. Pr: Barbet Schroeder. Dir & Sc: Jean-Luc Godard. Dir of ph: Albert Maysles. Ed: Jacqueline Raynal. Sd: René Levert. With: Joanna Shimkus, Philippe Hiquily, Serge Davri. 16mm, blown up to 35mm. 18 min.

Pierrot le fou 1965. Pr co: Rome-Paris Films/Dino de Laurentiis Cinematografica. Pr: Georges de Beauregard. Dir: Jean-Luc Godard. Asst dir: Philippe Fourastie, Jean-Pierre Léaud. Sc: Jean-Luc Godard; based on the novel *Obsession* by Lionel White. Dir of ph: Raoul Coutard. Ed: Françoise Collin. Sd: René Levert. Art dir: Pierre Guffroy. Mus: Antoine Duhamel. With: Jean-Paul Belmondo, Anna Karina, Dirk Sanders, Raymond Devos. 35mm. 110 min.

Masculin Féminin 1966. Pr co: Anouchka Films/Argos Films/Svensk Filmindustri/Sandrews. Dir: Jean-Luc Godard. Asst dir: Bernard Toublanc-Michel, Jacques Baratier. Sc: Jean-Luc Godard; based on the stories "La Femme de Paul" and "Le Signe" by Guy de Maupassant. Dir of ph: Willy Kurant. Ed: Agnès Guillemot. Sd: René Levert. Mus: Francis Lai, Mozart. With: Jean-Pierre Léaud, Chantal Goya, Marlène Jobert, Michel Debord. 35mm. 110 min.

Made in U.S.A. 1966. Pr co: Rome-Paris Films/Anouchka Films/SEPIC. Pr: Georges de Beauregard. Dir: Jean-Luc Godard. Asst dir: Charles Bitsch, Jean-Pierre Léaud, Claude Bakka, Philippe Pouzenc. Sc: Jean-Luc Godard; based on a novel by Richard Stark. Dir of ph: Raoul Coutard. Ed: Agnès Guillemot. Sd: René Levert, Jacques Maumont. Mus: Beethoven, Schumann, Mick Jagger, Keith Richard. With: Anna Karina, Laszlo Szabo, Jean-Pierre Léaud, Yves Afonso. 35mm. 90 min.

Deux ou Trois Choses que je sais d'elle [*Two or Three Things I Know about Her*] 1966. Pr co: Anouchka Films/Argos Films/Les Films du Carrosse/Parc Film. Dir: Jean-Luc Godard. Asst dir: Charles Bitsch,

Isabelle Pons, Robert Chevassu. Sc: Jean-Luc Godard; suggested by an idea in *Le Nouvel Observateur*. Dir of ph: Raoul Coutard. Ed: Françoise Collin, Chantal Delattre. Sd: René Levert, Antoine Bonfanti. Mus: Beethoven. With: Marina Vlady, Anny Duperey, Roger Montsoret, Raoul Lévy. 35mm. 90 min.

"Anticipation ou l'amour en l'an 2000" (sketch in *Le Plus Vieux Métier du monde*) 1967. Pr co: Francoriz/Les Films Gibé/Rialto Films/Rizzoli Films. Dir: Jean-Luc Godard. Asst dir: Charles Bitsch. Sc: Jean-Luc Godard. Dir of ph: Pierre Lhomme. Ed: Agnès Guillemot. Mus: Michel Legrand. With: Jacques Charrier, Anna Karina, Marilu Tolo, Jean-Pierre Léaud. 35mm. 20 min.

"Caméra-Oeil" (sequence in *Loin du Viêtnam*) 1967. Pr co: S.L.O.N. Dir & Sc: Jean-Luc Godard. Dir of ph: Alain Levent. With commentary by Jean-Luc Godard. 16mm. 15 min.

La Chinoise 1967. Pr co: Anouchka Films/Les Productions de la Guéville/Athos Films/Parc Films/Simar Films. Dir: Jean-Luc Godard. Asst dir: Charles Bitsch. Sc: Jean-Luc Godard. Dir of ph: Raoul Coutard. Ed: Agnès Guillemot, Delphine Desfons. Sd: René Levert. Mus: Stockhausen, Schubert, Vivaldi. With: Anne Wiazemsky, Jean-Pierre Léaud, Michel Semeniako, Lex de Bruijn. 35mm. 96 min.

"L'Aller et retour andate e ritorno des enfants prodigues dei figli prodighi" (sketch in *Amore e rabbia/vangelo 70*) 1967. Pr co: Anouchka Films/Castoro Film. Dir: Jean-Luc Godard. Asst dir: Charles Bitsch. Sc: Jean-Luc Godard. Dir of ph: Alain Levent. Ed: Agnès Guillemot. Sd: Guy Villette. Art dir: Mimmo Scavia. Mus: Giovanni Fusco. With: Nino Castelnuovo, Catherine Jourdan, Christine Guého, Paolo Pozzesi. 35mm. 26 min.

Week-end 1967. Pr co: Films Copernic/Ascot Cineraid/Comacico/Lira Films. Dir: Jean-Luc Godard. Asst dir: Claude Miller. Sc: Jean-Luc Godard. Dir of ph: Raoul Coutard. Ed: Agnès Guillemot. Sd: René Levert. Mus: Antoine Duhamel, Mozart, Guy Béart. With: Mireille Darc, Jean Yanne, Jean-Pierre Kalfon, Jean-Pierre Léaud. 35mm. 95 min.

Le Gai Savoir 1968. Pr co: Anouchka Films/Bavaria Atelier/O.R.T.F./Suddeutschen Rundfunk. Dir & Sc: Jean-Luc Godard. Dir of ph: Georges Leclerc. Ed: Germaine Cohen. Mus: Cuban revolutionary songs. With: Jean-Pierre Léaud, Juliet Berto. 35mm. 95 min.

Ciné-Tracts 1968. (Series of 2-to-4-minute shorts). Pr, Dir, Sc & Ed: Jean-Luc Godard and others. 16mm.

Un Film comme les autres [*A Movie like Any Other*] 1968. Pr co: Anouchka Films. Dir, Sc, Ph & Ed: Jean-Luc Godard and Groupe Dziga Vertov. 16mm. 100 min.

One Plus One (*Sympathy for the Devil*) 1968. Pr co: Cupid Productions, Inc. Dir: Jean-Luc Godard. Asst dir: Tim Van Rellim, John Stoneman. Sc: Jean-Luc Godard. Dir of ph: Anthony Richmond. Ed: Ken Rowles, Agnès Guillemot. Sd: Arthur Bradburn. Mus: The Rolling Stones. With: Anne Wiazemsky, Ian Quarrier, Danny Daniels, The Rolling Stones. 35mm. 99 min.

One American Movie (*One A.M.*) Abandoned during production in 1968; the footage shot, plus footage from a film being made about the original production, were released as *One P.M.* 1971. Pr co: Leacock-Pennebaker. Dir & Sc: Jean-Luc Godard and D.A. Pennebaker. Dir of ph: Richard Leacock, D.A. Pennebaker. Ed: D.A. Pennebaker. With: Richard Leacock, Jean-Luc Godard, Anne Wiazemsky, Eldridge Cleaver. 16mm. 90 min.

British Sounds (*See You at Mao*) 1969. Pr co: Kestrel Productions (for London Weekend Television). Dir: Jean-Luc Godard and Jean-Henri Roger. Dir of ph: Charles Stewart. Ed: Elizabeth Koziman. Sd: Fred Sharp. 16mm. 52 min.

Pravda 1969. Pr co: Centre Européen Cinéma Radio Télévision. Pr: Claude Nedjar. Dir, Sc, Dir of ph, Ed & Sd: Groupe Dziga Vertov (Jean-Luc Godard, Jean-Henri Roger, Paul Burron). 16mm. 58 min.

Vent d'est [*Wind from the East*] 1969. Pr co: Poli Film/Anouchka Films/Kuntz Film. Dir: Groupe Dziga Vertov (Jean-Luc Godard, Jean-Pierre Gorin, Gérard Martin). Sc: Jean-Luc Godard, Daniel Cohn-Bendit, Sergio Bazzini. Dir of ph: Mario Vulpiani. Ed: Jean-Luc Godard, Jean-Pierre Gorin. Sd: Antonio Ventura, Carlo Diotalleri. With: Gian Maria Volonté, Anne Wiazemsky, Paolo Pozzesi, Christiana Tullio Altan. 16mm. 100 min.

Luttes en Italie (*Lotte in Italia*) 1969. Pr co: Cosmoseion for RAI. Dir & Sc: Groupe Dziga Vertov (Jean-Luc Godard, Jean-Pierre Gorin). With: Christiana Tullio Altan, Anne Wiazemsky, Jérôme Hinstin, Paolo Pozzesi. 16mm. 76 min.

Vladimir et Rosa [*Vladimir and Rosa*] 1971. Pr co: Grove Press Evergreen Films/Telepool. Dir, Sc & Dir of ph: Groupe Dziga Vertov (Jean-Luc Godard, Jean-Pierre Gorin). With: Anne Wiazemsky, Jean-Pierre Gorin, Juliet Berto, Ernest Menzer. 16mm. 106 min.

Tout va bien 1972. Pr co: Anouchka Films/Vicco Films/Empire Film. Dir & Sc: Jean-Luc Godard, Jean-Pierre Gorin. Dir of ph: Armand Marco. Ed: Kenout Peltier. Sd: Bernard Ortion, Armand Bonfanti. Art dir: Jacques Dugied. Mus: Eric Charden, Thomas Rivat, Paul Beuscher. With: Yves Montand, Jane Fonda, Vittorio Caprioli, Jean Pignol. 35mm. 95 min.

Letter to Jane 1972. Pr co: Jean-Luc Godard and Jean-Pierre Gorin. Dir & Sc: Jean-Luc Godard and Jean-Pierre Gorin. 16mm. 52 min.

Ici et ailleurs 1974. Pr co: Sonimage/I.N.A. Dir & Sc: Jean-Luc Godard and Anne-Marie Miéville. Dir of ph: William Lubtchansky. Ed: Anne-Marie Miéville. From footage shot in 1970 by Groupe Dziga Vertov as *Jusqu'à la victoire*. 16mm. 60 min.

Numéro deux 1975. Pr co: Sonimage/Bela Prod./S.N.C. Dir: Jean-Luc Godard. Sc: Jean-Luc Godard, Anne-Marie Miéville. Dir of ph: William Lubtchansky. Vid: Gérard Teissedre. Tech collaboration: Milka Assaf, Gérard Martin. Sd: Jean-Pierre Ruh. Mus: Leo Ferré. With: Sandrine Battistella, Pierre Oudry, Alexandre Rignault, Rachel Stefanopoli. 35mm and video. 88 min.

Comment ça va 1976. Pr co: Sonimage/I.N.A./Bela Prod./S.N.C. Dir & Sc: Jean-Luc Godard and Anne-Marie Miéville. Dir of ph: William Lubtchansky. Mus: Jean Schwartz. With: Anne-Marie Miéville, M. Marot. 16mm. 78 min.

Six fois deux/Sur et sous la communication 1976. Part 1: Ya personne/Louison. Part 2: Leçons de choses/Jean-Luc. Part 3: Photo et cie/Marcel. Part 4: Pas d'histoires/Nanas. Part 5: Nous trois/René(e)s. Part 6: Avant et après/Jacqueline et Ludovic. Pr co: Sonimage/I.N.A. Dir, Sc & Ed: Jean-Luc Godard and Anne-Marie Miéville. Dir of ph: William Lubtchansky, Gérard Teissedre. Technical collaboration: Dominique Chapuis, Philippe Rony, Henri False, Joël Mellier, Louisette Neil. Video. Six parts, 100 min. each.

France/tour/détour/deux/enfants 1977–78. Program 1: Obscur/Chimie. Program 2: Lumière/Physique. Program 3: Connu/Géométrie/Géo-graphie. Program 4: Inconnu/Technique. Program 5: Impression/Dictée. Program 6: Expression/Français. Program 7: Violence/Grammaire. Program 8: Désordre/Calcul. Program 9: Pouvoir/Musique. Program 10: Roman/Economie. Program 11: Réalité/Logique. Program 12: Rêve/Morale. Pr co: I.N.A. for Antenne 2/Sonimage (Grenoble). Dir & Sc: Jean-Luc Godard and Anne-Marie Miéville. Dir of ph: Pierre Binggeli, William Lubtchansky, Dominique Chapuis, Philippe Rony. With: Camille Virolleaud, Arnaud Martin, Betty Berr, Albert Dray. Video. Twelve 26-min. broadcasts.

Scénario de Sauve qui peut (la vie) 1979. Pr: JLG Films. Dir: Jean-Luc Godard. Video. 20 min.

Sauve qui peut (la vie) [*Every Man for Himself*] 1979. Pr co: Sara Films/MK2/Saga Production/Sonimage/C.N.C./Z.D.F./S.S.R./O.R.F. Dir: Jean-Luc Godard. Sc: Anne-Marie Miéville, Jean-Claude Carrière. Dir of ph: William Lubtchansky, Renato Berta, Jean-Bernard Menoud. Ed: Jean-Luc Godard, Anne-Marie Miéville. Sd: Jacques Maumont, Luc Yersin, Oscar Stellavox. Mus: Gabriel Yared. With: Isabelle Huppert, Jacques Dutronc, Nathalie Baye, Cécile Tanner, Roland Amstutz. 35mm. 87 min.

Lettre à Freddy Buache 1981. Pr co: Film et Vidéo Productions. Dir & Sc: Jean-Luc Godard. Dir of ph: Jean-Bernard Menoud. Ed: Jean-Luc Godard. Sd: François Musy. In collaboration with Pierre Binggeli, Gérard Rucy. Mus: Ravel. Video transferred to 35 mm. 11 min.

"Changer d'image" (sequence for the broadcast *Le Changement a plus d'un titre*) 1982. Dir: Jean-Luc Godard. With: Jean-Luc Godard. Video. 9 min.

Passion 1982. Pr co: Sara Films/Sonimage/Films A2/Film et Vidéo Production SA/S.S.R. Dir, Sc & Ed: Jean-Luc Godard. Dir of ph: Raoul Coutard. Sd: François Musy. Mus: Mozart, Dvorak, Ravel, Beethoven, Fauré. With: Isabelle Huppert, Hanna Schygulla, Michel Piccoli, Jerzy Radziwilowicz, Laszlo Szabo. 35mm. 87 min.

Scénario du film Passion 1982. Pr co: JLG Films/Studio Trans-Vidéo/Télévision Suisse Romande. Dir: Jean-Luc Godard in collaboration with Jean-Bernard Menoud, Anne-Marie Miéville, Pierre Binggeli. Video. 54 min.

Prénom Carmen [*First Name: Carmen*] 1983. Pr co: Sara Films/Jean-Luc Godard Films. Dir: Jean-Luc Godard. Sc: Anne-Marie Miéville. Dir of ph: Raoul Coutard, Jean Garcenot. Ed: Suzanne Lang-Villar, Jean-Luc Godard. Sd: François Musy. Mus: Beethoven, Tom Waits. With: Maruschka Detmers, Jacques Bonnaffé, Myriem Roussel, Christophe Odent. 35mm. 85 min.

Petites Notes à propos du film Je vous salue Marie 1983. Pr: JLG Films. Dir: Jean-Luc Godard. With: Jean-Luc Godard, Myriem Roussel, Thierry Rode, Anne-Marie Miéville. Video. 25 min.

Je vous salue Marie [*Hail Mary*] 1985. Pr co: Pégase Films/S.S.R./JLG Films/Sara Films/Channel 4. Dir & Sc: Jean-Luc Godard. Dir of ph: Jean-Bernard Menoud, Jacques Firmann. Ed: Anne-Marie Miéville. Sd: François Musy. Mus: Bach, Dvorak, Coltrane. With: Myriem Roussel, Thierry Rode, Philippe Lacoste, Anne Gauthier, Manon Andersen. 35mm. 72 min.

Détective 1985. Pr co: Sara Films/JLG Films. Dir: Jean-Luc Godard. Asst dir: Rénald Calcagni. Sc: Alain Sarde, Philippe Setbon, Anne-Marie Miéville. Dir of ph: Bruno Nuytten. Ed: Marilyne Dubreuil. Sd: Pierre Gamet, François Musy. Mus: Schubert, Wagner, Chopin, Liszt, Honegger, Chabrier, Ornette Coleman, Jean Schwarz. With:

Nathalie Baye, Claude Brasseur, Stéphane Ferrara, Johnny Hally-day, Jean-Pierre Léaud, Laurent Terzieff. 35mm. 95 min.

Grandeur et décadence d'un petit commerce de cinéma 1986. Pr co: TF1, "Série Noire"/Hamster Prod./JLG Films. Dir & Sc: Jean-Luc Godard. Asst dir: Rénald Calcagni, Richard Debuisne, Marie-Christine Barrière. Dir of ph: Caroline Champetier, Serge Le François. Sd: François Musy, Pierre-Alain Besse. Mus: Bela Bartok, Leonard Cohen, Bob Dylan, Janis Joplin, Joni Mitchell. With: Jean-Pierre Léaud, Jean-Pierre Mocky, Marie Valera. 16mm. 52 min.

Soft and Hard (A Soft Conversation between Two Friends on a Hard Subject) 1986. Pr co: JLG Films/Channel 4. Dir: Jean-Luc Godard and Anne-Marie Miéville. With Jean-Luc Godard, Anne-Marie Miéville. Video. 48 min.

J.L.G. Meets W.A./Meetin' WA 1986. Pr co: Jean-Luc Godard. Dir: Jean-Luc Godard. With Woody Allen, Jean-Luc Godard. Video. 26 min.

"Armide" (sequence for *Aria*) 1987. Pr co: Lightyear Entertainment/Virgin Vision. Pr: Don Boyd. Assoc pr: François Hamel. Dir: Jean-Luc Godard. Asst dir: Rénald Calcagni, Jacques Lobeleux. Dir of ph: Caroline Champetier. Ed: Jean-Luc Godard. Mus: Jean-Baptiste Lully (aria "Enfin, il est en ma puissance"), sung by Rachel Yakar, Zeger Wandersteene, Danièle Borst. With: Marion Peterson, Valérie Allain, Jaques Neuville, Luke Corre. 35mm. 12 min.

King Lear 1987. Pr co: Cannon Films (Golan-Globus). Dir & Sc: Jean-Luc Godard. Dir of ph: Sophie Maintigneux. Ed: Jean-Luc Godard. Sd: François Musy. With: Burgess Meredith, Peter Sellars, Molly Ringwald, Woody Allen, Léos Carax. 35mm. 90 min.

Soigne ta droite [*Keep up Your Right*] 1987. Pr co: Gaumont/JLG Films/Xanadu Films. Dir & Sc: Jean-Luc Godard. Asst dir: Richard Debuisne, Marie-Christine Barrière, Rénald Calcagni, Hervé Duhamel, Guindollet, Benoît, Menidrey. Dir of ph: Caroline Champetier de Ribes. Ed: Jean-Luc Godard. Sd: François Musy. Mus: Rita Mitsouko. With: Jean-Luc Godard, Jacques Villeret, Philippe Rouleau, François Périer, Jane Birkin. 35mm. 82 min.

On s'est tous défilé 1988. Pr: JLG Films. Video. 13 min.

Puissance de la parole 1988. Pr co: Gaumont/JLG Films/France Télécom. Dir: Jean-Luc Godard. Dir of ph: Caroline Champetier, Pierre-Alain Besse. Sd: François Musy, Pierre-Alain Besse, Marc-Antoine Beldent. Mus: Bach, Bob Dylan, Beethoven, Cage, Richard Strauss, Franck, Ravel, Leonard Cohen. With: Jean Bouise, Laurence Cote, Lydia Andrei, Michel Iribarren. Video. 25 min.

"Le Dernier Mot"/"Les Français entendus par" (for the broadcast series *Les Français vus par*) 1988. Pr: Anne-Marie Miéville, Hervé Duhamel, Marie-Christine Barrière/Erato Films/Socpresse/Le Figaro/JLG Films. Dir: Jean-Luc Godard. Dir of ph: Pierre Bingelli. Sd: Pierre Camus, Raoul Fruhauf, François Musy. Mus: Bach. With: André Marcon, Hans Zichter, Catherine Aymerie, Pierre Amoyal. Video. 13 min.

Histoire(s) du cinéma 1989–. Program 1: "Toutes les histoires," "Une Histoire seule." Pr co: Gaumont/JLG Films/La Sept/FR 3/Centre National de la Cinématographie/Radio Télévision Suisse Romande/Véga Films. Dir, Sc & Ed: Jean-Luc Godard. Video. 100 min.

Le Rapport Darty 1989. Dir. Jean-Luc Godard and Anne-Marie Miéville. Video. 50 min.

Nouvelle Vague 1990. Pr co: Sara Films/Périphéria/Canal +/Véga Films/Télévision Suisse Romande/Films A2/C.N.C./Sofia Investimage/Sofia Créations. Dir & Sc: Jean-Luc Godard. Dir of ph: William Lubtchansky. Ed: Jean-Luc Godard. Sd: François Musy. Art dir: Anne-Marie Miéville. With: Alain Delon, Domiziana Giordano, Roland Amstutz, Laurence Cote. 35mm. 89 min.

"L'Enfance de l'art" (sequence for the film *Comment vont les enfants/How Are the Kids*) 1990. Pr: JLG Films/UNICEF. Dir & Sc: Jean-Luc Godard and Anne-Marie Miéville. 35mm. 8 min.

Allemagne année 90 neuf zéro [*Germany Year 90 Nine Zero*] 1991. Pr co: Antenne 2/Brainstorm Production. Dir & Sc: Jean-Luc Godard. Dir of ph: Christophe Pollock, Andréas Erben, Stépan Benda. Sd: Pierre-Alain Besse, François Musy. Art dir: Romain Goupil. Mus: Bryars, Scelsi, Liszt, Mozart, Bach, Stravinsky, Hindemith, Beethoven, Shostakovitch. With: Eddie Constantine, Hanns Zischler, Claudia Michelsen, André Labarthe, Nathalie Kadem. 35mm. 62 min.

Hélas pour moi (in production). Pr co: Les Films Alain Sarde/Véga Films. Dir: Jean-Luc Godard. With: Gérard Depardieu. 35 mm.

SELECTED BIBLIOGRAPHY

Compiled by
RONALD MAGLIOZZI

The following is a selective bibliography that focuses largely but not exclusively on material published in French and English since 1970. Further bibliographic information may be found in *The International Dictionary of Films and Filmmakers. Vol. 2, Directors/Filmmakers* (Chicago: St. James, 1991).

Books

Bellour, R. *L'Entre-Images: Photo. Cinéma. Vidéo*. Paris: La Différence, 1990.

Braudy, L., and M. Dickstein, eds. *Great Film Directors: A Critical Anthology*. New York: Oxford University Press, 1978.

Brown, R. S. *Focus on Godard*. Englewood Cliffs, N.J.: Prentice-Hall, 1972.

Cameron, I. *The Films of Jean-Luc Godard*. New York: Praeger, 1969.

Cerisuelo, M. *Jean-Luc Godard*. Paris: Lherminier/Quatre-Vents, 1989.

Collet, J. *Jean-Luc Godard: An Investigation into His Films and Philosophy*. New York: Crown, 1970.

————. *Jean-Luc Godard*. Rev. ed. by J. Collet and P. Fargier, Paris: Editions Séghers, 1974.

Deleuze, G. *L'Image-Temps*. Paris: Editions de Minuit, 1985.

Desbarats, C., and J-P. Gorce. *L'Effet-Godard*. Toulouse: Milan, 1989.

Estève, M., ed. *Jean-Luc Godard au-delà du récit*. Paris: Lettres Modernes, Collection Etudes Cinématographiques, 1967.

Giannetti, L. D. *Godard and Others—Essays on Film Form*. Rutherford, N.J.: Fairleigh Dickinson University Press, 1975.

Gibern, R. *Godard polémico*. Barcelona: Tusquets Editor, 1969.

Godard, J-L. *Godard on Godard*. Trans. and ed. T. Milne and J. Narboni. New York: Da Capo, 1986. Translations of texts by Godard from 1950 to 1968.

————. *Introduction à une véritable histoire du cinéma*. Paris: Editions Albatros, 1977.

————. *Jean-Luc Godard par Jean-Luc Godard*. Ed. A. Bergala. Paris: Cahiers du Cinéma/Editions de L'Etoile, 1985.

Goldmann, A. *Cinéma et société moderne*. Paris: Editions Anthropos, 1971.

Goodwin, M., and G. Marcus. *Double Feature*. New York: Outerbridge and Lazard, 1972.

Harcourt, P. *Six European Directors: Essays on the Meaning of Film Style*. Baltimore: Penguin, 1974.

Henderson, B. *A Critique of Film Theory*. New York: Dutton, 1980.

Kawin, B. F. *Mindscreen: Bergman, Godard and First-Person Film*. Princeton, N.J.: Princeton University Press, 1978.

Kreidl, J. *Jean-Luc Godard*. Boston: Twayne, 1980.

Lesage, J. *Jean-Luc Godard: A Guide to References and Resources*. Boston: G. K. Hall, 1979.

MacBean, J. R. *Film and Revolution*. Bloomington: Indiana University Press, 1975.

MacCabe, C. *Godard: Images, Sounds, Politics*. Bloomington: Indiana University Press, 1980.

Mancini, M. *Godard*. Rome: Trevi Editore, 1969.

Monaco, J. *The New Wave: Truffaut, Godard, Chabrol, Rohmer, Rivette*. New York: Oxford University Press, 1976.

Moulds, M., and others, ed. *1972–1990 International Index to Film Periodicals: An Annotated Guide*. 19 vols. London: International Federation of Film Archives.

Mussman, T., ed. *Jean-Luc Godard: A Critical Anthology*. New York: E. P. Dutton, 1968.

Roud, R. *Godard*. Rev. ed. Bloomington: Indiana University Press, 1970.

Toffatti, S., ed. *Jean-Luc Godard*. Turin: Centre Culturel Français de Turin, 1990.

Wollen, P. *Readings and Writings*. London: Verso, 1982.

Periodicals—Special Issues and Sections

"Spécial Godard." *Art Press* (Paris) 4 (Dec. 1984–Jan./Feb. 1985).

"Spécial Godard." *Avant-Scène* 323-324 (Mar. 1984). Includes scripts for *Prénom Carmen*, *Lettre à Freddy Buache*, *Scénario du film Passion*, and *Opération Béton*.

"Passion." *Avant-Scène* 380 (Apr. 1989). Includes script and critical commentary.

"Nouvelle Vague." *Avant-Scène* 396-397 (Nov.–Dec. 1990). Includes script for *Nouvelle Vague* and French film review extracts.

"Spécial Godard—Trente Ans depuis." *Cahiers du Cinéma* (Paris) (Nov. 1990).

Camera Obscura 8-9-10 (Fall 1982).

"Le Cinéma selon Godard." *CinémAction* 52 (July 1989).

"Dossier: Jean-Luc Godard." *Cinématographe* (Paris) 95 (Dec. 1983). On release of *Prénom Carmen*.

"Jean-Luc Godard: Le Cinéma." *Revue Belge du Cinéma* (Brussels) no. 22/23 (1988).

[Jean-Luc Godard] *Wide Angle* I/3 (1976), pp. 4–52. On methods of communication in various films.

Articles and Essays

Adair, G. "Gilbert Adair from London." *Film Comment* XVII/3 (May–June 1981), pp. 4, 6. On *Six fois deux/Sur et sous la communication* and *France/tour/détour/deux/enfants*.

Baron, A-M., and S. Garel. "Nouvelle Vague." *Cinéma* (Paris) 468 (June 1990), pp. 8–10. On press conference for *Nouvelle Vague*.

Bassan, R. "Jean-Luc Godard." *Revue du Cinéma* 390 (Jan. 1984), pp. 25–30. On theme of prostitution and *Prénom Carmen*.

Bergala, A. "Enfants: Ralentir." *Cahiers du Cinéma* 301 (June 1979), pp. 28–33. On *France/tour/détour/deux/enfants*.

Bergala, A., and L. Carax. "Jean-Luc Godard: *Sauve qui peut (la vie)*: Une Journée de tournage." *Cahiers du Cinéma* 306 (Dec. 1979), pp. 32–37.

Bergala, A., S. Daney, and S. Toubiana. "En attendant *Passion*: Le Chemin vers la parole." *Cahiers du Cinéma* 336 (May 1982), pp. 5–14, 57–60, 62–63.

Biette, J-C. "L'Encrier de la modernité." *Cahiers du Cinéma* 375 (Sept. 1985), pp. x–xi.

———. "Godard et son histoire du cinéma." *Cahiers du Cinéma* 327 (Sept. 1981), pp. v–vi. On film study courses given by Godard.

Bonitzer, P. "Jean-Marie Straub et Jean-Luc Godard." *Cahiers du Cinéma* 264 (Feb. 1976), pp. 5–10.

Bougut, M. "Voir un scénario." *Avant-Scène* 323-324 (Mar. 1984), pp. 77–89. On process of editing *Scénario du film Passion*; includes script.

Buache, F. "De Godard à Jean-Luc." *Revue du Cinéma* 14 (Winter 1985), pp. 50–62. On work since 1980.

Burgoyne, R. "The Political Topology of Montage: The Conflict of Genres in the Films of Godard." *Enclitic* VII/1 (Spring 1983), pp. 14–23. On montage, narrative, and signals.

Ciment, M. "Je vous salue Godard." *Positif* 324 (Feb. 1988), pp. 31–33. On Godard as modern jester, especially in *Soigne ta droite*.

Daney, S. "Le Thérrorisé (pédagogie godardienne)." *Cahiers du Cinéma* 262–263 (Jan. 1976), pp. 32–39. On work since 1968.

Durgnat, R. "Jean-Luc Godard: His Crucifixion and Resurrection." *Monthly Film Bulletin* LII/620 (Sept. 1985), pp. 268–71. On themes and periods of work.

Forbes, J. "Jean-Luc Godard: 2 into 3." *Sight and Sound* L/1 (Winter 1980/81), pp. 40–45. On *Sauve qui peut (la vie)* in the context of his video work.

Fox, T. C. "Looking for Mr. Godard." *The Village Voice*, Oct. 31, 1977, pp. 1, 41. On *Ici et ailleurs*, *Comment ça va*, and *Numéro deux* in the context of earlier work.

Gervais, M. "Jean-Luc Godard 1985: These Are Not the Days." *Sight and Sound* LIV/4 (Autumn 1985), pp. 278–83. On *Je vous salue Marie* and *Détective* in the context of earlier work.

Giavarini, L. "A l'ouest le crépuscule." *Cahiers du Cinéma* 449 (Nov. 1991). On *Allémagne année 90 neuf zéro*.

Giles, D. "Godard and Ideology." *Film Reader* 2 (Jan. 1977), pp. 169–78. On ideology in work since 1968.

Godard, J-L. "Colles et ciseaux." *Cahiers du Cinéma* 402 (Dec. 1987), pp. 14–19. On *Soigne ta droite*.

———. "La 9ème Symphonie." *Cahiers du Cinéma* 400, supplement (Oct. 1987), pp. 28–29. Illustrated letter of influential images.

———. "Les Dernières leçons du donneur." *Cahiers du Cinéma* 300 (May 1979), pp. 60–66. On concepts of cinema and TV.

Hachem, S. "Jean-Luc Godard, the Rebel without a Pause, Is Searching for a New Cinema Grammar." *Millimeter* IX/9 (Sept. 1981), pp. 187–88, 190–92.

Henderson, B. "Godard on Godard: Notes for a Reading." *Film Quarterly* XXVII/4 (Summer 1974), pp. 34–46. On Godard as a film critic.

Hoberman, J. "He-e-ere's Jean-ee: TV à la Godard." *The Village Voice*, Apr. 28, 1986, pp. 45–46. On the video works.

Hughes, J. "Atlantic City: John Hughes on Godard's *Made in U.S.A.*" *Film Comment* XIII/2 (Mar.–Apr. 1977), pp. 53–55. On transition to "post-Mao" period.

Kaplan, E. A., and J. Halley. "One Plus One: Ideology and Deconstruction in Godard's *Ici et ailleurs* and *Comment ça va*." *Millennium Film Journal* 6 (Spring 1980), pp. 98–102.

Lefèvre, R. "Je vous salue Myriem (Roussel)." *Revue du Cinéma* 404 (Apr. 1985), pp. 6–7.

———. "La Lettre et le cinématographe: L'Ecrit dans les films de Godard." *Image & Son* 317 (May 1977), pp. 75–82. On the use of text in films.

Lesage, J. "Looking at a Film Politically." *Jump Cut* 4 (Nov.–Dec. 1974), pp. 18–21. On *Vent d'est*.

Loshitzky, Y. "More than Style: Bertolucci's Postmodernism versus Godard's Modernism." *Criticism* XXXIV/1 (Winter 1992), pp. 119–42. On cinematic style in the early films.

Lovell, A. "Epic Theater and Counter Cinema." *Jump Cut* 28 (Apr. 1983), pp. 49–51. On Brechtian theory and Godard's work.

MacBean, J. R. "Filming the Inside of His Own Head: Godard's Cerebral *Passion*." *Film Quarterly* XXXVIII/1 (Fall 1984), pp. 16–24. On *Passion* and images from famous paintings.

———. "Godard and the Dziga Vertov Group: Film and Dialectics." *Film Quarterly* XXVI/1 (Fall 1972), pp. 30–44. On *Pravda*, *Lotte in Italia*, and *Vladimir et Rosa*.

Merrill, M. "Black Panthers in the New Wave." *Film Culture* 53-54-55 (Spring 1972), pp. 134–45. On *One Plus One* and the Black Power Movement.

Monaco, J. "Godard, Jean-Luc." In *World Film Directors. Vol. Two: 1945–1985*, pp. 392–400. New York: H. W. Wilson Company, 1988. Biographical essay, filmography, and bibliography.

Naremore, J. "Authorship and the Cultural Politics of Film Criticism." *Film Quarterly* XLIV/1 (Fall 1990), pp. 14–22. On the influence of his writing on film.

Neupert, R. "444,000 Images Speak for Themselves." *Wide Angle* IX/1 (1987), pp. 50–58. On photographic language and its code systems in his work.

Nicholls, D. "Godard's *Weekend*: Totem, Taboo, and the Fifth Republic." *Sight and Sound* XLIX/1 (Winter 1979/80), pp. 22–24. On *Weekend* in the context of other film and video work.

O'Pray, M. "The History of a Sign." *Monthly Film Bulletin* LVI/670 (Nov. 1989), pp. 327–28. On his influence on the British avant-garde.

Païni, D. "Cinéma prénom musique." *Cahiers du Cinéma* 356 (Feb. 1984), pp. vi–vii. On Godard's new definition of cinema.

Peary, G. "Jane Fonda on Tour: Answering *Letter to Jane*." *Take One* IV/4 (July 1974), pp. 24–26.

Poulle, F. "Sur les quatre Godard de la période chair de femme." *Jeune Cinéma* 166 (Apr. 1985), pp. 21–26. On *Passion*, *Prénom Carmen*, *Je vous salue Marie*, and *Sauve qui peut (la vie)*.

Powers, J. "Channel Crossings." *Los Angeles Reader*, Sept. 13, 1985, pp. 22, 25. On the U.S. premiere of the video work.

———. "*One Plus One*." *Los Angeles Reader*, Jan. 13, 1989, pp. 10, 12. On the radical nature of Godard's work in relation to contemporary African-American culture.

Prédal, R. "La Troisième 'Epoque' de Jean-Luc Godard." *Jeune Cinéma* 101 (Mar. 1977), pp. 23–26. On work since 1973.

———. "Godard, la télévision dans le cinéma." *CinémAction* 44 (June 1987), pp. 149–53. On combining film and television.

Prieur, J. and A. Bergala. [*France/tour/détour/deux/enfants*] *Cahiers du Cinéma* 301 (June 1979), pp. 24–33.

Quenin, F. "Canal + de Godard." *Cinéma* (Paris) 444 (June 1, 1988), pp. 19. On *Histoire(s) du cinéma*.

Rodchenko, H. A. "Bluejean-Luc Godard." *Film Comment* XXIII/6 (Nov.–Dec. 1987), pp. 2, 4. On ads made for French television.

Rosenbaum, J. "Jean-Luc, Chantal, Danièle, Jean-Marie and the Others." *American Film* IV/4 (Feb. 1979), pp. 5256. On French art cinema.

Roud, R. "Godard Is Dead, Long Live Godard/Gorin, *Tout va bien*!" *Sight and Sound* XVI/3 (Summer 1972), pp. 122–24.

———. "Jean-Luc Godard." In *Cinéma, a Critical Dictionary: The Major Film-makers, Vol. 1*, pp. 436–46. Edited by Richard Roud. New York: Viking, 1980. Critical biography.

Rowe, K. K. "Romanticism, Sexuality, and the Canon." *Journal of Film and Video* XLII/1 (Spring 1990), pp. 49–65. On treatment of women in *Passion*, *Je vous salue Marie*, and *Soft and Hard*.

Sarris, A. "Films in Focus: Godard and the Revolution." *The Village Voice*, Apr. 30, 1970, pp. 53, 61, 63–64. On the political content of his recent work.

Ségal, A. "Les Films 'invisibles' 1968–1972." *Avant-Scène* 171-172 (July–Sept. 1976), pp. 46–70. On the Dziga Vertov Group films.

Simon, J-P. "Les Signes et leur maître." *Ça* III/9 (1976), pp. 27–36. On *Ici et ailleurs*.

Sontag, S. "Godard." In *Styles of Radical Will*, pp. 147–85. New York: Farrar, Straus and Giroux, 1969.

Stam, R. "Jean-Luc Godard's *Sauve qui peut (la vie)*." *Millennium Film Journal*, nos. 10/11 (Fall/Winter 1981–82), pp. 194–99.

———. "*Numéro Deux*: Politics, Pornography and the Media." *Millennium Film Journal* 3 (Winter/Spring 1979), pp. 72–78.

Thomson, D. "The Great Godard: Films That Leave You Breathless." *The Boston Phoenix*, Mar. 4, 1980, section three, pp. 1, 3, 12, 14. On his place in film culture.

Walsh, M. "Godard and Me: Jean-Pierre Gorin Talks." *Take One* V/1 (Feb. 1976), pp. 14–17. On *Tout va bien*.

Weber, A. "Nouvelle Vague et nouveaux courants." *CinémAction* 23 (Nov. 1982), pp. 84–95. On the ideological nature of editing practiced by Nouvelle Vague filmmakers.

Whitaker, S. "Jean-Luc Godard." *Film Dope* (London) (Apr. 1980) Biofilmography.

Will, D. "Edinburgh Film Festival Notes 1: Godard's Second Comings." *Framework* 30/31 (1986), pp. 158–69. On sexual politics in recent work.

Wood, R. "Godard, Jean-Luc." In *The International Dictionary of Films and Filmmakers. Vol. 2, Directors/Filmmakers*, pp. 215–22. Chicago: St. James, 1991. Biographical essay, filmography, and bibliography.

———. "In Defense of Art." *Film Comment* XI/4 (July–Aug. 1975), pp. 44–51. On *Vent d'est* and Marxist cinema.

Interviews

Annaud, M. "Jean-Luc Godard: L'Important c'est les producteurs." *Film Français*, Mar. 14, 1975.

Baby, Y., and M. Even. "*Tout va bien*: Un Grand Film 'décevant.'" *Le Monde*, Apr. 27, 1972. Interviews with Godard and Gorin.

Bachmann, G. "In the Cinema, It Is Never Monday." *Sight and Sound* LII/2 (Spring 1983), pp. 118–20. On *Passion*.

———. "The Carrots Are Cooked: A Conversation with Jean-Luc Godard." *Film Quarterly* XXVII/3 (Spring 1984), pp. 13–19. On themes and *Prénom Carmen*.

Bergala, A., and S. Toubiana. "L'Art de (dé)montrer." *Cahiers du Cinéma* 403 (Jan. 1988), pp. 50–57. On *Soigne ta droite* and contemporary cinema.

Bergala, A., P. Bonitzer, and S. Toubiana. "La Guerre et la paix." *Cahiers du Cinéma* 373 (June 1985), pp. 60–65. On *Détective*.

Bougut, M. "Godard's Molotov Cocktail." *Lumière* 23 (May 1973), pp. 14–18. On *Tout va bien*.

Carcassonne, P., and J. Fieschi. "Jean-Luc Godard." *Cinématographe* 66 (Mar.–Apr. 1981), pp. 7–12. On Hollywood and his work.

Cott, J. "Godard: Born-Again Filmmaker." *Rolling Stone*, Nov. 27, 1980, pp. 32–36. On the craft and business of film.

Dieckmann, K. "Godard in His 'Fifth Period.'" *Film Quarterly* XXXIX/2 (Winter 1985–86), pp. 2–6. On Godard's life work, especially *Je vous salue Marie*.

Duras, M., and J-L. Godard. "Duras-Godard: Un Dialogue tendre et passionné." *Cinéma* (Paris) 422 (Dec. 1987), pp. 6–7. On writing, cinema, and TV.

Godard, J-L. "Conférence de presse de Jean-Luc Godard (extraits)." *Cahiers du Cinéma* 433 (June 1990), pp. 10–11.

Goldschmidt, D., and P. Le Guay. "Musique!" *Cinématographe* 108 (Mar. 1985), pp. 32–35. Interview with Agnès Guillemot on editing Godard.

Jousse, T. "La Splendeur dans l'herbe." *Cahiers du Cinéma* 433 (June 1990), pp. 6–11. Interview at 1990 Cannes press conference on *Nouvelle Vague*.

Kolker, R. P. "Angle and Reality: Godard and Gorin in America." *Sight and Sound* XLII/3 (Summer 1973), pp. 130–33. On their ideas on film technique and *Tout va bien*.

MacCabe, C. "Every Man for Himself." *American Film* IX/8 (June 1984), pp. 30–35, 71, 73. On *Prénom Carmen*.

Meisel, M. S. "An Interview Composed by Jean-Luc Godard." *Los Angeles Reader*, Jan 23, 1981, pp. 9–11. On *Sauve qui peut (la vie)*.

Narboni, J. "Jean-Luc Godard à Avignon: 'Laissez rêver la ligne.'" *Cahiers du Cinéma* 316 (Oct. 1980), pp. 8–17. On cinema, painting, and music.

Ranvaud, D., and A. Farassino. "An Interview with Jean-Luc Godard." *Framework* 21 (Summer 1983), pp. 8–9. On the video-scenario for *Passion* and on *Prénom Carmen*.

Rival, P. "Jean-Luc Godard: Je ne suis pas un prince, je suis un producteur." *Le Film Français* 2035 (May 3, 1985), pp. 32, 34, 137. On various aspects of current film production in France.

Rosenbaum, J. "Bringing Godard Back Home." *The Soho News*, Sept. 24, 1980, pp. 41–42. On *Sauve qui peut (la vie)*.

Sollers, P. "Godard/Sollers: L'Entretien." *Cinéma* (Paris) 314 (Feb. 1985), p. 36. On *Je vous salue Marie*.

Thomsen, C. B. "Filmmaking and History: Jean-Pierre Gorin Interviewed." *Jump Cut* 3 (Sept.–Oct. 1974), pp. 17–19. On Gorin's association with Godard.

Archives

Bois d'Arcy: Service des Archives du Film/Centre National de la Cinématographie, 7 bis, rue A. Turpault, 78390 Bois d'Arcy, France.

Lausanne: Cinémathèque Suisse, Case postale 2512, CH-1002 Lausanne, Suisse.

London: British Film Institute, Information Division, 21 Stephen Street, London W1P 1PL, England.

New York: The Museum of Modern Art, Film Study Center, 11 West 53 Street, New York, New York 10019, U.S.A.

Paris: La Cinémathèque Française, Palais de Chaillot, place du Trocadéro, 75116 Paris, France.

Toulouse: Cinémathèque de Toulouse, 3, rue Roquelaine, 31000 Toulouse, France.

Photograph Credits